CHURCH, STATE AND OPPOSITION
IN THE U.S.S.R.

GERHARD SIMON

Church, State
and Opposition
in the U.S.S.R.

*Translated by Kathleen Matchett in collaboration with
the Centre for the Study of Religion and Communism*

UNIVERSITY OF CALIFORNIA PRESS
Berkeley and Los Angeles

University of California Press
Berkeley and Los Angeles

ISBN: 0-520-02612-8

Library of Congress Catalog Card Number: 73-87754

German edition *Die Kirchen in Russland: Berichte, Dokumente* © 1970
Manz Verlag, München

This translation © 1974 C. Hurst & Co. (Publishers) Ltd.

Printed in Great Britain

Contents

Contents

Preface

Experts are convinced that the Soviet intelligentsia today is showing 'a growing interest in religious questions'.[1] Others declare that religion and Church are insignificant parts of contemporary Soviet society.[2] Both positions require discussion.

In the West there is a widespread lack of detailed knowledge concerning the situation of the Church in the Soviet Union, and what little is known is determined more by emotion than by objective information. Assessments range from, on the one hand, dismissal of the Russian Orthodox Church as a state Church frozen in its rituals and only tolerated because it pursues Soviet foreign policy goals abroad, to, on the other hand, adoration of the catacomb church, which in fact only exists in a very limited sense.

The three main events in the internal life of the Russian Churches over the last decade have scarcely been noticed: first, the wave of persecution under Khrushchev from 1959 to 1964, secondly, the internal Church oppositional movements, especially in the Russian Orthodox Church and among the Evangelical Christians and Baptists since the beginning of the 1960s, and thirdly, the present brutal persecution of a relatively large Baptist group, of whom at this moment about 200 leaders and supporters are known to be in labour camps. All these three factors are closely linked.

The movements of criticism and opposition have caused considerable upheaval in the Church communities, but at the same time have strengthened them in their inner life, although the criticism among the Baptists has led to a schism. The new independence and self-awareness in Church circles with respect to state, Party and their own Church leaderships has found expression since the mid-1960s in an abundance of letters, articles, petitions and reports, which cannot be formally printed in the Soviet Union but are passed from hand to hand. While the documents of the anti-Stalinist literary and political intelligentsia (Solzhenitsyn, Sakharov, Amalrik, Grigorenko and others) are being increasingly recognised in the West, the fact that there is a parallel movement in the Churches of the Soviet Union is barely known.

This movement is demanding the release of prisoners and the guarantee of rights which are proclaimed by the present Constitution but which cannot be realised. Thus the oppositional movement, like the liberal intelligentsia, fights for the overcoming of the 'accursed Stalinist past'.[3] The independent criticism in the Church demands religious tolerance and thus makes it clear that the 'most progressive country on earth', even today, has not implemented the intellectual advances of the eighteenth century.

Only a section of all congregations has been affected by the movement of recent years and these, like the Church as a whole, have to fight hard for their existence. The Churches today are a fringe phenomenon in Soviet society, but nevertheless one that is taken seriously by the atheist state. There is little reason to paint the future prospects of the Christian communities in bright colours, especially since it cannot be expected that Soviet state ideology will, in the foreseeable future, tolerate any pluralism in outlook without discrimination and repression. From this point of view, the hopes of the literary and Church opposition seem to be illusory. At the same time no one – not even the professional atheist – expects that the Church and religion will soon disappear as a social phenomenon. Atheist researchers have shown, better than anyone else, what strong roots the Churches of the Soviet Union have among the weary and heavy-laden. There is no immediate prospect of a national or state Church, but the continued existence of the community of those who believe and hope, and of their institutions, seems assured.

The continual pressure from outside makes internal Church renewal difficult. Although the Churches today emphatically support involvement in and for the world, nevertheless their reflections on modern Western theology are still in their infancy. But this problem does not appear to be particularly urgent, since the Soviet Union is a backward country in many other intellectual spheres also and such developments are still to come.

Some chapters of this book had been published before this work first appeared in volume form in German; however, they have been extended and revised. The first essay appeared in *Russlands Aufbruch ins 20. Jahrhundert*, ed. G. Katkov, E. Oberländer *et al.*, Freiburg/Breisgau, 1970, Walter Verlag, pp. 199–233. The chapter on Antoni Vadkovsky was printed in *Kirche im Osten*, XII, 1969, pp. 9–32, Verlag Vandenhoeck und Ruprecht, Göttingen. 'The Soviet State and the Church' appeared in *Aus Politik und Zeitgeschichte. Beilage zur*

Wochenzeitung 'Das Parlament', 15 February 1969, pp. 11–30, and the essay 'State Pressure and Church Resistance' was published in: *Osteuropa*, XIX, 1969, pp. 500–12. My thanks go to the publishers and editors for permission to reprint these essays.

All these writings were prepared in the Bundesinstitut für ostwissenschaftliche und internationale Studien, Cologne.

The English version has been prepared in co-operation with the Centre for the Study of Religion and Communism in London; my especial thanks here go to the translator, Miss Kathy Matchett. The text was revised and brought up to date for the English edition. The documentation has been almost completely revised.

GERHARD SIMON

Cologne, May 1970
London, July 1972

REFERENCES

1. *Religion and the Soviet State: A Dilemma of Power*. M. Hayward and W. C. Fletcher, (ed.), London, 1969, Chapters VI, IX.
2. L. Vladimirov, *The Russians*, New York, Washington, London 1968, p. 124.
3. *RCDA*, VII, 1969, p. 219.

A*

Note

Up to February, 1918, dates follow the Julian calendar which was then used in Russia.

Abbreviations

BV	*Bratsky Vestnik*
FAZ	*Frankfurter Allegemeine Zeitung*
Izv	*Izvestia*
JMP	Journal of the Moscow Patriarchate (*Zhurnal Moskovskoi Patriarkhii*)
KIO	*Kirche im Osten*
Mess	*Messager de l'Exarchat du Patriarche Russe en Europe Occidentale*
NZZ	*Neue Zürcher Zeitung*
O–P	*Ostprobleme*
öpd	*Okumenischer Pressedienst*
RA UdSSR	*Religion und Atheismus in der UdSSR*
RM	*Research Materials on Religion in Eastern Europe*
RCDA	*Religion in Communist Dominated Areas*
StO	*Stimme der Orthodoxie*
VRSKhD	*Vestnik russkogo studencheskogo khristianskogo dvizhenia*

I. Between Reform and Reaction

Church, State and Society on the Eve of the Russian Revolution

The present attitude of the Russian Orthodox Church to its social and political surroundings is characterised by two features: its unconditional loyalty to the Soviet state and its social involvement which, however, is almost exclusively theoretical. The demand for social justice, which is seen as a basic principle of the Christian ethic, places the Russian Orthodox Church on the side of the representatives of a 'theology of revolution', who justify violent political and social upheaval on the grounds of Christian responsibility to the world. The Russian Church therefore welcomes the social-revolutionary movements in the Third World, while any criticism of Soviet reality is unthinkable; in this respect the Church adheres solely to the principle of loyalty.

If one inquires about the historical antecedence of the above-mentioned two principles of the Church's work in the world – which incidentally *mutatis mutandis* apply also to the other religious denominations in the Soviet Union – there appear at first glance to be no links by which they might be traced back into pre-Soviet times. Social-ethical thinking before 1917 was completely undeveloped and the social action of the Church was utterly inadequate and haphazard. As far as the Soviet regime is concerned, it is well known that in the first years after the Revolution the Russian Orthodox Church attacked the Bolsheviks openly and uncompromisingly, anathematised them and forbade the believers to have any contact with enemies of the Church. In both cases, therefore, the present situation seems to have come about through a complete reversal of the positions existing roughly until the mid-1920s.

On closer study, however, other similarities come to light: one can look at the unquestioning submission of the Orthodox Church to the authority of the Soviet state as a continuation of the Church establishment before 1917. It is true that at that time the Orthodox Church was 'ruling'; but because of the privileges afforded it, it was forced into the embraces of the Tsarist state and had lost all independence; it had become a government department and had accepted absolute monarchy as a part of its doctrine. The state obedience of the Orthodox Church, therefore, if we follow this train of thought, appears to be a genuine continuum of Russian and Soviet history.[1] At the same time one must bear in mind that this dependence on the state had very different characteristics before and after the Revolution, and that submission to the frequently humiliating demands of the Soviet regime was the price the Church had to pay to retain its legal status. There is hardly any room for doubt that there would be no legal Church communities in the Soviet Union today if they did not proclaim their unconditional loyalty to the state.

In the social involvement of the Church, as vehemently proclaimed today, one may detect an obvious discontinuum in Russian Church history. But here too it becomes apparent that many roots of this new social-ethical position reach back into the time before 1917, when the consciousness of responsibility for social conditions was awakening both in the Church leadership and among radical circles of the clergy and the intelligentsia.

In any case, the development in the last two decades before the Revolution is of particular significance in understanding the present Church situation in the Soviet Union. This development was affected on the one hand by a Church establishment, for centuries frozen in set forms and outwardly magnificent, and on the other hand by the drive for reforms and a bursting of the state Church fetters.

The Russian State Church

The close relationship of Church and state in modern history is a general European phenomenon, and the bond between the Orthodox Church and Russian absolutism since Peter the Great must be evaluated and de-dramatised, as not being specifically Russian state of affairs. However, the intertwining of state and Church interests in Russia particularly worked out to the detriment of the Church; it forfeited its independence as a warning prophet alongside the state power and neglected its secular tasks in the social and educational field, in order to preach solely 'on heaven and heavenly things'.[2] In principle, however, these consequences of Church establishment are to be seen in other European countries also, and the state Churches of the nineteenth century very much identified themselves with the nationalist euphoria and the conservative *status quo*. In every place they had only a small part in the diagnosis and cure of the social question and, not least for this reason they lost the support of the newly forming classes of workers and intellectuals. Thus it corresponds totally to historical experience that the Orthodox Church became one of the last and most reliable supports of the Russian autocracy and saw the main tasks of its secular work as that of defender against liberalism and socialism.

The Russian Orthodox Church may be seen as a prototype of the state Church; nevertheless, the frequently repeated criticisms that in 1900 it was an institution frozen into enforced ritualism are only partly true. The Russian Church was certainly in a position to develop strong reforming urges and to accept impulses towards the reformation of its attitude to the world. It is necessary to give greater diversity to the picture of an institutionalised Church, as it is to show light and shade even in a painting with a dark background.

But first we must sketch in this background. The control and tutelage exercised over the Orthodox Church by the state manifested itself in the phenomenon of extraordinary privileges accorded to the state Church. In the basic laws of the Russian Empire, the Orthodox Church was called 'the first and ruling'.[3] It alone had the right to proselytise; until 1905 it was impossible for a member to leave the state Church, and defection was a criminal offence. In defence of Orthodoxy the Church could command civil and police authorities, who were obliged on their own account or at the request of the clergy to take action against attacks upon the Church – even if only verbal – and against defection to the Old Believers or the sects. Religious instruction in the Orthodox faith was obligatory in all general and many higher schools; costs in relation to this were borne by the state.

The Orthodox Church also received considerable grants from state funds, which were used largely to maintain the theological schools and academies, and from the 1890s to pay the clergy and finance the rapidly expanding system of Church elementary schools. Corresponding to the explosive growth of the state budget, grants to the Church from state funds rose from 19·8 million roubles in 1897 to 29·3 million roubles in 1905 and 53·9 million roubles at the beginning of the First World War.[4] These figures, however, become relative when one remembers that the grants to the Orthodox Church never exceeded two per cent of the state's outlay, and that part of this money in the case of the elementary schools was used for interdenominational purposes. The state funds also supported other denominations, such as the Evangelical Lutheran and Roman Catholic Churches, so that at the end of the nineteenth century the clergy of these denominations in the Baltic lands, Finland and Poland were economically and socially considerably better off than, for example, the Orthodox clergy in rural central Russia.

The prominent position of the state Church found its expression particularly in its close relationship with the Tsarist autocracy. The basic laws of the Empire required the Emperor, the heir to the throne and their wives to be members of the Orthodox Church. This condition preserved in rudimentary form the claim of the medieval Church to watch over the orthodoxy of the Ruler and to reject him as Ruler if he left the Orthodox faith. The Church raised the Emperor by 'holy coronation' far above the mass of the faithful and declared him to be the 'anointed of God'. The Ruler for his part accepted the role as 'chief defender and maintainer of the dogmas of the ruling faith and preserver of Orthodoxy'.[5] In this sense he was sometimes referred to as 'head of the Church', without possessing any clerical rank according to canon law. In fact, however, the Emperor or his appointed authorities had unlimited power over the Church during the last century before the Revolution in the fields of administration, finance and appointments; Nicholas II and his wife actually demanded from the Holy Synod certain canonisations, and thus interfered in the spiritual government of the Church in the most intimate way.

The will of the monarch in the mind of the official Church became more and more identified with the will of God, to whom absolute obedience belonged. The increasing dependence of the Church upon state authorities, which grew continually more powerful during the two centuries following Peter the Great, went hand in hand with the shrinking of Church influence on state interests and political decision-making. The Church finally lost its influence with the mass of the peasants too, since in all secular matters it was no more than the direct promulgator of state interests. On this matter even the apparently impressive statistical details on the established and controlled Church cannot deceive us.

In 1904 the Russian Orthodox Church had an official membership of 88 million, that is, about 70 per cent of the population of the Empire. For the administration and spiritual care of the believers there existed sixty-one dioceses, the number of which had been increased by 1917 to sixty-seven. In many bishoprics, which were divided according to state boundaries, there were one or several vicar-bishops alongside the diocesan bishop, who acted as assistants and deputies for the latter. During the last century of the Russian Empire only the bishops of St. Petersburg, Moscow and Kiev bore the title of Metropolitan;

however, there was no such thing as a Metropolitan's jurisdictional district comprising several bishoprics. In 1904 there were about 40,000 parishes, with 106,620 clergy (47,743 priests, 14,701 deacons and 44,176 cantors). The number of monasteries and convents in 1914 reached exactly 1,025, in which lived 94,629 monks and nuns as well as lay brothers and sisters; more than three-quarters of these were the nuns and lay sisters. Although the number of churches, clergy and monasteries during the time of the Synod was almost constantly increasing according to absolute statistics, nevertheless, this growth during the whole of the eighteenth and nineteenth centuries remained far behind the increase in population. While in 1738 there were 106 churches for every 100,000 Orthodox inhabitants, in 1890 there were only fifty-six. At the beginning of the First World War there were several hundred fewer monasteries than in 1700.[6]

Only the Church elementary schools experienced a sudden expansion at the end of the nineteenth century, thanks to the initiative of the Oberprokuror of the Holy Synod, Pobedonostsev. In the parish schools over two or three winters the eight- to eleven-year-old peasant children learnt the initial basics of reading, writing and arithmetic. In the centre, however, stood religious instruction, with the greatest number of lesson hours. The concept of the Church schools was from the very beginning questionable, being pedagogically old-fashioned, and thus it met with mistrust from the liberal zemstvo circles and the intellectuals. In an enlightenment-oriented Russian society it necessarily evoked opposition, when the children in these schools had to learn to read with Church Slavonic texts and Church music took the place of nature study and geography. Instruction was given by clergy and by badly trained and badly paid secular teachers, mostly women. Nevertheless, the contribution of the Church schools to the fight against illiteracy was not insignificant, and at the peak of their development, 1·9 million pupils attended the 43,407 schools. The number of Church schools in the 1890s – although not that of their pupils – actually exceeded the number of secular elementary schools, which came under the Ministry of Education (in competition with the Church).[7]

The above details show that the state Church disposed of an extensive apparatus that had to be administered and constantly adjusted to meet new demands. At the same time the self-government of the Church during the eighteenth and nineteenth centuries had been more and more whittled away in favour of state control, so that it was only from the level of the bishoprics downwards that it was possible to speak of an independent competence on the part of Church bodies.

Since the Ecclesiastical Regulation of Peter the Great (1721), the Holy Synod had stood at the head of the Church, instead of a Patriarch. The former was a collegiate clerical body, comprising seven or eight bishops at the end of the nineteenth century. This was after the representatives of the parish and monastic clergy, who in the eighteenth century had also had a place and a voice there, had been excluded. Standing members of the Synod were the three Metropolitans and the Exarch of Georgia; the Emperor then arbitrarily summoned three or four diocesan bishops to St. Petersburg as temporary members. The Synod decided all important administrative and spiritual questions, and beyond that it had to deal with an excessive quantity of purely routine matters. At the same time the Church government had no autonomous competence in any important administrative or legal action, for its decisions had to be submitted to the Emperor for ratification. Every episcopal appointment naturally required imperial approval.

The rulers in the nineteenth century, however, were no longer able to govern the Church personally, although legally this was quite possible; they entrusted this to an official, the Oberprokuror of the Holy Synod. From the beginning of the nineteenth century he became the sole mediator between Emperor and Church and increasingly the real head of the state Church. The Oberprokurors, who in the eighteenth century had exercised scarcely more than a controlling function, extended their authority and area of competence during the nineteenth century to an almost ministerial position. At the end of this development, during the rule of Oberprokuror K. P. Pobedonostsev (1880–1905), initiatives and Church policy-making had passed exclusively into the hands of the Oberprokuror and his colleagues. It is true that the college of the Synod still made formal decisions in all matters laid before it by the Oberprokuror, but it had sunk to the role of a rubber-stamping body incapable of independent action, and its functions had passed to the imperial official: a development which had not been intended by Peter the Great to have this radical consequence. Only the Chairman of the Synod, as a rule the Metropolitan of St. Petersburg, was able in some cases to make his will felt; this was mostly in connection with appointments.

The administration of the institutionalised Church was strongly centralised, so that the Oberprokuror's bureaucracy could reach directly down to the level of the local parishes. The instrument of the

Church leadership in the dioceses was the secretary of the episcopal consistorium, who received his orders direct from the Oberprokuror. In fact the bishops also (although not officially) were appointed at the suggestion of the Oberprokuror, and against all canon law were moved every few years from one diocese to another. The frequent episcopal translations allowed the Oberprokuror to show fine degrees of favour and disfavour to the bishops and this made them dependent, helpless, servile to their master and tyrannical towards their subordinates.

Despite his dependence on the Church leadership, the bishop was still endowed with considerable power in his own diocese. Laden with excessive bureaucratic duties and competence, he was often not the prime spiritual father in his bishopric, but an impersonal overlord enthroned high above the faithful and the clergy. Since almost all the bishops were the sons of parish priests, they had behind them a marked social climb which they did not by any means always owe to their special abilities, but rather to their superior theological education at one of the four Theological Academies and above all to their monastic state. Because at the end of the nineteenth century there was very little new blood among educated monks, most young monks made a rapid career, leading them fairly easily to the episcopate. The shared origin, the deep social divide and the hierarchical gap sharpened the ever-existing tensions between the 'black' monastic clergy and the 'white' or 'worldly' clergy, who had to be married and who had no prospect of ever participating in the responsible leadership of the Church.

Since the 1860s the parish clergy indeed no longer constituted a closed estate by law, but the flow of new priests still continued to come almost exclusively from the clergy itself; only in occasional cases did young Russians of different origin choose the scarcely attractive profession of parish priest. On the other hand in the last decades before the Revolution the sons of clergy went increasingly into secular jobs. Only a small proportion of graduates of the seminaries took their vows; very many aimed at the universities or took jobs in public administration, so that in many of the dioceses there was a noticeable lack of new priests, and candidates were ordained with inadequate theological education, or sometimes none at all.

Village clergy and congregations suffered particularly through the need for Church reform. The priest and his deacon and cantor were dependent on a domineering bishop and an ineffective consistorium.

They had an abundance of sometimes meaningless bureaucratic obligations to fulfil; a host of books had to be kept and continual reports written about trifles; at the same time the clergy had always had the responsibility of keeping the civil registers, which brought with it many associated tasks. There was hardly time or strength left for work in the congregation apart from Sunday and occasional services.

The parish clergy traditionally derived its income from two main sources: Church land and the free-will or previously regulated gifts of the congregation. The land which belonged to almost every village church had to be either worked by the clergy themselves or leased out to peasants. The duty of maintenance on the part of the congregation derived from a time when the congregation itself elected its priest, and it was justified on those grounds. However, the Church, with its strict hierarchical orientation, had already suppressed this practice in the seventeenth century and regarded the local priest exclusively as the tool with which it directed the congregation. The double dependence on the episcopal power and on maintenance by the congregation frequently brought parish clergy into desperate straits. Arguments with members of the congregation over the fee for baptisms, weddings and funerals were commonplace, and the priest who extorted the last chicken from the peasants determined the image of the village clergy.

Relief and economic security for the clergy in this situation could only be obtained through a fixed salary, which, after initial trials under Nicholas I, had been introduced in more and more parishes since the 1890s. In 1904 exactly 27,000 parish churches together received 11·5 million roubles from state funds; by 1916 this sum had been raised, against the sometimes considerable opposition of the Duma, to 18·8 million roubles, in which 31,000 of the more than 41,000 parishes shared. Even then adequate economic security for parish clergy, which would have made possible the renunciation of Church land and all gifts from the congregations, was still far from realisation. In 1910 the Synod calculated that an additional yearly grant of 75 million roubles from state funds would be necessary.[8] At the demise of the Empire, therefore, the parish clergy were still economically insecure and only partly in a position to attend to their true function. Feared or avoided by the peasants, mocked by the landowners or decried as a protector of reaction by the liberal intelligentsia, the parish clergy formed an isolated social group whose influence on the people had sharply declined and who had no link with the upper social strata.

The local congregations, which should be at the centre of attention for any Church leadership, had become merely the object of Church government. Inside and outside the Church it was agreed that the activation of parish life must be one of the principal objects of any Church reform. However, despite amazing sacrificial giving, the participation of the people in Church life was often restricted to the observance of centuries-old rituals, done hastily, fragmentarily and without inner participation. Complaints that the people were unaware of even the most elementary aspects of Christian doctrine never disappeared from the columns of the Church press. 'The "Christ-loving" people not only do not love Christ, they do not even know him: that is the ancient tragedy of our Russian reality,' said the official organ of the Synod in the summer of 1917.[9]

The Revolution and Preparation for a Council

In the years immediately after the turn of the century the state Church, despite this depressingly negative picture, became drawn along in the general mood of fresh beginnings, and found the strength to attempt a thoroughgoing reform. Failures were acknowledged and conclusions were drawn. The inner life forces which came to light then have in fact also enabled the Orthodox Church to continue its existence under an atheist regime.

The Revolution of 1905 and the preceding restless years helped self-criticism in the Church, encompassing all areas of Church life, to come to an abrupt breakthrough. Criticism from the professorial staff of the Theological Academies, the parish clergy and the episcopate made the public aware of how far the Church had failed in its own tasks.

People were agreed that the chief principle and point of departure for all reforms should be a return to the canonical self-government of the Church. From here followed two main demands: the removal of tutelage by the state authorities and the convocation of a Russian Local Council (pomestny sobor: a national assembly of the Russian Orthodox Church) to decide Church reforms in all areas. At first no one thought of a separation of Church and state; the state Church wanted to retain its privileges, but to use them independently and without strings. Many circles expected the Council, as the crowning point of a renewed canonical Church government, to restore the Patriarchate – a demand, however, which from the beginning aroused misgivings among a part of the 'white' clergy, who favoured a democratisation of Church institutions at all levels.

From 1902 onwards discussion of reform took up much space in Church periodicals and reached its peak in the years after 1905, when censorship was suspended for a short time. But suggestions for reform also found a lively echo in the secular press; in the spring of 1905 particularly, the liberal press welcomed the Church progressives as allies in the struggle against autocracy. It was overlooked that political liberalism and the desire for Church reform emanated from quite different sources, and that among the higher clergy at least, no one questioned the existing social and political system in Russia.

The ideas for reform centred rather on an inner revitalisation of the state Church, to be achieved primarily by a return to the canonical traditions. The representatives of the 'white' clergy in particular raised the demand for election of priests by the congregations and of the bishops by the clergy and laity of a diocese. An altogether greater participation of the laity in Church life was generally held to be essential. It was expected that the congregations would receive far-reaching autonomy (distinct from the administration of the consistorium), and the rights of a person at law. Many writers demanded that in future not only should there be regular all-Russian councils, but that in every diocese permanent congresses of clergy and laity should be organised. It is clear that this would have meant a reduction in episcopal power and a considerable activation of the existing diocesan clergy meetings. Hitherto these diocesan meetings had been completely dependent on the whim of the bishop; they had only an advisory status and did not even have the right of convening regularly.

In the plans for reform, the social and political role of the clergy and the Church frequently came under discussion. There was an almost unanimous drive for a greater and more responsible participation by the clergy in state-political life. They should be represented on all public bodies from the zemstva up to the Duma and the government, in order to win back the lost social positions of the Church.

Again and again the sharpest criticism was directed against the theological schools, especially the seminaries, which for some time had not been fulfilling their role of training new priests. The seminaries were an anachronistic mixture of general school for the priestly class and theological training centre where enlightenment-oriented sons of priests, who were looking towards careers in the universities, were supposed to be led to a spiritual vocation through Church music, long services and a discipline of terror. The result was the gradual internal decay of the seminaries from the 1890s. Antiquated teaching material, incapable teachers and a wretchedly strict and stifling boarding life led every year to seminary unrest in several of the sixty institutions in the Empire. There were strikes, violence and assassination attempts against rectors and teachers, and revolutionary circles were discovered more and more frequently in the seminaries. Relief here could only be achieved by radical action, and many suggestions for reform therefore urged the dissolution of the seminaries in their existing form; they should be replaced, for priestly candidates only, by open theological schools no longer needing to take any account of the class origin of the seminarists.[10]

The lively public discussion of necessary reforms in the state Church bore its first tangible fruits when at the beginning of 1905 an extraordinary conference of the Committee of Ministers considered the introduction of freedom of conscience in Russia. The sessions were led by the President of the Committee, S. Yu. Witte, who drew the Metropolitan of St. Petersburg, Antoni (Vadkovsky), into the debates – which already represented a violation of the prerogative of the Oberprokuror, and in an important matter gave the Church the opportunity of speaking and acting on its own behalf. The Committee of Ministers started from the premise that 'the religious convictions of a person are not subject to the control of the state. . . .' The Metropolitan of St. Petersburg emphasised that any forcible conversion or compulsion to return to the Orthodox Church was far from the Church's desire, and he supported the release from the state Church of those who only belonged to it on paper, but who in fact had abandoned all connection with it. He rejected administrative and police measures in the struggle against the sects. Thereby the chairman of the Holy Synod abandoned significant basic principles of Church policy during the previous decades and introduced a new relationship of the Church to the state and to the heterodox.[11]

The result of the debates in the Committee of Ministers was the law 'On the Establishment of the Principles of Religious Tolerance' of 17 April, 1905.[12] For the first time it made departure from the state Church legal and made possible the joining of other denominations or sects. Significantly, defection from any denomination was not provided for in the law at all. The state Church still remained the privileged 'first' and 'ruling' Church, and the missionary veto for all other denominations was still guaranteed by law and administratively enforced.

At the same time, after 1905 the Orthodox Church stood in a

completely new relationship to the other denominations, because no one could any longer be prevented from breaking with it openly. By May 1909, therefore, according to official statistics, 301,450 'Orthodox' had left the Church, having previously been unable to declare their different allegiance openly. More than half of these were Christians united to Rome, particularly from the Kholm district, who in the nineteenth century had been forcibly converted to the state Church; these went over to the Latin rite of the Catholic Church. There was also the departure of 'Orthodox' Muslims in the Volga region and the reconversion of Estonian and Latvian peasants in the Baltic lands to the Lutheran Church. The evangelical sects and the Old Believers also expected a large influx.[13]

The Extraordinary Conference of the Committee of Ministers at the beginning of 1905 did not confine itself in its deliberations to the preparation of the law on tolerance, but it was willing, at the suggestion of Metropolitan Antoni, to consider the whole question of a new regulation of Church–state relations as well as the problems of internal Church reform. The intervention of Pobedonostsev with the Emperor in fact prevented this; nevertheless, both Metropolitan Antoni and Witte had already laid before the Committee of Ministers their working papers, which had been drawn up with the help of professors from the St. Petersburg Academy.

Metropolitan Antoni in his paper began with the suggestion that the Old Believers and the sects were now, through the law on tolerance, in a 'more favourable position' than the state Church, because they had been granted 'autonomy in their Church affairs', while the Orthodox Church was hindered and cramped by the state authority. He therefore put the question whether it was not time for 'that continual protectorate and over-careful control of the secular authority over Church life and the activity of the Church leadership to be removed or at least somewhat relieved; for in this way the Church is robbed of its independence and initiative, and its field of activity is almost entirely confined to the performance of Sunday and occasional services, while her voice remains completely unheard both in private and in public life.' Even though Antoni stressed the need for caution in his concrete demands for Church reform, such programmatic declarations on the part of the leading Metropolitan, putting in question the state's right of patronage, were unheard of in the age of Pobedonostsev.[14]

The paper which Witte laid before the Committee of Ministers went further still in its criticism of the state Church. It repeated the words of Dostoyevsky, that the Church since Peter the Great was in a 'state of paralysis'; he said it had lost the principle of conciliation and had become a bureaucracy and police-ruled state institution. Church life, said Witte, had become 'frozen and cut off from the questions which now concern society'.[15]

It is true that the Emperor did not permit the Committee of Ministers to discuss all these problems and transferred them to the Synod, but even the college of bishops, in the general atmosphere of revolutionary unrest and ferment, was unwilling to remain silent. The Synod conferred on Church reform in March 1905 and the three Metropolitans (circumventing the Oberprokuror) were given the unusual opportunity of informing the Emperor personally about the results. In the written report, the Synod requested the Emperor to give his consent to the convocation of a Russian Council to elect a Patriarch and carry through important Church reforms. First-mentioned among these were decentralisation of Church administration, reorganisation and debureaucratisation at diocesan level, as well as congregational and school reform.

Through this swift and unexpected action by the Synod and the lively public approval, the impression was created in Church and society that the restoration of the Patriarchate by a Russian Local Council was in the immediate offing. But all hopes for self-renewal by the Church in the near future were dashed when the Emperor in his resolution on the report of the Synod, 31 March, 1905, declared that 'in the present time of unrest' he considered it 'impossible' to undertake 'such an important matter'. The convocation of a Council was promised 'at a convenient time'.[16]

Nevertheless, the Synod was able at first to set in motion preparations for the Council, until reaction put an end to this also. All bishops were requested to state their opinion and they unanimously approved the convocation of a Council as well as the election of a canonically ruling Patriarch. Even the hierarchs, beyond this, made surprisingly free criticisms of the whole of Church life and produced an abundance of suggestions for improvement. At the same time the different reforming positions among the conservative episcopate, on the one hand, and in the progressive Church press as well as from the 'white' clergy, on the other, could not be overlooked. While, for example, the latter raised the demand for equal participation by clergy and laity in the Council, most of the bishops wanted the complete voting right in any future Council to be reserved for them alone; both sides appealed (as was often the case) to the practice or the spirit of the Fathers.

For the working out of concrete structures for the Council, which were to be based on the recommendations of the bishops, the Synod appointed a Committee for the Preparation of the Council. Its work, however, came under increasing suspicion in the growing atmosphere of reaction. The committee, which consisted of ten bishops, twenty professors and a number of other experts and personalities from public life, under the presidency of Antoni (Vadkovsky), was therefore only able to sit from March to June and from November to December 1906, when it was suspended by order of the Emperor. The work of the committee nevertheless, produced valuable results, although they clearly bore the stamp of the conservative reform positions in the episcopate and projected the image of a self-ruling episcopal Church with close links, as before, with the autocracy. Thus part of the progressive Church press, which was demanding much more wideranging changes, labelled the work of the committee as unsatisfactory.

The preparatory committee resolved to give voting rights at the future Council only to the bishops; representatives of the lower clergy and of the laity were to participate in the discussions only in an advisory capacity. It is true that the people were given the opportunity to propose candidates from the clergy and laity to take part in the Council. However, the choice – from a large number of suggested candidates – lay solely with the diocesan bishop.

The committee wanted to set a Patriarch at the head of the Church, to be assisted in Church government by a standing Synod of twelve bishops. The Church was prepared, as before, to present all important resolutions of the Council, the Patriarch and the Synod to the Emperor for his decision (*blagousmotrenie*); only this, according to the committee, should be done by the Patriarch and not by an Oberprokuror, whose competence was to be reduced once more to a merely supervisory function. The liberal Church press here had demanded the complete abolition of the Oberprokurors. The committee's plans for reorganisation of the dioceses and congregations[17] also lagged behind the press demands for democratisation and participation of the laity in Church life.

After the dissolution of the preparatory committee by the Emperor, despite energetic pressure from 'white' clergy, the more vocal sections of the Duma and society, preparations for a Council came almost to a standstill and were not taken up again for the duration of the Empire; a 'pre-conciliar conference' of the Synod in 1912 should be regarded more as an alibi. After its experience with the Duma, the imperial regime clearly did not wish to run the risk of creating a new forum for criticism of autocracy in the form of a Council, especially since this criticism, though moderate, would have come from one of the last props of absolute autocracy.

Right-wing Radicalism and Socialism

The state Church felt the reaction after 1905 very swiftly and sharply. In any case, the Church leadership of its own accord swung without resistance over to the new course; of the hopeful plans and ideas hardly any were realised. Instead of the urgently necessary reform of the seminaries for priests, the Synod in 1908 and 1909 decreed a stricter religious training, the removal of secular education from the seminaries and new punishments against revolutionary acts by students.

Instead of the academies being granted the internal autonomy and academic independence which had been demanded for years, the theological schools remained, (according to the new statute of 2 April, 1910) as firmly bound as before to the diocesan bishop and the Synod. In this statute for the first time it was mentioned that the academies were to awaken in the students 'submissivness to throne and fatherland'. The Church leadership did not dare to lay the draft of this statute before the Third Duma, even though it was ruled by conservative parties; it obtained the force of law solely through the Emperor, on the basis of the often used exception clause in the basic laws. As a consequence, there were sharp recriminations by the Duma against the Synod and the refusal to pass state grants for the theological schools in the following financial year.[18]

The chance to put parish life on a new footing was equally unexploited, although all parties had seen the necessity for action. Parish reform was postponed for years by Church and parliamentary bodies, and finally in 1915 removed from the agenda of the Duma, because the hierarchy refused to accept the bill, supported most of all by the Octobrists, which provided for the election of the priest by the congregation, which was to receive the legal rights of an individual.[19]

Just as the opportunities for reform in all fields remained unused, so criticism of the Orthodox monasteries died without echo. The monasteries were not in a position to place their sometimes considerable wealth and property at the service of public works; care of the sick, schools and care for social failures and outcasts by the monasteries were still the exception.

Instead of an inner renewal of the Church, the years after 1906 brought an increasing identification of the official Church with political reaction. Progressive forces were pushed aside and – in a polarisation process – sometimes into extreme positions. In this way the state Church continued to undermine its own foundations and brought itself to the brink of a schism. It was therefore unable to be a stabilising element in a land torn by unrest.

The alignment of the Church with reaction happened partly in the name of complete political neutrality. Men like Antoni (Vadkovsky) clung to the illusion of a Church standing above political parties and interests, and failed to see the fact that in this way the Church was accepting the political *status quo* – that, in other words, it was assisting the reaction that stemmed from the Emperor. Other Church circles went further and declared openly that the state Church must take up its position on the side of an endangered autocracy and against the conspiracy of constitutionalism, socialism and Jewry.

Metropolitan Vladimir (Bogoyavlensky), in his struggle against the Revolution, appealed to all believers in the capital, describing strikes and unrest as an 'insane and unbridled conspiracy' by 'monstrous human beings who have abandoned God'. The Metropolitan called on his 'beloved sons' to rise up and be ready to defend themselves against the social democrats, directed from abroad, who wanted to 'enslave the whole world'. 'Be prepared to die for the Tsar and for Russia!'[20] It is significant, however, that at this moment, while internal Church reform discussions were in full swing, not only the Moscow city Duma but even the Synod itself criticised the Metropolitan and warned him against inciting acts of violence.[21]

One indication of the increasingly extreme political orientation of the Church was its attitude to the right-wing radical 'League of the Russian People'. While Metropolitan Antoni in November 1906 still refused to take part in a meeting of the League and to consecrate the flags of this monarchist-reactionary conspiratorial group, at the same time in many dioceses bishops and clergy were already beginning to work actively with the League of the Russian People and other 'patriotic' organisations. At first, in reply to individual requests by bishops, the Synod declared several times that there was no objection to clergy co-operating with the League of the Russian People. But under pressure from leaders of the League, it then made on 15 March 1908 the much more far-reaching decision to inform the bishops openly that 'they should permit and bless participation of the Orthodox clergy under their jurisdiction in the work of the League of the Russian People and other monarchist, patriotic societies. . . .'[22]

The hierarchy, however, did not content itself with the furtherance of right-wing radical groups, but condemned at the same time any co-operation of Church representatives with parties of the left. In the First and Second Dumas, to the indignation of the Church leadership, several deputies from the Orthodox clergy joined socialist parties. When in May 1907 five priests in the Duma made their anti-monarchist sympathies clear, the Synod stepped in and declared that it was incompatible with the priestly office to belong to parties which 'strive to overthrow the state, the social order or even the authority of the Tsar'. Only one deputy, however, gave way to the demand of the Synod to leave his party; ecclesiastical court cases were instigated against three members of the *Trudoviki* ('Workers' Party') and one social-revolutionary.[23]

The correspondingly manipulated franchise led in the same year to a preponderance of conservative parties in the Third Duma, and the area of conflict between Church and parliament seemed at first to have been removed. One of the sharpest spokesmen of the reactionary episcopate, Archbishop Antoni (Khrapovitsky) of Volhynia, who wanted to save Russia through a restoration of the Patriarchate and a monastically controlled state Church, celebrated the election result in Zhitomir cathedral as if it were an Easter festival. 'Our holy Russia has been raised up again.' No longer, he said, could the 'monstrous human beings' 'give themselves out as spokesmen for the will of the people'. The newly elected 'true spokesmen' knew that 'the shaking of the Tsarist autocracy meant the beginning of the destruction of all Russia. . . .'[24]

Meanwhile, the personal and factual interweaving of the state Church and political extremism had become increasingly close. Many local branches of the League of the Russian People were led by clergy and the League met in churches and Church buildings. Priest-monk Iliodor (Trufanov), who operated from the Pochaev monastery in Volhynia and later from Tsaritsyn, became notorious for his inflammatory propaganda on behalf of the Black Hundreds (right-wing action groups); for a time he had a close relationship with Rasputin. He wrote and preached against Jews, Poles and revolutionaries and called the people to self-defence against these 'Mongol bands'. He defended terror from the right and whipped the people up to pogroms against the Jews, in order to free itself from its 'tormentors'. This anti-semitic campaign was at the same time a cynical attempt to win support among the Russian peasants by pushing all social problems on to a scapegoat against which revenge was permitted. The Synod was unable to check Iliodor.[25]

The linking of the Church with monarchism and reaction did not mean that in the state Church the social question was completely ignored – as had largely been the case before 1905. Particularly in 1905, the year of revolution, and immediately afterwards, demands were raised in all circles of the Church, ultraconservative and liberal, for social improvement for the workers and peasants, shorter working hours and social security. For the institutional Church, however, these remained largely proclamations, and the real controversy regarding Russian life was played out almost entirely within the apologetic against socialism. On the other hand the progressive-minded Church press (including *Tserkovny Vestnik, Tserkovno-Obshchestvennaya Zhizn*) showed that a considerable part of the clergy was prepared to work actively on the solution of social problems. Thus many parish clergy between the revolutions looked after peasant savings banks, took part in the struggle against alcoholism by founding teetotal leagues and undertook other welfare work. The Church as an institution, however, did not strive to participate in the overcoming of the ever-sharpening social conflicts either by persuasion or by example.

All the more intensive was the Church's controversy with socialism after 1905, as it had been surprised by the impact and inroads of atheistic socialism among the workers and intellectuals. The Church periodicals and newspapers printed a large number of articles on socialism; popular and academic brochures were printed; discussion evenings were arranged in many city parishes, and the Synod sent its synodal missionaries into the workers' suburbs. From the Oberprokuror V. K. Sabler, who wrote a two-volume work on socialism, to the provincial Church news-sheets, the danger of revolutionary socialism was the centre of attention.[26] The Fourth Missionary Conference at Kiev, in 1908, concerned itself primarily with socialism, and the Church leadership introduced at the seminaries and academies a 'course on the history and true nature of socialism'. The intensive controversy revealed a fairly sophisticated knowledge of Marxism and socialism, and it probably contributed significantly to the propagation of socialist ideas. The Church apologists confined themselves almost entirely to German, French and English socialist thinkers. The Russian social-democrat writers obviously remained largely unknown to the Church authors and the Bolsheviks were completely ignored.[27]

The Church writers unanimously recognised the need for social improvement, but in the main they defended the existing social order. One of the chief anti-socialist polemicists, the synodal missionary Archpriest Ioann Vostorgov, declared at the Missionary Conference in Kiev that the strength and success of socialism were determined 'by the lack of a thoroughgoing and effective Christian ordering of our mutual relationships' and 'by the imperfection of our social life as expressed in poverty and the extremes of capitalism'.[28]Oberprokuro Sabler deplored the 'difficult living conditions of the workers' and 'the ruthless exploitation of the workers by rich capitalists'.[29] For the promotion of 'moral and material well-being' he recommended the organisation on the Western European model of co-operatives, agricultural trading societies and the introduction of savings banks and loan institutions. Sabler even went so far as to demand, for the longer-term future, worker participation in production 'as partners or shareholders'.[30] Such ideas, however, remained only declamatory and acquired no binding power; other Church authors defended poverty as God-given: it must be maintained, in order that Christians should have the opportunity to practise charity. The right to property was justified by reference to the New Testament, and at the same time it was declared that Christ 'paid only minimal attention to the external needs of man'.[31] The 'difficult life of the poor and the secure well-being of the rich' likewise corresponded to the 'will of God'. Theologically the social problem was pushed to one side, for poverty 'was rooted in the sinful nature of man'.[32]

In the foreground for all Church writers stood the incompatibility of Christianity and socialism. 'Socialism appeals for class struggle and for enmity, Christianity on the other hand for unity and love.'[33] Socialism wanted to destroy the present state and social order by a violent revolution, while the Church wanted, by an appeal to conscience and by moral influence, to produce charity and social reforms. While socialism promised merely to liberate people from material poverty, Christ had not come to rescue the world from 'the power of the capitalists . . . and the slavery of a despotic regime, but from the slavery of sin and death'.[34] Socialism wanted to change social conditions, while the root of all evil lay solely in the moral pollution of man; man must be renewed by Christian faith, then the social order would automatically change.[35] Socialism was concerned with society, Christianity with the individual.

Besides this, the Church writers carried on a mostly very searching controversy with socialist plans for the future, which were characterised as utopian and dangerous. In a socialist society the individual would lose his value and dignity and would be oppressed by an all-powerful state apparatus. Family, patriotism and tolerance could no longer exist. The prophecy of the removal of alienation in socialist society was rejected. 'There are no grounds for believing that with the dawn of a new age, men will completely change.'[36] For all those reasons, the Church rejected any form of 'Christian socialism' as an attempt to build bridges between irreconcilable opposites.

The polemic against Christian socialism occupied such a large space because there were many attempts on the fringes of the state Church to bring about progressive political commitment from Christian convictions, to overcome apologetics and to become practically involved. With the cognisance of Metropolitan Antoni there was formed at the beginning of the century the 'St. Petersburg Union of Russian Factory Workers', which by the beginning of 1905 had more than 10,000 members and was led by the doubtful figure of the priest Georgi Gapon (1870–1906). This was a new attempt to guide the revolutionary movement of the workers into controlled paths and to supervise it; nevertheless Gapon represented genuine social-liberal demands and he created a type of trade union which was by no means prepared to be a puppet in the hands of the authorities. On 9 January, 1905, at the height of the strike movement early in that year, Gapon organised a demonstration march of the St. Petersburg workers, carrying icons and church banners. The idea was to present a petition to the Tsar, demanding freedom of the press, a constitutional parliament, an eight-hour day and the distribution of the land to the peasants. The workers were met in front of the Winter Palace with salvoes from the guard. Apparently it was only after the fiasco of 'Bloody Sunday' that Gapon came into open contact with the police, and in March 1906 he was shot by social revolutionaries as a police agent.

More profitable for a social-Christian involvement than this discredited attempt to create a Christian trade union movement were the discussions of the 'Religious-philosophical Meetings' in St. Petersburg in 1901–3. Here representatives of the Church and of the religious intelligentsia, who became known as 'God-seekers' (bogoiskateli), met to seek a common language for the pressing problems of the time. However, the gatherings, initiated by the writer Dmitri Merezhkovsky and his wife Zinaida Hippius, soon revealed how far the mystically inclined religious speculations of the writers departed from traditional Orthodox theology. Nevertheless, the attempt was made here to bridge the now yawning gap between the Church and the intelligentsia, even though only a small number of scholars interested in religion inspired chiefly by V. Solovyov, participated. A common social-ethical ideal was to reunite Orthodoxy and the intellectuals. Both sides were concerned to restore influence on social life to a modernised Church.

'The lack of a religious-social ideal among churchmen is the real cause of this hopeless situation,' said the theologian and writer V. A. Ternavtsev in his introductory paper on aims. The Church had forgotten her earthly tasks and the intellectuals in their service to the community were now fulfilling 'Christ's demands of service to men'. This wishful notion of religious inspiration and of unconscious or subconscious Christianity on the part of the revolutionary intelligentsia played an important role in the attempt to bring Church and intellectuals nearer in the common pursuit of social-ethical action, and it also determined the writings of the authors of *Vechi*. 'God is among the intelligentsia,' declared V. V. Rozanov at the St. Petersburg meetings, and Ternavtsev expressed the hope that 'the intelligentsia would . . . surely come through rationalism and back to the Christian faith'.[37] In reality, however, the barrier of language and thought between even the religiously committed part of the intelligentsia and the Church often proved insuperable.

It is more appropriate to speak of a return to Orthodoxy in the case of a number of other intellectuals who, after the turn of the century, came into the Church. These included, among others, the circle around P. A. Florensky and the intellectuals who had been disappointed by Marxism: S. N. Bulgakov, N. A. Berdyaev, S. L. Frank and P. B. Struve, who were the central figures in the writing team which in 1909 launched the collection *Vechi* ('Signposts').[38] If the 'Religious-philosophical Meetings' were concerned to appeal to the Church to recognise her social responsibility, the authors of *Vechi* called on the doctrinaire and revolutionary intelligentsia to consider afresh a programme of social and political reforms on the basis of Christian and humanist awareness of responsibility. A Christian view of the world and of man was for many of the *Vechi* writers the point of departure for their critique of the intelligentsia which believed in materialism and progress. Thus these contributions belong also to the series of attempts to base a political and social involvement on Christian convictions.

The former Marxists Berdyaev and Bulgakov held fast, even after their return to Orthodoxy, to many social-political demands of Marxism, and from this standpoint they sharply criticised the state Church for its lack of responsibility and action. Bulgakov founded a 'League of Christian Politics', which demanded national equality and socialisation of the means of production. Bulgakov based himself on the idea that the first Christians had put socialist ideals into practice in their communities, and had thus set this as a goal for Christianity. Christianity must therefore lead to 'political liberation and religious renewal'.[39] Bulgakov was already described by the contemporary press as the founder of Christian socialism in Russia, although his decidedly anti-revolutionary opinions brought him into ever sharper conflict with the socialist parties.

On the other hand, there were groups of Orthodox clergy who felt more and more aligned with the socialist parties, and who adopted a considerable part of their programme. They aroused extraordinary public interest and did not remain unnoticed among the clergy, especially the 'white' priests. One germ cell of this Christian socialism, in the stricter sense of a left political orientation, was the 'Group of Thirty-two' St. Petersburg priests, which was formed during the troubles of 1905. Many of these had taken part in the 'Religious-philosophical Meetings'. On 17 March, 1905, the group handed the Metropolitan of the capital a memorandum urgently demanding steps towards Church reform; further petitions followed. This group also campaigned for a democratisation of the Church, for the reduction of episcopal power and for the autonomy of the parishes. In a declaration of 1906, the group went further and declared that it was the task of the clergy to protect the workers against capital, to sympathise with the peasants, and to campaign for a speedy solution to the land problem. One of the spokesmen for the 'Group of Thirty-two', Father Grigori Petrov, acknowledged in his writings the 'fathers' of the revolutionary intelligentsia, Herzen and Belinsky; he expected a basic reordering of all social relationships and the end of exploitation of man by man. Petrov was elected as a Constitutional Democrat deputy to the Second Duma, although he already stood under severe pressure from right-wing churchmen because of his 'anti-Christian socialist teachings', and had been sentenced by the Synod to three months' confinement in a monastery on account of his sharp criticism of social conditions and of Church–state relations. Later this extraordinarily popular priest, who not only had access to the aristocratic salons but also spoke in the working-class districts, was stripped of his priestly office by the Church leadership.[40]

Petrov was not the only priest who came into sharp conflict with the Church leadership as a Duma member. Of the six priests in the First Duma, four expressed definitely progressive views. In the Second Duma there were thirteen deputies from the Church, of whom only the two bishops and two priests joined conservative parties. Three belonged to the Cadets and three to the *Trudoviki*, and one was a social-revolutionary. The most outspoken was Father Fedor Tikhvinsky (*Trudoviki*); he spoke in the Duma demanding not only a ministry responsible to parliament but the nationalisation of all land, which was to be handed over to the peasants for cultivation.[41] The electoral law of 1907 and the agitation of the Church leadership ensured that in the Third and Fourth Dumas there were no more clergy members on the parliamentary left wing.

The group of thirty-two St. Petersburg priests also had to cease its activity in the years of reaction; nevertheless the problem of combining Christianity and socialism continued to be discussed. The Professor at the St. Petersburg Theological Academy, Archimandrite Mikhail (Semenov), published in 1907 the brochure *How I became a People's Socialist*; he had chosen the title explicitly in connection with *How a Minister Became a Social Democrat* by Pastor Paul Goehre who, together with Chr. Blumhardt, joined the S.P.D. (Socialist-Democratic Party of Germany) in 1900. Archimandrite Mikhail in his booklet stated that a solution to social problems was possible only through the abolition of private property and a complete reordering of social structures. In 1906 the Professor for Church Law had written a *Programme of the Russian Christian Socialists*, which demanded a constitutional monarchy and a radical set of labour laws. Mikhail later lost his position in the academy and the priesthood. An adventurous life led him eventually to the Old Believers, where he rose to Bishop after the Revolution.[42]

A similar development of ideas was expressed by Nikolai Smirnov, who made a significant contribution to the clarification of the concept of Christian socialism. He argued that the social-Christian and charitable movement of the nineteenth century from Wichern to Stoecker and Naumann, with its appeal to the goodwill of the individual, had not been in a position to solve the social question because it had not made the step from the individualist-Christian ethic to the social ethic. But the conflicts arising with industrialisation and the formation of the proletariat could not be overcome, according to Smirnov, by a

B

'complete inner reorientation of the individual' – as in the last analysis the social-Christian movement always imagined – on the contrary, this contemporary crisis could only be overcome 'by reorganising outward forms, the structure of society and production'. Christianity and socialism must therefore meet social problems together, with social-political measures aimed at the 'rule of the working proletariat and the dissolution of all other classes within it; . . . not only does the socialist ideal not lie outside the scope of Christian hope, but on the contrary it is in present conditions the most desirable, perhaps the only desirable thing in the interest of the work of Christ.' This identification of Christian and socialist hopes for the future, moreover, was made explicitly with reference to German revisionism; in Smirnov's opinion, atheism and materialism no longer formed integral parts of the political programme of the latter.[43]

The ideas of Smirnov and others were further radicalised by a 'League of democratic Orthodox clergy and laity', formed after the February Revolution of 1917 in Petrograd, among whose founders were the remainder of the 'Group of Thirty-two'. The League supported the political programme of the social revolutionaries, demanded the distribution of the land to the peasants, the handing over of the factories to the workers and the 'liquidation of capital in the name of Christ'. The League therefore campaigned for a socialist revolution which was expected in the near future.[44] A straight line led, after the October Revolution, from the League of Democratic Clergy, to which A. I. Vvedensky and B. V. Titlinov also belonged, to the 'renewal movement' (obnovlenchestvo) and the 'Living Church' (zhivaya tserkov – a schismatic movement which arose in the 1920s, favouring accommodation with the state). A further forerunner of the renewal movement before the Revolution may be seen in the 'Social Christian Workers' Party' (after 1919 the 'Christian-Socialist Workers' and Peasants' Party'), which was founded in June 1917 by F. I. Zhilkin and I. I. Glazunov, and which had a political programme close to that of the social revolutionaries. Among the leading figures in this group was N. D. Kuznetsov, who later played an important role in the renewal movement. A similar group, likewise with only a limited sphere of activity, was formed in 1917 in Kiev under the title 'League of new Christian Socialists'.[45]

At the beginning of the 1920s the renewal movement came into sharp conflict with the patriarchal Church. It greeted the Bolshevik Revolution as the fulfilment of Christian hopes and presented itself as the means to complete this revolution within the Church. One of the forerunners and leaders of the movement, A. I. Vvedensky, took the identification of Christianity with socialism a long way: 'The present so-called Marxism is the gospel reprinted in atheist language.'[46] The politically loyal position of the renewal movement *vis-à-vis* the Soviet power was adopted by the patriarchal Church from the mid-1920s.

The League of democratic clergy and similar organisations, like the monarchist reactionaries, appealed to the New Testament. Each side accused the other of un-Christian, political motives and itself claimed to stand outside and above politics, its actions being answerable to the Christian faith alone. Because no one was prepared to approach political questions in political terms, an extreme polarisation occurred within the Russian Church, which led after the October Revolution to a schism. There was no feasible middle way.

From the Triumph of Reaction to the Patriarchal Election in Red October

The shake-up in the state Church and the loss of authority suffered by the Church leadership became more and more visible in the years before and during the First World War. Through the dependence of the Church leadership on the *Starets* and (in the words of Nicholas II) 'bearer of the true faith' – Grigori Rasputin – the signs of crisis took on an ever more threatening aspect. Metropolitan Antoni of St. Petersburg and Oberprokuror Lukyanov tried in vain to remove the 'wise one' from the court. With Lukyanov's successor, V. K. Sabler (May 1911–June 1915), the office of Oberprokuror was taken over by someone who was completely under the influence of the Rasputin group, and who moreover reintroduced the Pobedonostsev type of Church regime, whereas in the preceding years, with a succession of swiftly changing Oberprokurors unfamiliar with Church matters, the Synod had achieved greater independence. Sabler on the other hand had been Pobedonostsev's deputy in 1892–1905, and now he made use of the undiminished powers of a leader of the state Church in order to prevent the modernisation of the Church. Through Sabler's help, Rasputin made the Synod subservient to himself; the Siberian peasant, 'through whom God directs' (Empress Alexandra Fedorovna), enthroned and dismissed bishops and annulled synodal decisions. The Synod was forced to appoint the semi-illiterate Varnava (Nakropin) Archbishop of Tobolsk and to call Rasputin's friend Pitirim (Oknov) to St. Petersburg to assume the first bishopric of the empire. Sabler's successor A. D. Samarin (July–September 1915), who tried to resist the worst consequences, left the job after only a few weeks, due to intervention by Rasputin and the Empress. These events in themselves were humiliating enough for the Church; they led, however, to a catastrophic loss of authority, because the endless series of Rasputin scandals was discussed in detail in public, in the press and in the Duma. Particularly sharp attacks on Rasputin and the Church leadership in its submission to him came from the conservative parties, who were forced to look on while the state Church, as one of the last supports of the old order, was being compromised and disgraced by an occult wonder-worker.[47]

Sabler in particular came under crossfire in the Duma because he tried as far as possible to circumvent parliament, and rejected the most modest proposals for urgent reforms in the Church which came from the moderate parties. The nationalist deputy V. M. Purishkevich declared in a debate in March 1912: 'Neither the leftists nor the revolutionaries, neither the social democrats not the *Trudoviki* – no one has harmed the Orthodox Church so much in the last three, four, ten years as the present Oberprokuror.'[48]

In the Duma elections of 1912, the state Church led by Sabler intervened in the electoral struggle more openly and insistently than before on behalf of the Octobrists and parties to the right of them. The bishops instructed their clergy to stand as electors and deputies for the conservative parties. This electoral agitation compromised both the Church and the right-wing parties and it was to some extent sharply rejected by them. The result, however, was that forty-six clergy entered the Fourth Duma. It is true that there were already forty-five in the Third Duma; however, their party affiliation now revealed a clear move to the right. The very furthest to the left were two priests in the Progressive Party and two with the Octobrists; forty others, however, stood with the right-wing parties.[49]

Nevertheless, criticism of the Church did not cease in the Fourth Duma: it frequently came precisely from the parish clergy members. It is significant for the isolation of the Church leadership and the shake-up of the state Church that even those priests, who on Sabler's initiative had become deputies of the right-wing parties, launched bitter attacks on the Oberprokuror from the parliamentary platform. They claimed that the leader of the state Church continued to rule autocratically, without respecting the will of the bishops and clergy;

he summoned bishops arbitrarily to the Synod, which, moreover, was often unable to decide technical matters because it had been inadequately informed by the Oberprokuror. If any decisions by the Synod did not correspond to the Oberprokuror's ideas, they were either ignored or only nominally put into practice.

After the departure of Sabler, which was welcomed from all sides (including *Moskovskie Vedomosti*), a group of Duma deputies from the lower clergy presented his successor with a memorandum subjecting the Church situation to a comprehensive criticism. The deputies scourged the Church administration as well as arbitrary action on the part of the bishops and consistories. The bishops were portrayed as careerist young monks looking down contemptuously on the 'white' clergy and without any capacity for directing or caring for their flock. In many bishoprics, they said, the practice of frequently and lightly transferring priests from one parish to another had reached fantastic proportions. This group of priests demanded a restriction on episcopal powers and the strengthening of the meetings of diocesan clergy which in many bishoprics, for fear of the parish clergy, were simply no longer called. It said that the parishes must be made more independent, and that they should do more welfare and educational work. The priestly members of parliament assessed the influence of the Church on the people very pessimistically and spoke of a 'drop in religious feeling' and the 'well-known cool distance towards the Church': 'The authority of the clergy seems to be dwindling more and more . . .' Only the swift convocation of a Council, they said, could prevent further decay.[50]

There can be no doubt that the Orthodox Church lost considerable ground in the decade before 1917; the Church leadership was politically isolated even from the conservative parties, the Church press made continual complaints about the lack of influence of the clergy upon the peasants, and the progressive intelligentsia, with few exceptions, looked down with contempt on the priesthood. The Rasputin scandals, the interference of the Emperor and Empress in the most intimate Church matters, and above all the reforms which had been overdue for more than a decade, led everyone, in the years of the First World War, including the episcopate, to the realisation that the state Church had reached an impasse.

When therefore the Romanov dynasty came to an end in February 1917, no hand was lifted in the Church to save the monarchy or to prevent the Revolution. If any proof were needed that by 1917 the empire had already been largely undermined, it could be found in the fact that even the state Church welcomed the fall of the monarchy. The Synod refused on 27 February to condemn the Revolution, as the Oberprokuror in office, N. P. Rayev, had suggested. Some months later, in a proclamation on 13 July, 1917, it acclaimed the events of February as 'the hour of general freedom for Russia; the whole land... rejoiced over the bright new days of its life. . . .'[51]

In all important political questions the Orthodox Church stood behind the Provisional Government. The Church supported the prolongation of the war by appeals and collections of money and wanted to postpone all social-economic decisions until the convention of the National Assembly. In the summer, when the country began to sink further and further into anarchy and chaos, the Church leadership and Church institutions called again and agian for internal peace in the face of the external enemy. The fatherland was in danger, they said, so strikes and class hatred must cease; it was vital for the people to unite again, despite the barriers of class and political parties. All these well-meant but scarcely effective proclamations by the Church showed the lack of understanding on the part of those with responsibility of the real causes of the 'troubled times'; they had long since lost contact with political reality. However, the danger of Bolshevism, which could exploit the chaos, was recognised. The struggle of the Orthodox Church against Bolshevism was tied up in the approaching electoral fight with proclamations in favour of the Cadets, who by now had lost their grip on revolutionary events.[52]

The fall of the monarchy led to unrest in many dioceses. Stormy meetings were held; in some dioceses the clergy declared the bishops to be deposed. In June 1917, at the insistence of the new Oberprokuror V. N. Lvov, the Synod introduced election of the bishops by clergy and laity of the diocese. Most incumbents were then confirmed by election. The liberal clergy also campaigned in many cases for the distribution of the land to the peasants and for progressive labour laws.

At the same time, revolutionary unrest in the country did not stop at the clergy. Very often the peasants took over Church and monastic land, some priests were driven out of their villages, salary agreements were annulled, and acts of violence were even committed against a few priests. Nevertheless, it cannot be claimed that the unrest was specifically anti-Church in character, as the peasants were concerned more about the land than about the priests.

Although the Church and the Provisional Government agreed over essential political questions, tensions nevertheless soon arose, when it became clear that the Provisional Government regarded itself as a 'power of purely secular character' – 'which on principle stood outside religious denominations'. Its policy moved in the direction of a separation of Church and state, even though at first the reality remained far from this.[53] Even this tendency was enough for conservative circles in the Church to attack the new government as 'godless'.[54] The sharpest conflict arose over the Orthodox Church schools, which on 20 June, 1917, the Provisional Government placed under the Ministry of Education, thus withdrawing them from Church administration. Thus the unification of the primary school system, which had been contested for decades, was resolved against the Church, whose anti-modernist schools found little support even among the conservatives.

The Provisional Government appointed as Oberprokuror the Nationalist deputy V. N. Lvov. In the Third and Fourth Dumas he had led the 'Committee for the Affairs of the Orthodox Faith', and had been among the sharpest critics of the Church in its need for reform. After the Revolution Lvov joined the 'Living Church'. He immediately set about suggesting comprehensive reforms to the Synod, with a new energy, but no less autocratically than the previous Oberprokurors. While his programme was widely welcomed among the diocesan clergy, the hierarchy showed resistance, whereupon, at the beginning of April 1917, the all-powerful Oberprokuror summarily dismissed the Synod and formed a new one; among its members were four 'white' clergy including two professors from the Academies. The chief task of the new Synod was the preparation of the Council, which was now carried out with vigour.

On 2 August, 1917, in the presence of Alexander Kerensky, the Prime Minister, the All-Russian Local Council met in Moscow; it had not been convened for more than 200 years. It was a consequence of the Revolution that the composition of the Local Council corresponded much more to liberal hopes than to the proposals of the Committee for the Preparation of the Council of 1906. Alongside the bishops there were two elected representatives of the clergy and three of the laymen from each diocese; these had full voting rights in the Council. Thus about half of the council members, who numbered almost 600, were laymen. The right of veto, however, was given to a two-thirds majority of the bishops.

The Oberprokuror A. V. Kartashev, who had been appointed a few days previously, made it clear at the opening of the Council that the Provisional Government for the time being continued to claim all prerogatives concerning the Church and retained the right to approve the proposals of the Council for a new regulation of Church-state relations. On 5 August Kartashev, a member of the Cadets, changed the Oberprocuracy into a 'Ministry for Religious Faiths' – which, however, was only an apparent concession to the autonomy of the Church, since only the name was altered.

While the country sank further into chaos, the Council tried to raise its voice for the salvation of Russia. In one appeal it said: '. . . Listen to the voice of the Church. The homeland is perishing.' 'Do penance . . . purify yourselves by fasting and fill the churches with those who are praying.' And to the soldiers: 'Sacrifice your lives.'[55] The ruin of Russia and the tensions with the Provisional Government led to the anti-liberal forces in the Council gaining the upper hand more and more, and finally manoeuvring the Council into an unrealistic political position. While the attempted counter-revolutionary coup by Korni-lov, the Commander-in-Chief, won considerable sympathy from the episcopate, a number of liberal priests and laymen left the Council in protest. Even after the Bolshevik coup the Council held fast to its concept of the 'ruling' role of Orthodoxy. In its recommendations to the Constitutional Assembly it also claimed for the future the inviolable and tax-free property situation of the Church, the recognition of Church marriage and divorce laws, obligatory religious instruction in all general schools and financial support from the state. Thus the Council flatly rejected a separation of Church and state.

While the Bolshevik Revolution swept such resolutions aside, one important achievement of the Council – the restoration of the Patriarchate – has survived up to the present. In the lively debates preceding the election, various speakers from the laity and 'white' clergy stood out against the appointment of a Patriarch, saying that the Church should be ruled solely on the principle of conciliarity. Then the Council decided, within earshot of cannons thundering for the Revolution, to put a Patriarch at the head of the Church, and on 31 October elected three candidates, all with clear conservative leanings: Archbishop Antoni (Khrapovitsky), Archbishop Arseni (Stadnitsky) and Metropolitan Tikhon (Belavin). Tikhon, the candidate with the least votes, was elected Patriarch by lot on 5 November.

Although the Patriarch and the Council openly declared their anti-Soviet position, the Sobor was able to remain in session until September 1918; through its further decisions the Patriarch was given an extra-ordinarily strong position within the Church – decisions which proved

themselves in the coming years of persecution. The remaining reforms
of the Council had come too late, and did not survive the first years of
Church conflict.[56]

The Old Believers and the Protestant Sects between the Edict of Tolerance and the October Revolution

The Old Believers and the Russian sects are those religious groups
which in the course of history have broken away from the Orthodox
Church. Since they owed their existence to what was, according to
theological tradition and Russian law, an illegal act, it was only after
years of long persecution that state and Church were prepared to
recognise the breakaways' right to exist. Under the empire they never
achieved equal rights; it was only the Soviet persecutions of the Church
which for the first time made no distinction between Orthodoxy,
Old Believers and sects.

The Old Believers, who at the turn of the century claimed several
million members, formed by far the largest religious group outside
the state Church. At the same time the Protestant sects, which did not
arise until the 1860s, had achieved considerable importance because
they spread very rapidly throughout the whole empire, chiefly in the
Ukraine, thus attracting massive persecution from the state and state
Church.

The law of tolerance of 17 April, 1905, brought relief to the evangelical sects above all, because the decree of 1894 forbidding the 'Stundists'
(a Protestant movement, its name derived from the German Stunde,
an hour) to meet was abolished. It was under this nickname, which they
gave themselves but later dropped, that Church propaganda lumped together the Russian Baptists, Evangelical Christians and others as
'rationalistic' and 'Protestant' groups. The 'Stundists' were described
in a circular of the Minister for the Interior (1894) as 'one of the most
dangerous and harmful sects to the Church and the state', particularly
because they allegedly preached 'socialist principles'.[57] The untruth
of such allegations soon became evident and was confirmed by the
Ministerial Committee of 1905, where Metropolitan Antoni (Vadkovsky) of St. Petersburg lamented that the Orthodox clergy in
unworthy zeal had let themselves be drawn into repressions against
the 'Stundists'.

After the 1905 law on tolerance many secret Old Believers and
sectarians were able to declare openly their departure from the state
Church. This gave great impetus to missionary zeal, especially among

B*

the Protestant sects. Important concessions in the law now permitted these denominations to open churches, monasteries, prayer halls, schools and charitable institutions. Public meetings, which had formerly been strictly forbidden, were now permitted. In the years of reaction, however, this concession was gradually withdrawn by the government on the grounds that the Old Believers and sects were evangelising among the Orthodox population, which under the law was still expressly forbidden.

Further to this law, an *Ukaz* of 17 October, 1906 regulated the formation and activity of these congregations, which received the legal rights of a person. At the same time the authorities retained wide powers of overseeing the Old Believers and sects and limiting their activity. This was achieved by various means, including the necessity for all communities and for clergy or presbyters to register with the government authorities.

In spite of the continuing inequality between Orthodoxy and other denominations the years after 1905 were for the dissidents the most successful and the least disturbed in their history. All groups became intensely active. Many newspapers and periodicals were founded, whereas up to then all printed matter had had to be smuggled in from abroad; a large number of books and brochures could be published, and local and all-Russian congresses followed one another in quick succession. The liveliness of these communities was in sharp contrast to the frozen tradition of Orthodoxy, for these Church congregations were built up from the grass roots and not by the administration. Participation of the laity in Church responsibility, election of the clergy and leaders by the congregations, and close human contact between the believers were a matter of course for the dissidents. Human solidarity and a rigorous daily ethic which did not tolerate drunkenness, cruelty and dissipation were the chief attractions of the evangelical sects.

The Old Believers in these years attempted to overcome the divisions by which they had been splintered into many different groups. By far the most important, the 'Belaya Krinitsa Concord' which in the nineteenth century had formed its own episcopal hierarchy from Austrian Bukovina, was able to strengthen its position further and to win back a part of those believers who had split off after the 'Circular Letter' of 1862. The priestless Old Believers, too, tried on the initiative of one of their groups, the *Pomortsy*, to overcome their differences, and in 1906 and 1912 they held all-Russian conferences of all priestless groups. On more than one occasion (1906 and 1917) there were even combined councils of priestly and priestless groups. Although the hopes awakened here were only in very small part fulfilled, nevertheless such gatherings created a new solidarity, and contributed to the reduction of the group fanaticism which had formerly been prevalent. The leading force continued to be the 'Belaya Krinitsa Concord', which between 1905 and 1914 was able to build more than 200 new churches. In 1912, at its headquarters of the Rogozhsky Cemetery, Moscow, it opened an Old Believer institute for the training of priests and teachers. The work of this, the largest Old Believer community, was aided by the fact that it included among its members a group of very successful factory-owners and employers who brought it the necessary financial and political security.[58]

The liveliness and activity of the Old Believers between the Revolutions was outstripped by the missionary zeal of the evangelical sects. The 'League of Russian Baptists', which had existed illegally since the 1880s, was able (under the leadership of D. I. Mazayev and V. G. Pavlov) to call its all-Russian conferences regularly, and even to maintain a missionary society from 1907 to 1910, in which year it was dissolved by the authorities as being against the law. The rival group of Evangelical Christians in 1909 formed itself into the 'All-Russian League of Evangelical Christians' which for twenty years was overshadowed by the strong personality of I. S. Prokhanov. Although more than one attempt was made from both sides, personal and theological differences prevented a union of the Evangelical Christians and Baptists from ever being achieved. The Evangelical Christians were much freer both in doctrine and organisation, and it was only gradually, after 1905, that they introduced a regular organisation and permanent presbyters in the communities. In spite of these differences, which were accentuated by tensions within each group itself, a certain affinity remained, and the Evangelical Christians and Baptists sent a joint delegation to the Second International Baptist Congress in Philadelphia (1911), which elected Prokhanov Vice-President of the Baptist World Union.

Successful evangelisation in Russia resulted, by 1917, in a membership of about 200,000 for the evangelical sects, including more than 30,000 Evangelical Christians. A quarter of all Evangelical Christians and Baptists had been baptised after 1905. Particularly large numbers of converts were won in the Ukraine and in Siberia among peasants who had migrated to virgin lands. The sects also carried on successful work among industrial workers, and counted a number of employers among their members. Traditionally the peasant element was stronger among the Baptists, and the urban element among the Evangelical Christians. A number of publications were used in pastoral work and for communication (including *Khristianin*, *Slovo Istiny*, *Gost*, *Utrennyaya Zvezda*); the largest of these, *Baptist*, had a circulation of 104,000 in 1910.

Alongside the two large groups of Baptists and Evangelical Christians, the Adventists and Pentecostals remained only small communities even after the turn of the century. The Adventists had come to Russia in the 1880s under the impetus of German Adventists in Hamburg; the Pentecostal movement began in Finland in about 1908, the ground having been prepared by American Methodist preachers.

The political position of the Old Believers, as of the evangelical sects, had given rise variously to speculation, hope and suspicion, and to massive repression on the part of the state. The revolutionary intelligentsia saw in the dissidents 'political protest in religious disguise',[59] and the social democrats decided at their Second Party Congress to campaign for their programme among the sects. However, the periodical *Rassvet* ('Dawn'), which was founded in 1904 for this express purpose, only reached nine issues. The Old Believers and sects were always suspected both by the state and by the state Church of sympathising with the revolutionaries, or at least with the liberals. Orthodoxy justified its persecution of sectarians largely by the argument that they were a danger not only to the state Church but to the state and the autocracy. The Russian Revolutions proved that neither the hopes of the intelligentsia nor the suspicions of the Establishment were justified.

It is true that during the strikes and peasant unrest of 1904–5 there was an inclination in a few communities to take part in revolutionary activity and forced expropriation of the land, but the leading figures of the Baptists and Evangelical Christians gave stern warnings against deeds of violence, and exercised a moderating influence on their members. After the October Manifesto there arose a short-lived political party consisting of Mennonites, Baptists and Evangelical Christians on the edge of the Constitutional Democrats: the 'League of Freedom, Truth and Peace' had its headquarters in Sevastopol and was led by the Mennonite P. M. Frizen. The programme of the League included equal rights for all denominations, universal equal suffrage, free schooling without class distinction and so on. The Party supported a constitutional monarchy and rejected a national assembly for the purpose of proclaiming a constitution. Despite their impressive programme, the religious groups were clearly unfitted for effective and lasting political work, as they were theologically and politically divided even among themselves.

After this first attempt had failed, the dynamic and inventive I. S. Prokhanov in 1908 founded a Russian evangelical league that was to stand above the denominations; progressive Orthodox circles were also invited to participate. Prokhanov hoped by this initiative to bring about a 'reformation' in Russia and so stave off the growing threat of 'bloodshed of elemental and continual revolutions'. Legal reforms and above all 'the moral regeneration of every individual' were to replace revolution and the class struggle.

The political position of the evangelical sects was clarified by some statements of Pavlov in 1917, when he spoke of his allegiance to 'Christian' socialism of the traditional type, consisting of welfare work and the appeal to the conscience rather than the manipulation of social conditions. 'The solution of socio-economical problems according to Gospel teaching must first pass through a preparatory stage – the spiritual revolution.'[60]

The social-political views and actions as outlined above also convinced the Tsarist authorities; the Ministry of the Interior as well as various police cases confirmed again and again that there was no connection between the evangelical sects and the revolutionary parties.[61]

The same went for the Old Believers. Although there were groups among them (particularly among the workers) who actively participated in revolutionary strikes and sympathised with the socialist parties, Archbishop Ioann (Kartushin), head of the Belaya Krinitsa Concord, declared in December 1905 that the October Manifesto had been forcibly obtained from the Emperor, any further limitation of whose will must be prevented. On 21 January, 1906, a delegation of Old Believers from the most differing groups handed the Emperor a most submissive declaration of allegiance with more than 76,000 signatures, in which the Old Believers thanked the autocrat for ensuring religious and political freedom.

An extraordinary congress of Belaya Krinitsa Old Believers in January 1906 rejected both the extreme right- and the extreme left-wing parties, and formulated a political programme similar to that of the Cadets and Octobrists. The programme called for a constitutional monarchy, civil rights, suspension of all class privileges and distribution of the land to the peasants with compensation for the previous owners. This liberal platform chiefly determined the political opinions of the Old Believers up to the February Revolution of 1917.

Looked at soberly, therefore, the Old Believers and sects gave the Tsarist government no cause to regard them as dangerous opponents; on the contrary, with clever handling these groups could very easily have become reliable supports for a constitutional monarchy. But reaction rejected constitutionalism and in its blindness alienated the religious dissidents more and more from the state and the monarchy.

In the provinces reaction often set in before the Pobedonostsev policy had even been changed, because the local authorities simply did not enforce the law on tolerance; instead they continued to break up 'Stundist' meetings, imprison and sentence presbyters or close and confiscate Old Believer chapels. From about 1908 the central imperial authorities also went back again to repressive and discriminatory measures. Although the Old Believers were also affected by this – for example, according to a circular from the Minister of the Interior of January 1914 they could not be employed as teachers in general schools – nevertheless the evangelical sects formed the main target for the reaction, because these communities were continually growing at the expense of Orthodoxy.

Two decrees of the Ministry of the Interior in 1910 were particularly important in the suppression of public meetings and evangelisation. The 31 March regulations for the religious congresses of the sects were supposed to take away from them the 'character of propagandistic meetings'. In future every conference of Baptists and Evangelical Christians including the programme of the event and the list of participants had to be approved by the Minister of the Interior; worship services at such meetings were strictly forbidden, and a representative of the Ministry of the Interior had to be present on all occasions. Money collections could not be made at congresses – a completely petty regulation.

The regulations on sectarian worship meetings of 4 October, 1910 introduced even further limitations. According to these, all meetings that were not specifically for worship – such as discussion evenings, readings, lectures and organisational meetings – had in each individual case to be approved by the competent official. Children's services and catechismal instruction for children were completely forbidden. The new regulations also prescribed that at every gathering – even at prayer meetings – a police agent had to be present.[62]

These decrees made the work of the evangelical sects very difficult in the following years; they were aimed at limiting the activity of the communities exclusively to worship services, preventing public meetings and evangelisation, and forbidding religious instruction of children. These principles of the imperial Ministry of the Interior correspond in detail to those of Soviet religious policy – a continuum of Russian history that would repay a closer examination.

In spite of all this discrimination, the wave of patriotic enthusiasm at the outbreak of war in 1914 embraced the Old Believers and sects, but even that did not deflect the obdurate reaction from its course. On the contrary, repressions against the Baptists and Evangelical Christians reached their height during the war. These groups, because of their former close contact with German Protestant settlers in Russia, were suspected of friendliness towards Germany and accused of conspiracy with the enemy. Because of the conscientious objectors who existed among them, they were all considered pacifists and traitors.

Reaction led to the situation where the Old Believers and sects, which only ten years before had firmly supported the monarchy, unanimously welcomed the fall of the Romanov dynasty. Thus the Provisional Government, especially under Kerensky, was able to count on the active support of the Protestant sects.

REFERENCES

1. This thesis was put forward above all by J. S. Curtiss in *Church and State*, in C. E. Black (ed.), *The Transformation of Russian Society, Aspects of Social Change since 1861*, Cambridge, Mass. 1960, pp. 405–25.
2. Metropolitan Antoni Vadkovsky, *Rechi, slova i pouchenia*, St. Petersburg, 1912, p. 259.
3. *Svod zakonov* I, 1, Article 40.
4. *Tserkov v istorii Rossii* (IX cent. – 1917). *Kriticheskie ocherki*, Moscow 1967, p. 262; I. Smolitsch, *Geschichte der russischen Kirche 1700–1917*. Vol. I, Leiden 1964, p. 700.
5. *Svod Zakonov* I, Article 42.
6. *Vsepoddaneishy otchet Ober-prokurora Sv. Sinoda po vedomstvu pravoslavnago ispovedania za 1903/04*, St. Petersburg 1909, Statistical Appendix; I, Smolitsch, op. cit., pp. 705 ff.; P. Milyukov, *Ocherki po istorii russkoi kultury;* Vol. II, Paris 1931, p. 210.
7. G. Simon, *K. P. Pobedonoscev und die Kirchenpolitik des Heiligen Sinod 1880–1905*, Göttingen 1969, pp. 139 ff.
8. *Otchet 1903/04;* N. M. Nikolsky, *Istoria russkoi tserkvi*, Moscow-Leningrad 1931, p. 337.

9. *Vserossiisky tserkovno-obshchestvenny vestnik*, No. 95, 1917, quoted from A. Vvedensky, *Tserkov i gosudarstvo. Ocherk Vzaimootnoshenia 1918–1922*, Moscow 1923, p. 57.
10. J. S. Curtiss, *Church and State in Russia. The Last Years of the Empire 1900–1917*, New York 1940, pp. 211 ff.; I. Smolitsch, 'Der Konzilsvorbereitungsausschuss des Jahres 1906: Zur Vorgeschichte des Moskauer Landeskonzils 1917/18', in *Kirche im Osten*, VII, 1964, pp. 59–64; I. V. Preobrazhensky (ed.), *Tserkovnaya reforma: Sbornik statei dukhovnoi i svetskoi pechati po voprosu o reforme*, St. Petersburg 1905.
11. V. I. Yasevich-Borodaevskaya, *Borba za veru*, St. Petersburg 1912, pp. 421–96, here pp. 427, 441–2.
12. 3. *Polnoe sobranie zakonov Rossiiskoi imperii*, Vol. XXV, No. 26, 126.
13. G. Simon, op. cit., p. 252.
14. Antoni's essay in *Tserkovnaya reforma*, pp. 133–6, quotations pp. 133–4.
15. The essays by Antoni and Witte are printed with a bitter attack by Pobedonostsev and a reply by Witte in A. P., *Istoricheskaya perepiska o sudbakh pravoslavnoi tserkvi*, Moscow 1912.
16. The Synod's presentation to the Emperor and the latter's resolution are published in N. D. Kuznetsov, *Preobrazovania v Russkoi tserkvi*, Moscow 1906, pp. 59–61, 63.
17. The most important decisions of the plenary meeting of the Committee for the Preparation of a Council in *Vsepoddaneishi otchet Oberprokurora . . . za 1905/07*, St. Petersburg 1910, pp. 53–64; I. Smolitsch, *Der Konzilsvorbereitungsausschuss*, op. cit., pp. 74–93.
18. Curtiss, op. cit., pp. 306–8; Smolitsch, *Geschichte der russischen Kirche*, op. cit., pp. 681–3; B. V. Titlinov, *Tserkov vo vremya revolyutsii*, Petrograd 1924, p. 28.
19. Nikolsky, op. cit., pp. 356–8.
20. The most important passages of the message in English in Curtiss, op. cit., pp. 259–60.
21. ibid., p. 239.
22. ibid., pp. 270–2, the quotation from the Synod's decision pp. 271–2; M. Galkin, *Mitropolit Antoni*, St. Petersburg 1913, pp. 33–6.
23. Curtiss, op. cit., p. 215.
24. Wording of Antoni (Khrapovitsky)'s sermon in Nikon (Relitsky), *Zhizneopisanie blazhenneishego Antonia, mitropolita Kievskago i Galitskago*, Vol. II, New York 1957, pp. 174–7.
25. Curtiss, op. cit., pp. 255–6, 265, 336–9, 372.
26. V. Sabler, *O mirnoi borbe s sotsializmom*, 2 vols., 2nd ed., Sergiev Posad 1911; A. I. Babi, 'Borba pravoslavnoi tserkvi s nauchnym sotsializmom v Moldavii v kontse xix- nachale xx veka', in *Izvestia Akademii nauk Moldavskoi SSR. Seria obshchestvennykh nauk*, 1/1968, pp. 20–30.
27. The controversy of the Church with socialism, like 'Christian socialism' in Russia, to be discussed later, has been largely unresearched. See F. Haase, *Russische Kirche und Sozialismus*, Leipzig–Berlin 1922; J. Chrysostomus, 'Die Russische Orthodoxie angesichts der zeitgenossischen sozialen Strömungen am Vorabend der Revolution von 1917', in *Ostkirchliche Studien*, XVII, 1968, pp. 297–314. The most recent publications from the

Soviet side: E. F. Grekulov, *Tserkov, samoderzhavie, narod (2-ya polovina xix - nachalo XX v)*, Moscow 1969, pp. 93–101, and M. M. Sheinman, *Khristiansky sotsializm. Istoria i indeologia*, Moscow 1969, pp. 126–66. The dissertation of W. Kunze (Göttingen), now in preparation, will also deal with these problems.

28. Nikon (Relitsky), op. cit., Vol. III, p. 243.
29. Sabler, op. cit., Vol. II, p. 69.
30. Ibid., p. 86.
31. I. P. Pokrovsky, *Sotsializm s drevneishikh vremen i khristianskoe verouchenie*, Perm 1910, pp. 20–2, 27–8.
32. N. Stelletsky, 'Sotsializm, yego istoria i kriticheskaya otsenka s khristianskoi tochki zrenia', in *Trudy Kievskoi dukhovnoi akademii*, June 1905, p. 230; same author, *Noveishi sotzializm i khristianstvo*, Kharkov 1912, p. 78. Both quoted from Sheinman, op. cit., pp. 148, 154.
33. Sabler, op. cit., Vol. I. See VII.
34. Pokrovsky, op. cit., p. 14.
35. I. Galakhov, *Sotsializm i khristianstvo*, Chernigov 1913.
36. Sabler, op. cit., Vol. II, p. 39.
37. P. Scheibert, *Die Petersburger religiös-philosophischen Zusammenkünfte von 1902 und 1903*, in *Jahrbücher für Geschichte Osteuropas*, N. F. XII, 1964, pp. 513–60, quotations pp. 526–8.
38. N. Zernov, *The Russian Religious Renaissance of the 20th Century*, London 1963, pp. 90–110; G. Oberländer, 'Die Vekhi-Diskussion (1909–1912)', (Thesis, Cologne 1965).
39. Quoted from *Tserkov v istorii Rossii*, op. cit., p. 255. – The 'new religious awareness' (Bulgakov), which is characteristic of the first decade of the new century and – as shown – led to a rapprochement of some circles of the intelligentsia to Christianity and the Church, had certain echoes in the Russian social democratic movement. The 'god-builders' (*bogostroiteli*) around A. V. Lunacharsky understood socialism as a new religion without God and proletarian man as a deeply religious being. Lenin also noted the religious feeling of the age, and in 1909 he indignantly registered an 'interest in everything to do with religion' (V. I. Lenin, *Werke*, Vol. XV, Berlin 1962, p. 404.
40. Vvedensky, op. cit., pp. 24–30 (quotation p. 25); Curtiss, op. cit., p. 199; G. S. Petrov, *Dumy i vpechatlenia*, St. Petersburg 1907, pp. 9–13, 38–9; same author, *Tserkov i obshchestvo*, St. Petersburg 1906, pp. 58 ff.
41. Curtiss, op. cit., pp. 202–4. The repressions of the Synod against the left-wing deputies have been discussed on pp. 17 ff.
42. Arkhimandrit Mikhail, *Kak ya stal narodnym sotsialistom*, Moscow 1907, pp. 1, 25; Sheinman, op. cit., pp. 137–9.
43. N. Smirnov, *Iz sovremennykh problem, Khristianstvo i sotsializm*, Moscow 1908, quotations pp. 193, 196, 202.
44. Vvedensky, op. cit., pp. 32–9 (quotation p. 39).
45. The renewal movement itself reckoned among its ancestors the Slavophiles, Dostoevsky, Solovev, Tolstoy, the 'God-seekers', etc. (B. V. Titlinov, *Novaya tserkov*, Petrograd–Moscow 1923, pp. 41 ff.) This arc appears to be extraordinarily extended, but Soviet research even today holds to

this interpretation. (Cf. in particular: N. S. Gordienko – P. K. Kurochkin, 'Liberalnoobnovlencheskoe dvizhenie v russkom pravoslavii nachala XX veka', in *Voprosy Nauchnogo ateizma*, VII, 1969, pp. 313–40).

46. Sheinman, op. cit., p. 181.
47. M. W. Rodzjanko, *Erinnerungen*, Berlin (1926), pp. 14–60; Curtiss, op. cit., pp. 369–76, 390–409.
48. Quoted from Smolitsch, *Geschichte*, op. cit., p. 324.
49. Curtiss, op. cit., pp. 341–3; A. N. Naumov, *Iz utselevshikh vospominanii 1868–1917*, Vol. II, New York 1955, pp. 226–7.
50. Curtiss, op. cit., pp. 290–304, 387 (the quotations from the latter).
51. Vvedensky, op. cit., p. 49.
52. Ibid., pp. 36–47; J. S. Curtiss, *Die Kirche in der Sowjetunion (1917–1956)*, Munich 1957, pp. 26–8.
53. A. Kartaschew, 'Die Provisorische Regierung und die russische Kirche', in *Orient und Occident*, Heft, 1934, p. 4.
54. Vvedensky, op. cit., pp. 104–5.
55. Ibid., pp. 93–5.
56. A. A. Bogolepov, 'Church Reforms in Russia 1905–1918', in *St. Vladimir's Seminary Quarterly*, X, 1966, pp. 44–66; Curtiss, *Die Kirche in der Sowjetunion*, op. cit., pp. 14–44; J. Chrysostomus, *Kirchengeschichte Russlands der Neuesten Zeit*, Vol. I, Munich–Salzburg 1965, pp. 67–112.
57. Yasevich–Borodaevskaya, op. cit., p. 560.
58. V. F. Milovidov, *Staroobryadchestvo v proshlom i nastoyashchem*, Moscow 1969, pp. 61–76; J. Chrysostomus, 'Die Lage der Altgläubigen vor dem Ersten Weltkrieg', in *Ostkirchliche Studien*, XVIII, 1969, pp. 3–15.
59. Lenin, *Werke*, Vol. IV, Berlin, 1960, p. 238.
60. A. I. Klibanov, *Istoria religioznogo sektantstva v Rossii (60e gody XIX v. – 1917 g.)*, Moscow 1965, pp. 264, 270, Note 440 (Prokhanov quotations), p. 279 (Pavlov quotations).
61. Klibanov, op. cit., pp. 225–79; A. Blane, 'The Relations between the Protestant Sects and the State, 1900–1921', (Ph.D. thesis, Duke University, Durham, N.C. 1964), pp. 48–67; L. N. Mitrokhin, *Baptizm*, Moscow 1966, pp. 64–70.
62. Both regulations in Yasevich–Borodaevskaya, op. cit., pp. 625–9, 635–9.

II. Antoni (Vadkovsky), Metropolitan of St. Petersburg

On the eve of the Russian Revolution the Metropolitan of St. Petersburg had a kind of honorary primacy among the bishops of the Russian Orthodox Church;[1] as a rule he was the 'first' (*pervenstvuyushchi*) member of the Holy Synod. Even during the time of the greatest concentration of power in the hands of the Oberprokuror, as connected above all with the names of Pratasov (1836–55) and Pobedonostsev (1880–1905), the Metropolitan of St. Petersburg always exercised a certain influence on Church government, although the guidelines of Church policy were laid down by the Oberprokuror and his officials.

Antoni (Vadkovsky) deserves attention simply because of his position as first hierarch of the Russian Orthodox Church, and the more so since he held the St. Petersburg office during the decisive years before and after 1905 when the Church was undergoing so much political unrest. For a short time in the years 1905 and 1906, supported and pressurised on all sides by the reform movement, he became the spokesman of the desire for renewal in the Russian Orthodox Church. But when, during the years of reaction after 1906, conservative circles both inside and outside the Church raised considerable protest against any reformation of the Church, Antoni could not find the courage and strength to continue with his programme. Being deeply convinced that 'it does not behove the servant of God to fight',[2] and repelled by the struggle of factions and interests, he could not see that there is no politics, even Church politics, without party strife and conflict of interests. In his unworldliness, which in its equanimity bordered on resignation and indifference, Antoni was completely within the Orthodox tradition of the post-Petrine era which saw its task 'in preaching not about the earth and earthly things but about heaven and heavenly things'. In spite of this political failure, Antoni as a personality was certainly one of the most attractive of the bishops on the eve of the Russian Revolution; his life stands out, full of contrasts, from the grey background of a Church in dire need of reform.

Alexandr Vasilevich Vadkovsky was born on 3 August, 1846,

in the village of Shiringusha, Spassk district, Tambov province.³ He came from a typical family of Russian provincial clergy. His father, Vasili Iovlevich, spent his whole life as priest and later archpriest in Shiringusha village, and exercised a patriarchal rule over his large family; as well as the children there were always unmarried relatives living in the house. The family's living standard was very modest. The father had no particular intellectual or political interests and he read no literature beyond his liturgical books. On the other hand the mother, Olga Nikiforovna, seems to have been a lively, open-hearted woman, with whom Alexandr had a close and warm relationship until her death in 1901. She was the sister of the archpriest (*kafedralny protoierei*) in the cathedral at Vyatka, S. N. Kashmensky, who by founding a missionary school led the way in improving relations with the non-Russian peoples in the Orthodox Church and in missionary work among the Old Believers.

Of Alexandr Vasilevich's five brothers, two (Sergei and Vasili) became priests, two others (Yakov and Vladimir) took up the medical profession, while the fifth, Konstantin, was physically and mentally retarded and remained as cantor in the father's village church.

Alexandr himself, growing up as one of a large family in a strong Church atmosphere, was intended for the ministry from his earliest youth; even in the 1860s it was the rule in the priesthood for sons to follow the profession of their fathers and for the daughters of priests also to marry priests.

Alexandr Vasilevich graduated from the Tambov Theological Seminary in 1866 and entered Kazan Theological Academy, where on the basis of his good work he was accepted as a free scholar. But his grant was small and the students lived in very poor circumstances. The gifted, conscientious and inconspicuous student Vadkovsky often did not even have the money to buy himself tea and in winter he was unable to leave the academy building, where the students lived as well as worked, because he had no coat. Because of his extraordinary achievements he remained at the academy as a graduate after completing his four years' study in 1870 and in October of that year he was appointed lecturer in the history of homiletics. This immediate jump from the scholars' bench to the teaching staff was a frequent and in many respects unhealthy occurrence in the academies, whereby the young scholars were usually appointed without the suitability of their training and interests being considered.

Nevertheless, after his promotion to Master of Theology in 1871,

Vadkovsky regarded homiletics as his field of study, and in the following years he wrote a number of scholarly works on the history of preaching in the old Slavonic and old Russian Church times. Vadkovsky devoted more than ten years to study and teaching at the Kazan Academy. From 1875 he collaborated with the Commission for the Cataloguing of the Manuscripts of the Solovetsky Monastery, for the first volume of which he wrote lengthy contributions. He published most of his historical-homiletical essays in the organ of the Kazan Theological Academy, *Pravoslavny Sobesednik*; the editing, which was laborious and poorly paid, was in his hands from 1879 to 1882. Vadkovsky later published the most important of his writings of the 1870s and early 1880s as a collected edition, for which the Kazan Academy in 1893 awarded him the degree of Doctor of Church History.[4] At that time he already belonged to that group of prominent bishops to whom the title of Doctor of Theology, which was given somewhat rarely and involved considerable responsibilities, fell more easily.

With the small salary of an academic lecturer – he was only appointed senior lecturer in 1883 – Vadkovsky could only think of a modest standard of living; still at the beginning of the 1870s he founded his own family. On 30 October, 1872, he married Elizaveta Dmitrievna Penkovskaya, the sister of a colleague. This gentle and constantly ailing wife represented a fateful turning-point in Vadkovsky's life; married to her, he had hoped to lead a peaceful and ordered life as a quiet academic, but on 3 December, 1879, after a long illness, his wife died of tubercolosis, leaving behind two small children: Boris, born in 1873, and Lidia, two years younger. Near to despair, the father nevertheless found strength in the task of providing for the future of his children. But even this stay was taken from him when within a week, on 8 and 15 November, 1882, both children died of diphtheria.

After difficult months of inner searchings, the 36-year-old Alexandr then decided upon a step that set his life in a new direction: on 4 March, 1883, he took his monastic vows before Palladi (Rayev), Archbishop of Kazan, and two days later he was ordained as a priest-monk. As such he received the name Antoni.

There is no doubt that Vadkovsky personally felt the entry to the monastic state as a rejection of the world and as a loss, although at the same time it was to give his life a new meaning in the service of God. On the other hand he must have fully realised that this was the beginning of a professional career that he could scarcely escape. For the

Russian Church in the last decades of the nineteenth century suffered a noticeable lack of monks with scholarly theological education, who alone could provide the next generation of higher clergy. It is significant that in 1883 Antoni was the only monk among the professors and students at the Kazan Academy. In this situation almost every student of a Theological Academy who resolved to take monastic vows could count on sooner or later becoming a bishop. It is clear that among such an episcopate there were a number of careerists, and that the tension, which was in any case always latent, between the episcopate and the 'white' clergy, who were denied all access to the responsible positions in the Church, thereby increased considerably. Antoni (Vadkovsky) certainly did not belong to the careerists, and it was easier for him – not coming directly from the 'white' clergy but still having been a husband and father – to build a bridge towards them than it was for many other bishops.

After some months Antoni began his new life as head of a small monastery in Kazan, and after his elevation to archimandrite he was appointed Inspector of the Kazan Academy on 12 December, 1884. Thereby the whole field of educational work with the students, which with the passing of a new academy statute in the same year received a particular emphasis, was put into his hands. Antoni's systematic patron in Kazan and later also in St. Petersburg was Archbishop Palladi (Raev), who in 1885 appointed him as one of the secretaries to the Bishops' Conference in Kazan. Such regional gatherings of bishops to discuss Church-political matters of common interest occurred several times in 1884 and 1885 on the initiative of Oberprokuror Pobedonostsev. On this occasion in Kazan the Oberprokuror got to know Antoni better. He made a powerful impression on Pobedonostsev and the latter quickly summoned him to St. Petersburg.[5]

We do not know precisely why Pobedonostsev, from the first close acquaintance, was particularly fond of the Kazan Inspector; but it is certain that Palladi (Rayev), of whom the Oberprokuror also had a high opinion,[6] played a part here. For the rest, Antoni's piety and strictly churchmanlike attitude, along with an unpretentious and natural manner, corresponded to Pobedonostsev's idea of a future hierarch. Also Vadkovsky possessed an excellent theological and particularly patristic education, without however having any concrete Church-political ideas or being ruled by a reforming zeal in any respect. He must therefore have given the Oberprokuror, who had the initiative in all important Church appointments, the impression of a man who could be an example to the lower clergy and could easily be guided in all important political questions.

So from 1885 Antoni had protection in high places, which he retained for two decades. In August 1885 he was appointed Inspector of the Theological Academy in St. Petersburg and left Kazan for ever; he was to remain within the confines of the capital for the whole of the second half of his life. Just two years later, on 15 April, 1887, he assumed the headship of the St. Petersburg Academy as Rector, and at the same time, on 3 May, he was consecrated bishop. The elevation of rectors of academies to the episcopate, which became the rule at the end of the nineteenth century, is linked with the extension of their competence at the cost of the professorial staff and with the general strengthening of the authoritarian principle in the Church. Antoni became assistant Bishop of St. Petersburg, and as Bishop of Vyborg he took over the care of the Orthodox communities in Finland.

His main task, however, was the direction of the St. Petersburg Academy, which he set about with great skill. The new academy statute of 1884, which was greeted with widespread distrust on the part of the professors because it put considerable limits on academic freedom and research, corresponded with Antoni's inclinations in many respects. It pleased him that more emphasis was now being placed on moral education and the initiation of the students into churchmanlike piety. Antoni particularly encouraged a more intensive practical homiletic training. After becoming Rector, he founded preaching circles with the students, outside the normal courses of lectures. Their members preached in the churches of the capital after the services, organised discussions, invited people to debates with the Old Believers and sects, and went into the poor areas in order to make contact with the working class, which was moving farther and farther away from the Church. The work of the preaching circles went on within the framework of the 'Society for the Spreading of Moral and Religious Enlightenment in the Spirit of the Orthodox Faith', founded in 1881, with whose internal missionary and charitable work Antoni remained closely linked all his life.[7]

As Inspector and later as Rector he always tried to maintain discipline among the students not by means of punishment but by exhortation and Christian-moral appeals. This was far from normal at a time when the theological schools – the seminaries, at least, more than the academies – were filled with internal and external unrest, which towards the end of the century took on a political character. The young and inexperienced monks who were mostly in charge of the seminaries often tried to meet the insubordination and demands of the students with strict disciplinary measures, thus provoking the students to actual revolt. Antoni was convinced that terror and reprisals were quite the wrong method for overcoming the crisis in the theological schools, and that the Christian life could rest only 'on a lively feeling of sacred duty, but not on fear'.[8]

By this attitude and by a bearing which was far from any hierarchical arrogance, Antoni had a personal influence on many students, which he sometimes used to encourage students towards the monastic life. During his five-year rectorate in St. Petersburg he consecrated at least twenty men – including eighteen academy students – as monks; twelve of these later became bishops. But when Antoni encouraged young men to become monks, he was not thinking primarily of the ecclesiastical duties of future hierarchs, but rather of the monastic ideal of inner perfection. He exhorted the young monks to strive for the highest virtues – of obedience, humility and self-denial – and, on the other hand, warned them plainly of the sacrifices, the loneliness and popular lack of understanding of the monastic life.[9]

Thus Antoni belongs among those men who worked for a renewal and strengthening of the body of educated monks. The most fiery advocate for this was Antoni (Khrapovitsky), one of the most outstanding Russian bishops at the turn of the century. However Vadkovsky never went as far as Khrapovitsky, who believed that monasticism alone would bring about the reform of the Church and the salvation of the Russian Empire. On the contrary, Vadkovsky was convinced that in the theological schools the profane sciences and secular teachers also had an important role, and he did not share the fear of the anxious conservatives in the Church that faith and piety would be endangered by intellectual training and enlightenment.[10]

Antoni's effectiveness as rector won Oberprokuror Pobedonostsev's full recognition; he stated that Antoni had succeeded 'in a short time in completely renewing . . . the spirit (of the Academy) and awakening churchmanship in it'.[11] Pobedonostsev therefore did not hesitate to offer Antoni a still wider field of competence. In October 1892 he was raised from assistant bishop to archbishop; at the same time the Orthodox communities in Finland were separated from the St. Petersburg diocese and made into an independent diocese. With his release from the rectorate, Antoni became the first independent Orthodox bishop in Finland and thereby retained his original diocese. At a time when most bishops were being translated every couple of years from one diocese to another, this was a real distinction. But Antoni did not only make the jump from assistant bishop to archbishop; at the same time he was summoned as an attendant member (*prisutstvuyushchi*) to the highest organ of the Church, the Holy Synod, to which he belonged for the remaining twenty years of his life. The degree of trust that Antoni enjoyed with the Church leadership may be judged by the fact that he belonged to the Synod for six successive years as attendant member – that is as representative of the provincial episcopate appointed by the Emperor – while normally bishops were only called to the Synod for one year or at most two years. After his elevation to Metropolitan of St. Petersburg, he then belonged to the highest Church authority by virtue of his office.

The creation of an independent bishopric in Finland and the appointment to it of a man who clearly enjoyed the confidence of the Church leadership is, of course, connected with the Church's sense of a Russian national apostolate, which saw in Finland a contemporary missionary field, and with the incipient russification measures in the grand-duchy generally. Finland was the smallest diocese in the Empire; at the beginning of the 1890s the Orthodox bishop, who like the former assistant bishop had his seat in Vyborg, had the oversight of only twenty-three parishes, whose Orthodox believers, numbering approximately 50,000, lived mostly in Karelia and were cared for there by twenty-eight priests.[12]

The appointment of Antoni as spiritual overseer of these diaspora communities was, from the point of view of the Russian Church's interests, a happy choice, because Antoni's Russian patriotism was certainly strong, and yet not of that aggressive type which was later to poison Russo–Finnish relations irreparably. As an admirer of the political and theological views of Khomyakov, an early nineteenth-century Slavophile philosopher, he represented a Slavophilism with a strongly Russo-centric accent, which at the end of the nineteenth century often determined the political horizon of conservative and above all clerical Russia. With this background, the victory of Peter the Great over Sweden could sometimes become for Antoni a crusade-like event,[13] and in his great enthusiasm he sometimes missed the distinction between Slavdom and Orthodoxy.[14] In his patriotic rhetoric the Russian people became the 'holy nation', the 'new Israel', called to 'enlighten (*prosvetit*) and renew the face of the earth'; such lyrical self-admiration always contained the originally quite un-

Orthodox idea that the Russian people were the true bearers of Christianity.[15]

In the case of Antoni, however, this imperious nationalism was mellowed by Christian self-awareness, which regarded the non-Russian and the heterodox as neighbours, and by his natural reticence in concrete political affairs. Thus Antoni saw his task in the Finnish diaspora as 'purely missionary', and did his best to make the Orthodox minority, which was largely Finnish-speaking, aware of its uniqueness; at the same time, however, he avoided any open hostility towards the Finnish Lutheran community;[16] he considered it his task to prevent the Finnish and Russian minorities from being assimilated by their surroundings. Even though it later fell to his lot to celebrate N. I. Bobrikov and V. K. Pleve, the protagonists of russification in Finland who both suffered political assassination in 1904, as martyrs for the national cause,[17] Antoni's own work in the grand-duchy was only a prelude to the aggressive russification measures that set in after his removal in 1899.

Let us look briefly at his administration in more detail. He achieved an increase in the number of parishes and clergy in Finland. In 1901 there were thirty-three priests, which allowed for a more intensive care of the scattered Orthodox population in the rural areas of Karelia. Antoni also succeeded in obtaining state grants for the building of churches and schools and the opening of a number of new Church schools. On the other hand, it was impossible to achieve any sure success in the important question of the material support of the rural Orthodox clergy – the clergy in the towns had enjoyed an adequate state salary since 1883.

Over the language question Antoni tried as far as possible to avoid conflict. In his many journeys to the Orthodox communities, he saw that most parishioners spoke only Finnish and did not even understand Russian; he therefore began to learn Finnish himself. The Church publishing and translation work, which was in the hands of the Brotherhood of SS. Sergi and German, was expanded in both Russian and Finnish during Antoni's period of office.[18]

During his ten years of office in the grand-duchy, Antoni on the whole succeeded in raising the level of self-awareness among the Orthodox and in procuring for them a certain publicity in Russia, but he did not manage to raise the small and poor communities to the cultural and material level of the Lutherans. The years of unconcealed russification in Finland after 1899 destroyed Antoni's modest achievements, and severely compromised the Orthodox Church in Finland. The consequence was that after 1905 about half of the Karelian Orthodox went over to Lutheranism or at least sympathised with it.[19]

In December 1898 Metropolitan Palladi (Rayev) of St. Petersburg died. It was he who had ordained Antoni as a monk in Kazan, and who had supported and sympathised with him through his whole church career. According to the way such things were usually reckoned, Ioanniki (Rudnev), the strict, proud and unloved Metropolitan of Kiev, could now count on being called to the capital see. But this was prevented by the Oberprokuror and his deputy, V. K. Sabler, who influenced the Emperor at Christmas 1898 to appoint Antoni (Vadkovsky), who for some time had been familiar with the Church leadership as well as with the capital, as Metropolitan of St. Petersburg. It was, however, impossible to avoid appointing Ioanniki, who was twenty years Antoni's senior, as chairman of the Holy Synod (*pervenstvuyushchi chlen*), although this office was normally held by the Metropolitan of St. Petersburg; Antoni did not receive it until Ioanniki's death in 1900.[20]

It cannot be supposed that the Oberprokuror and his closest associate Sabler had selected the Archbishop of Finland for the office of the first hierarch because of his particular Church-political ability, for the leading officials of the Synod continued to reserve for themselves the political decisions. On the other hand, Antoni's awareness of his spiritual role as a bishop may have been decisive in the eyes of the Oberprokuror. At the farewell banquet in his honour in Vyborg January 1899 he declared: 'I have never been a politician (*politicheski deyatel*) and never will be.'[21]

Although Antoni carried out the duties of his office until 1905 with this attitude strongly in evidence – 'peaceful and quiet', as he himself expressed it – still his work was characterised by an unchanging personal style. It was in accordance with his modesty and personal frugality that he considerably reduced the extravagant style of life in the Metropolitan's residence at St. Petersburg. The frequent banquets and the six-horse carriages of the Metropolitan were abolished. Antoni also simplified ceremonial, and forbade the clergy to greet the Metropolitan of St. Petersburg with a bow down to the ground. He addressed even the cantors, who stood at the very bottom of the hierarchical ladder, as *vy* (formal address), and generally tried to make close contacts with the clergy. Among the petitioners who constantly thronged his reception room, besides the lower clergy, there often appeared peasants in footcloths, who had come to lay before the first bishop of Russia their worries and needs or ask his advice.[23] This accessibility of a Russian Metropolitan was exceptional at a time when most bishops considered that their office demanded a noble bearing and that they should sit in state high above the lower clergy and the people.

Antoni repeatedly warned young bishops at their induction against pride and pious self-sufficiency, and he himself was deeply aware of his own weakness, possessing nothing in which to glory (2 Cor. 12:5).[24]

Since he held the view that 'works of love and mercy stand higher than prayer and fasting',[25] Antoni tried to intensify the charitable work of the Church, which he considered wholly inadequate. He involved himself among other things in the work of the Brotherhood of the Queen of Heaven (*Bratstvo vo imya tsaritsy nebesnoi*) in St. Petersburg, which from 1903 onwards founded homes all over Russia for sick children, especially the mentally sick.[26] He continued to give particular attention and support to the All-Russian Temperance Brotherhood (*Vserossiiskoye bratstvo trezvosti*), which arose in 1898 within the Brotherhood of the Queen of Heaven, dedicated to the spreading of religious and moral enlightenment, and which in 1905 had about 3,000 branches throughout Russia, combating alcoholism among the people.[27] Antoni also co-operated in a number of other welfare societies and he was President of the Imperial Philanthropic Society. He gave almost all the money that came to him personally as Metropolitan of St. Petersburg to good causes, and died leaving no fortune, being in this respect unique among the Russian bishops.[28]

Antoni's practical Christian orientation also found expression in his conviction that Christians should be found among criminals in the prisons; they should go to the outcasts in a spirit of love.[29] Although in this Antoni was adopting a turn of thought that had always been alive in popular piety, nevertheless it caused a stir when in 1900 he personally organised a spiritual ministry to the prisons in St. Petersburg. Every year at Easter he visited the prisons and brought the prisoners the Easter greeting, and after much controversy with the authorities, he even succeeded in penetrating the political prisons of the Fortress of SS. Peter and Paul and Schlüsselburg, where he knew that many of the prisoners were by no means believing Christians. Antoni achieved several amnesties or shortened sentences, and he even appealed on behalf of political prisoners.[30]

Hence, in his activity as a Christian in the world, Antoni went far beyond what was expected of an Orthodox bishop. But even he, like the Church as a whole, was unable to see that the social problems of Russia were not to be solved by charity.

In a description of Antoni's activity before 1905, mention must be made of the foreign contacts of the Russian Church which were largely developed through the Metropolitan of St. Petersburg. As far as we know, relations with Constantinople and the Eastern Patriarchaates did not depart from the usual course during Antoni's term of office. Mutual greetings telegrams were exchanged, Constantinople was occasionally consulted in canonical questions of detail, and the Orthodox brethren of the East expected material assistance from Russia.[31]

Antoni personally was more heavily involved in contacts between the Orthodox Church and the Old Catholics, who from the beginning of the 1870s had been holding unity discussions with the Orthodox and Anglicans. In 1893 and 1897 as Archbishop of Finland, he headed a Synodal Commission to examine the theological basis for a Church union with the Old Catholics. Although he was much interested in the unity question and also sought personal contact with the Old Catholics, he was not prepared theologically for a meeting half way. He agreed with the majority of Russian theologians that the Old Catholics should have to join Orthodoxy and not vice versa because only the Eastern Orthodox Church had preserved the fullness of Christian truth. These fundamental differences in ecclesiology and other theological difficulties meant that Antoni did not share the optimism of the main proponents of union on the Russian Orthodox side, Archpriest I. L. Yanyshev and General A. A. Kireyev, who prophesied a speedy reunion of the Old Catholics and the Orthodox.[32]

Besides its contacts with the Old Catholics, the Russian Orthodox Church at the end of the nineteenth century already had a certain tradition of good relations with the Anglican Church, which Antoni was interested in preserving. He had a special opportunity for putting this into effect when he travelled to England as the official representative of the Russian Church at the Diamond jubilee of Queen Victoria in June 1897. He was received in England with great honour, receiving honorary doctorates at Oxford and Cambridge, and mutual expression was given to ecumenical feelings. In the following years too the Metropolitan of St. Petersburg maintained various contacts with English churchmen.[33]

Antoni's character and his attitude to the world and people marked him as a man who preferred the middle way to all extremes and who was therefore able to mediate between hostile groups. He avoided touching burning issues when it could be foreseen that doing so would involve unrest and confusion.

In almost all areas of Church life there had been for some time dissatisfaction with existing conditions. Criticism was, however, seldom expressed openly, and was completely suppressed among the Church leadership. By 1900 the theological seminaries had reached a severe crisis point, which found expression in ever more frequent seminary revolts. The parishes lacked vitality and there was too little participation by the laity in Church life generally. The lower clergy and the bishops were weighed down by Church bureaucracy. Above all, many bishops and committed Orthodox Christians found the administration of the Church by the Oberprokuror and the secular Synodal bureaucracy more and more intolerable; they no longer accepted the Church as being one among many state bodies without an effective spiritual head. Not until the revolutionary disturbances of 1904–5 was there a broad discussion of the urgently needed Church reforms, and the Metropolitan of St. Petersburg for a short time became one of the exponents of this movement.

For Antoni as well as most of the clergy the revolutionary upheavals came as a complete surprise, and they invaded the life of the Church like a primeval flood. The Metropolitan was only able to see the events in the categories of traditional theological interpretation of history and on 23 January, 1905, he declared before the rioting workers of the Putilov factory in St. Petersburg: 'The just judgment of God has come upon us suddenly.' At the same time he appealed for repentance and penance without understanding that in this way, although his attitude might seem to have theological justification, he could make no contribution to the understanding or overcoming of the political crisis.[34]

Antoni was like most churchmen in his limited understanding of the causes of the 'troubled times'. He had already spoken on this theme in 1887 in abstract cultural-critical terms: the spiritual degeneration of the present time had its roots in man's turning away from God and the Christian Church, and he sharply criticised his contemporaries for being ruled by their concern for their own material well-being instead of caring about the salvation of their souls.[35]

It was the threat of revolution at the beginning of the century which brought this dilemma to light within the Church. A number of theologians and laymen concluded that in future it would be necessary to restore to the Church greater weight and influence in public life, and above all to heal the rift between the Orthodox Church and the Russian intelligentsia. Both these questions were at the heart of the discussions of the Religious-Philosophical Society between 1901 and 1903, the work of which Antoni regarded with favour.[36]

Although these reform discussions began at the turn of the century, it was not until 1905 that the Metropolitan, shaken by the Revolution of that year, turned energetically to the internal reform of the Church – which alone could ensure that Orthodoxy would contribute to the solution of Russia's urgent contemporary problems. The public discussion of Church reform in all areas reached a high point in March and April 1905, when a public declaration was made by thirty-two clergy of the capital. Antoni had approved the programmatic declaration in advance. In it the priests demanded freedom for the Church from state oversight and guardianship so that it could take up its social tasks again and exert a fruitful influence 'on all areas of human life'. The priests also adopted in their programme the two most important points of the reformers: they demanded the convocation of a Local Council and the restoration of the Patriarchate in Russia. It is significant here, as of Church reform discussion generally, that the renewal of the Church was understood as a return to canonical self-government.[37]

The reform movement questioned the whole post-Petrine absolutist state Church structure, and often assumed a liberal guise – this was particularly true of its demand for freedom from state guardianship – but it did not start from genuinely liberal principles. The discussion was usually accompanied by an intensive preoccupation with the canons of the ancient Church, and through them alone justified the far-reaching reform demands. The positive echo and the lively participation of the liberal press in the discussion of Church reform should not deceive the observer into thinking that there was within the Church any real disposition towards political liberalism. Neither Antoni nor the whole episcopate ever questioned the Tsarist autocracy or the social structure of Russia.

Antoni made his main contribution to the reformation of the Church through his work in the Committee of Ministers and later in the Synod, when at the beginning of 1905 both these bodies were occupied with questions of Church reform. A Special Conference of the Committee of Ministers consulted (during six sessions) between 25 January and 1 March, 1905 – with the additional co-operation of the Metropolitan of St. Petersburg – on a Law of Tolerance which was then passed on 17 April and at last introduced freedom of conscience in Russia over matters of belief. The Russian state Church ceased to be an institution of obligation, and its members were allowed for the first time to move to other denominations.[38]

The very participation of the Metropolitan in the consultations of the Committee of Ministers was unusual and it became even more significant when the Oberprokuror completely withdrew from them. For Pobedonostsev must have realised in the first session that Antoni, in deference to his Christian conscience and his canonical training, was putting forward princples that betrayed premises of Church policy that had been regarded as essential over the last two decades.[39] Antoni advised the release from the Orthodox Church of all those who were kept in it only through police and administrative methods, but who according to conscience were no longer in any sense Orthodox Christians. He also called for a repeal of the harsh repressive measures against the sects, in particular the annulment of the Stundist law of 1894, which had forbidden any kind of worship meetings to be held by this rapidly spreading revival movement. But above all the Metropolitan demanded that Orthodox priests be freed from all police duties, as for example the denunciation of sectarians. Force and repression, he declared, could not be advocated from a Christian point of view in questions of faith and conscience.[40]

The Law on Tolerance of 17 April, 1905, in which Antoni's views were to some extent realised, came as a great surprise to the Orthodox clergy and completely altered the relationship between the state Church and the other denominations. There was therefore no lack of criticism in the Church to the effect that the state had now removed its protective hand from the Church. But Antoni declared his pleasure over the new law which, he said, had 'freed the Church from an external shield'; but she would never forfeit her invincibility.[41]

In all the Church reform discussions, the new regulation of Church–state relations was of central importance for Antoni. This becomes clear if we return once again to the above-mentioned conference of the Committee of Ministers. For it was on the initiative of Antoni and of S. Yu. Witte, President of the Committee, that the consultation on the Law of Tolerance broadened into a thorough debate on the reorganisation of the Russian Church leadership. The lively simultaneous discussion in the press probably acted as an extra stimulus.[42]

Both Antoni and Witte submitted a memoir as a working basis for the ministers and heads of department.[43] The Metropolitan had worked out his memorandum, *Questions of the Desirable Reforms in the Organisation of the Russian Orthodox Church*, in collaboration with some professors of the St. Petersburg Theological Academy. The point of departure here was that after the promulgation of a Law on Tolerance, the Old Believers and sects would find themselves in a 'more favourable situation' than the Orthodox Church, which was designated in law as 'ruling', for the state did not interfere in 'their internal and – in the true sense – ecclesiastical life'. The Old Believers and the sects were able to regulate the organisation of their congregational life, the election or appointment of both lower and higher clergy, and many other things, with autonomy and direct responsibility, while the Orthodox Church was constantly hemmed in and controlled by the state in all its activity. So that the Orthodox Church should not lose its influence among the people, the memoir said, it was time 'to abolish or at least to relieve somewhat that constant oversight and that all too watchful control by the secular authority over the life of the Church and the activity of the Church leadership'. The Orthodox Church could 'become an irreplaceable support for the Orthodox state' only 'through a renewed moral authority'.

Antoni was, in accordance with his nature, very reserved and careful in making concrete demands. In his essay he spoke only of the necessity for reorganising the parishes and decentralising Church government, without mentioning directly the Local Council or the restoration of the Patriarchate.

On the other hand, the proposals submitted by Witte to the Special Conference of the Committee of Ministers went much further in content and tone, and the ministers together with the Metropolitan of St. Petersburg set about preparing a completely new regulation of Church–state relations. This was prevented at the last minute by Pobedonostsev, who had absented himself completely from the consultations, and who curtly rejected in writing Antoni's and Witte's suggestions.

Through an interview with the Emperor in 13 March, 1905, the Oberprokuror had responsibility for Church reform removed from the Committee of Ministers and transferred to the Synod alone.[44] But under the influence of the revolutionary events in the nation, and through the pressure of opinion within the Church, even the Synod, with Antoni at its head, was resolved to act and for the first time to exclude the Oberprokuror, who was strictly opposed to a restoration of canonical self-government by the Church.

C

Before the three decisive sessions of the Synod on 15, 18 and 22
March, rumours were already loud in the press that a Local Council
had already been fixed for May. However, it achieved its first success
by obtaining for the three Metropolitans an audience with the Emperor.
In this way Antoni and the other bishops obtained, for the first time in
a century, right of access to the Emperor to inform him about Church
matters. The Metropolitans were later received again by Nicholas II
on 17 December, 1905, 25 January, 1907 and 11 April, 1907.

During their first audience with the Emperor, the hierarchs presented
a petition from the Synod, asking for the convocation of a Local
Council and for the restoration of the Patriarchate. However, Nicholas
rejected the convocation of a Council 'in the present, troubled times'
and thus dashed all hopes for a speedy and thoroughgoing renewal
of the Church. On the other hand he did not put any difficulties in
the way of preparations for a future Council.[45]

Through this decisive action in the critical weeks of February and
March 1905, Antoni inadvertently came under the crossfire of conflict-
ing opinions among a politically aroused public. The liberal press
gave unconditional approval to Antoni and to all plans for Church
reform, and acclaimed the swift decision of the Synod to call a Council
and the disarming of the Oberprokuror, who had long been a symbol
of reaction. The liberals felt satisfaction that the Orthodox Church
was at last on the move, and they saw the Metropolitan of St. Petersburg as a kindred spirit. In so doing, however, they completely overlooked the fact that his ideas of a free Church were rooted solely in
Orthodox theology of conciliarity and canonical self-government.[46]
But on the conservative-reactionary side as well, people were not
prepared or even able to see this connection, and so they for their part
attacked the Metropolitan as a liberal, because of the Synod's over-
hasty decisions in March. He was even suspected of personal ambition,
and the ultra-conservative newpaper *Moskovskie Vedomosti* reported
ironically that his election as Patriarch had clearly been a foregone
conclusion.[47]

But Pobedonostsev felt deeply injured by his former protégé and
felt no inhibition about expressing his bitterness in private letters:
'The local Metropolitan has become unbearable to us and has disgraced
the Church; we feel only contempt towards him. . . . [He] not only
has no shame, but seems to sink deeper and deeper into lies.'[48] Yet,
between March 1905 and his retirement in October, the Oberprokuror
scarcely interfered again in the affairs of Church government. The

preparations for a Russian Council reached a definite stage when, at the request of the Synod, the bishops presented their opinions on questions of Church reform, and in March 1906 when a Committee for the Preparation of the Council began work under Antoni's leadership.

It was characteristic of Antoni and different from most bishops that in drafting his report on Church reform he should have consulted a number of clergy and professors. It was equally significant that the essays of various professors, which Antoni appended to his report, concerned themselves primarily with Ancient, Byzantine and pre-Petrine Church organisation; this was how the twentieth-century reform was to orientate itself.[49]

Antoni demanded that in the future a Local Council should meet regularly as the supreme legislative organ of the Church, and in this most bishops agreed with him. A major task of the Council was to be the election of a Russian Patriarch. According to the Metropolitan, Church life was to be much more broadly and more democratically based than before, and he therefore suggested that alongside the bishop, who was endowed with comprehensive powers, a diocesan council should be set up consisting of elected representatives of the clergy and laity. At the same time the bishop did not need to be absolutely bound by its decisions. Antoni did however want to give this standing council, at diocesan level, the right to elect episcopal candidates, and a corresponding organ at parish level, the parish meeting, should elect candidates for the priesthood. With these views on the responsible participation of the laity in Church life and the broad application of the elective principle, Antoni went much further than most bishops were willing to go in reducing the hierarchical principle. The Oberprocuracy, which had no foundation in canon law, was not even mentioned in Antoni's essay.

It must be reckoned as a shock reaction to the Revolution, but also as a foolish avoidance of reality that Antoni should have suggested that only the upper classes be admitted to the parish meeting in the towns, while in the country all men over twenty-five were to have a seat and a vote in it.

The comments by the diocesan bishops which reached the Synod formed the basis for the consultations of the Committee for the Preparation of the Council which, under Antoni's presidency, did important work in a relatively short time (8 March–10 June and 1 November–15 December, 1906).[50] In his opening speech Antoni emphasised how closely the idea of a Council corresponded to the will of the Emperor, and thus revealed that neither he nor the whole episcopate understood the restoration of canonical Church government in the sense of separation of Church and state.[51] The Church was striving only for internal autonomy; in its unshakeable monarchistic attitude it was still prepared to make all Church political decisions dependent on the Emperor's ratification.

In this spirit, and with the help of first-rate experts, the Committee elaborated plans for the composition and conduct of the future Council and on the reorganisation of Church government, at the head of which was to be a Patriarch elected by the Council. On the other hand, the plans for reform at diocesan and parish level were of a temporary, sketchy nature. All the decisions of the Committee bore a decidedly compromise character, and in many points they fell short of Antoni's ideas; this, for example, was the case over the participation of the laity in the diocesan meeting, which the Committee expressly rejected. Nevertheless, a Council at the end of 1906 would have had an excellent working basis.

However, even before the consultations ended, the growing pressure of reaction was making itself felt upon movements for Church reform. After its catastrophic experience with the Duma, the Tsarist regime was clearly not prepared to risk a Council which would include among its working members representatives of the lower clergy and the laity. It was already doubtful in the summer of 1906 whether the Preparatory Committee would be able to continue with its work, and it was probably due to Antoni's personal intervention that it was able to meet again in November and December. In any case the Synod had to decide in advance to put an end to the Committee's deliberations before the end of the year.[52]

With this the work of reforming the Russian Church from its roots and giving it strength to meet contemporary demands, which had begun with so much enthusiasm under Antoni's leadership, had practically speaking come to a full stop. Some years later, it is true, another Commission for the Preparation of a Council was set up, but it did no original work, only watering down the 1906 proposals in a reactionary way. For example, there was to be an Oberprokuror alongside the Patriarch with equal rights. After a year's existence, the Commission was dissolved again in April 1912.[53]

Thus Church reform very quickly fell victim to reaction, as the result of which Antoni almost entirely withdrew from politics again. In spite of this, he could not avoid being the target after 1905 of a continual opposition from right-wing radical circles within the Church, and the political parties of that persuasion. He bore the awful label of liberal, because he had collaborated over the Law on Tolerance, showed solidarity with the far-reaching demands of the 'Thirty-two', and spoken unconditionally on behalf of a thorough Church reform. Besides this, and in contrast to most clergy, he had separated himself from the right-wing radical 'League of the Russian People' and its terrorist actions. Thus in November 1906, despite repeated requests from the party leaders, he refused to take part in a meeting of the League and to dedicate the flags of the party organisations. Thereupon the 'Black Hundred' initiated a vitriolic press campaign against the Metropolitan, culminating in a pamphlet by A. I. Dubrovin that appeared on 5 December, 1906, in *Russkoye Znamya*, the organ of the League. In it Antoni was accused of supporting liberal bishops and clergy and of having turned the St. Petersburg Academy into a 'breeding-place of revolutionaries'. The writer even made the ridiculous charge that the Metropolitan had behaved in a defeatist manner during the war with Japan.[54]

The whole liberal press felt a duty to defend Antoni, and the clergy of St. Petersburg spontaneously expressed its love and respect for him. Dubrovin retracted his libellous statements, but the Metropolitan's relations with the monarchist right-wing parties and groups remained permanently tense. But he did not ally himself with the socialist parties or even the Constitutional Democrats. He believed that he could keep the Church out of political opinion-forming and party strife. The Church was to be utterly outside politics, and it was therefore logical in 1906 for Antoni to surrender his mandate in the state council, to which he had only recently been summoned. 'It is not the affair of the clergy to be involved in political questions and the building of the state,' he said in the Synod in 1912; 'their immediate duty is the care of the Church and the salvation of the souls of believing Christians.'[55]

How far Antoni clung to an illusion in his idea of an apolitical Church is clear from the fact that in May 1907 the Synod declared that membership of a left-wing party was incompatible with priestly dignity and initiated an ecclesiastical case against the four clerical members in the Duma (Brilliantov, Arkhipov, Kolokolnikov, Tikhvinsky), who did not abandon their parties.[56] On the other side, Antoni (Khrapovitsky), who had many political followers in the episcopate,

described the right-wing radical League of the Russian People as 'the
first and so far the only truly popular, peasant (*muzhytskoye*), democratic institution in all Russia'.[57]

Although after 1906 the Orthodox Church identified itself fatally,
and more and more consciously, with reaction, it did so against the
wishes of the Metropolitan, who, at the beginning of 1906, had already
stated in an official letter to Bishop Vladimir of Kishinyov that priests
should not join political parties. On the contrary, the Synod had said
several times since 1906 that there was no objection to collaboration
by priests in the League of the Russian People. In March 1908, after
pressure from the League, the Synod finally stated publicly that
priests were permitted to take part in the work of the League 'and
other monarchist, patriotic societies'.[58]

It soon became clear that in more and more other Church matters
also the voice of the Metropolitan was going unheeded. In vain did
he warn the missionaries at the Fourth Missionary Conference at
Kiev in July 1908 not to call for state measures and repressions in
disputes with the Old Believers and sects, the only way to conduct
missions being that of love and peace. But the missionaries continued
to demand administrative vetoes and state support in their work.[59]

Thus after failure to achieve Church reform, the Metropolitan of
St. Petersburg could no longer make his authority felt in the Synod.
At this point he must have resigned himself: will-power and deter-
mination had never been his strong point, and he had often spoken
of the boring, prosaic 'business sphere [which] is completely foreign
to my nature'. 'I would willingly live continually . . . as a contempla-
tive.'[60] After 1906 he sought God more than ever not in the storm or
the struggle, but in the blowing of the still wind (1 Kings 19:10 ff.).[61]

Antoni's retirement from Church-political decisions was speeded
up by increasing physical weakness. Since the turn of the century his
state of health had made it necessary for him to visit the spa of Kislovodsk every year, but the disputes over Church reform and the opposition against him visibly weakened his powers of resistance. After 1910
he was seriously ill and almost completely incapable of working. He
died in St. Petersburg on 2 November, 1912, shortly after returning
from the Caucasus.[62]

It is characteristic of the Church and domestic political situation
of the time that his successor should have been Metropolitan Vladimir
(Bogoyavlensky) of Moscow, who had never made any secret of his
sympathy with political right-wing radicalism.

REFERENCES

1. Our faulty knowledge of Russian Church history is even mentioned and deplored by Soviet sources, cf. A. N. Sakharov's detailed and critical discussion of the compilation *Tserkov v istorii Rossii* (IX v. – 1917 g.). *Kriticheskie ocherki*, Moscow 1967, in *Voprosy istorii*, 1968, No. 6, pp. 167–78.

2. Mitropolit Antoni (Vadkovsky), *Rechi, slova, i pouchenia*, St. Petersburg 1912, p. 107; the following quotation ibid., p. 259.

3. The biographical details were assembled from M. B., *Antoni, Mitropolit S.-Peterburgsky i Ladozhsky* (Petrograd) 1915, pp. 13 ff.; *Almanakh sovremennykh russkikh gosudarstvennykh deyatelei*, St. Petersburg 1897, see 'Antoni Vadkovsky'; Tserkovny vestnik, 1912 No. 45, pp. 1411 ff.; M. V. Vadkovsky, 'Moi vospominania o m. Antonii', in *Istorichesky vestnik*, 1916 No. 1, pp. 199 ff.; V. Talin, 'Antoni, mitropolit S.-Peterburgsky i Ladozhsky', in *JMP* 2/1963, pp. 65–72.

4. Antoni Vadkovsky, *K istorii khristianskoi propovedi. Ocherki i issledovania*, 1892, 1895. There is a bibliography of Vadkovsky's publications from the time of his academic activity between 1872 and 1885 in M. B., *Antoni*, pp. 23–5 and Ya. A. Bogorodsky, 'Mitropolit Antoni (Vadkovsky) v Kazansky period yego zhizni i deyatelnosti', in *Pravoslavny sobesednik*, 1913, No. 2, pp. 267–9.

5. M. B., *Antoni*, p. 47.

6. K. P. Pobedonostsev, *Pisma k Alexandru III*, Vol. 2, Moscow 1926, p. 265, of 9 September 1892.

7. The *Obshchestvo rasprostranenia religiozno-nravstvennago prosveshchenia v dukhe pravoslavnoi very* was founded to counter the pietistic, revivalist movement of Colonel Pashkov. On Antoni's relations with the society see M. B., *Antoni*, pp. 229 ff.

8. Mitropolit Antoni (Vadkovsky), *Rechi, slova, i pouchenia*, St. Petersburg 1912, p. 328.

9. Antoni, *Rechi*, pp. 411–64: twenty addresses by Antoni to monks consecrated by him between October 1887 and October 1892; M. B., *Antoni*, p. 70.

10. M. B., *Antoni*, pp. 246 ff.; Antoni (Vadkovsky), *Iz pouchenii vysokopreosvyashchennago Antonia*, St. Petersburg 1895, pp. 77–8.

11. V. S. Markov, *K istorii raskola-staroobryadchestva vtoroi poloviny XIX stoletia*, Moscow 1914, p. 508 (Letter of Pobedonostsev to N. I. Subbotin).

12. *Pravoslavnaya tserkov v Finlandii, napechatano po rasporyazheniu G. ober-prokurora Sv. Sinoda*, St. Petersburg 1893, *Prilozhenia*, pp. 46–7.

13. Antoni, *Rechi*, pp. 116 f.

14. Letter of Antoni to Metropolitan Mitrofan of Montenegro of 11 June 1909 (*Pravoslavny sobesednik*, 1914, No. 5, p. 925).

15. Antoni, *Rechi*, pp. 342–3.

16. M. B., *Antoni*, p. 161 (Antoni's farewell speech at a banquet in his honour in Vyborg in January 1899); ibid., *Prilozhenia*, p. 42 (Letter of Antoni to his parents of 21 June, 1888; quotation here).

17. Antoni, *Rechi*, pp. 509–12.

18. M. B., *Antoni*, pp. 116, 118–19, 153; Brokgauz-Efron, Vol. 70, St. Petersburg 1902, p. 995.

19. *Vsepoddaneishi otchet ober-prokurora Sv. Sinoda po vedomstvu pravoslavnago ispovedania za 1905/07* gg., St. Petersburg 1910, p. 147.

20. K. P. Pobedonostsev, *Pisma k Alexandru*, p. 265, of 9 September, 1892; V. S. Markov, *K Istorii raskola – staroobryadchestva*, p. 270, note 111.

21. M. B., *Antoni*, p. 160.

22. Ibid., *Prilozhenia*, p. 184 (Letter of Antoni's to O. S. L. of 19 February, 1900).

23. M. Galkin, *Mitropolit Antoni*, St. Petersburg 1913, pp. 59–60; M. B., *Antoni*, pp. 73 ff., 184.

24. Antoni, *Rechi*, pp. 250–4, 276, 278–9, 293, 319–20.

25. M. V. Vadkovsky, 'Moi vospomiania o mitropolite Antonii', in *Istoricheski vestnik*, 1916, No. 2, p. 491.

26. M. B., *Antoni*, pp. 179–80; *Tserkovnie vedomosti*, 1912, No. 45, p. 1832.

27. M. B., *Antoni*, pp. 233–4.

28. Ibid., pp. 173, 182–3; *Tserkovny vestnik*, 1912, No. 51/52, col. 1614.

29. Antoni, *Iz pouchenii*, p. 112.

30. M. B., *Antoni*, pp. 174 ff.; Galkin, *Mitropolit Antoni*, pp. 45–6; Antoni, *Rechi*, pp. 112, 212–15; M. V. Vadkovsky, *Moi vospominania*, pp. 481–2.

31. A. Dmitrievsky, 'V Bozhe pochivshi mitr. Peterburgsky Antoni i yego snoshenia po delam tserkovnym s pravoslavnym Vostokom', in *Pravoslavny sobesednik*, 1914, No. 4, pp. 598–606; No. 5, pp. 920–31.

32. V. A. Kerensky, 'Mitropolit Antoni (Po povodu knigi M. N. "Antoni, mitropolit S.-Peterburgsky i Ladozhsky")', in *Istorichesky vestnik*, 1916, No. 6, pp. 729–30; Antoni, *Rechi*, p. 459; on relations between the Old Catholics and the Russian Orthodox Church generally, Steinwachs, 'Die Unionsbestrebugen im Altkatholizismus', in *Internationale kirchliche Zeitschrift*, I, 1911, pp. 169–86, 471–99.

33. M. B., *Antoni*, pp. 123 ff., 191–2; M. V. Vadkovsky, *Moi Vospominania*, pp. 489–90.

34. Antoni, *Rechi*, pp. 89–91.

35. Ibid., pp. 350 (quotation from here), 395–6, 401, 478 ff.

36. G. Florovsky, *Puti russkago bogoslovia*, Paris 1937, pp. 470 ff.; M. B., *Antoni*, p. 245.

37. I. V. Preobrazhensky (ed.), *Tserkovnaya reforma: Sbornik statei dukhovnoi i svetskoi periodicheskoi pechati po voprosu o reforme*, St. Petersburg 1905, pp. 1–6.

38. 3. *Polnoe sobranie zakonov XXV*, No. 26126 (of 17 April, 1905).

39. S.Yu. Witte, *Vospominania*, Vol. 2, Moscow 1960, pp. 360, 362.

40. V. I. Yasevich-Borodaevskaya, *Borba za veru*, St. Petersburg 1912, p. 427; M. B. Antoni, p. 195; *Otchet 1905/07*, pp. 16–20.

41. Antoni, *Rechi*, p. 288.

42. S.Yu. Witte, *Vospominania*, pp. 363–4.

43. Cf. above pp. 12–13.

44. 'Iz tserkovnykh bumag K. P. Pobedonostseva', in *Krasny arkhiv*, 18, 1926, p. 205.

45. *Otchet 1905/07*, pp. 37–8, 64–5; the petition of the Synod to the Emperor

and his resolution of 31 March 1905 are printed in Nikon (Rklitsky), *Zhizneopisanie blazhenneishego Antonia, mitropolita Kievskago i galitskago*, Vol. 3, New York, 1957, pp. 27–30 (quotation from p. 30); I, Smolitsch, *Geschichte der russischen Kirche 1700–1917*, Leiden 1964, pp. 316–19. The quotation in Smolitsch on pp. 320–1, supposedly from a conversation of the Emperor with Antoni on 27 December, 1905, actually comes from an imperial rescript of the same day; there was no audience with the Metropolitans that day (*Otchet 1905/07*, p. 39).

46. Preobrazhensky, *Tserkovnaya reforma*, pp. 23, 47, 116–17, 432–3 and passim.

47. Ibid., pp. 73–6, 190–3, 286.

48. 'K. P. Pobedonostsev v dni pervoi revolyutsii (Neizdannie pisma K S. D. Voytu)', in *Na chuzhoi storone*, 8, 1924, p. 186, No. 18, p. 188, No. 20. (Letters of 16 March and 7 April, 1905).

49. Antoni's paper in *Otzyvy yeparkhialnykh arkhiereev po voprosu o tserkovnoi reforme*, Vol. 3, St. Petersburg 1906, pp. 83–175 (pp. 100–75 essays of various professors on individual questions). Comparison with the positions of other bishops may be made through *Svodki otzyvov yeparkhialnykh preosvyashchennykh po voprosam tserkovnoi reformy*, St. Petersburg 1906. General presentation of the bishops' memoranda in I. Smolitsch, 'Der Konzilsvorbereitungsausschuss des Jahres 1906. Zur Vorgeschichte des Moskauer Landeskonzils von 1917/18', in *Kirche im Osten*, 1964, VII, pp. 64–74, and N. Zernov, *The Russian Religious Renaissance of the 20th Century*, London (1963), pp. 70 ff.

50. On the Committee for the Preparation of the Council compare the extensive essay by Smolitsch mentioned in Note 49. The most important decisions of the Committee are in *Otchet 1905/07*, pp. 53–64.

51. Antoni, *Rechi*, pp. 94–97.

52. Ibid., pp. 97–101.

53. Nikon (Rklitsky), *Zhizneopisanie Antonia*, pp. 197–201.

54. Galkin, *Mitropolit Antoni*, pp. 33–6; M. B., *Antoni*, pp. 224–5; content of the article by Dubrovin given in J. Sh. Curtiss, *Church and State in Russia. The Last Years of the Empire 1900–1917*, N.Y. 1940, p. 210 (quotation here also).

55. Galkin, op. cit., p. 70. The authenticity of these words of Antoni rests solely on oral tradition.

56. Curtiss, *Church and State*, pp. 205, 242.

57. Letter of Antoni (Khrapovitsky) to N. A. Berdyaev of the year 1909 in reply to the collection *Vekhi* in which Berdyaev was co-editor (Nikon (Rklitsky), *Zhizneopisanie*, Vol. II, p. 189.

58. Curtiss, *Church and State*, pp. 270–2 (quotation from the Synod's declaration ibid., p. 272).

59. Galkin, *Mitropolit Antoni*, pp. 29–30; N. B., *Antoni*, p. 242.

60. Letter from Antoni to O. S. L. of 31 July 1890 (M. B., *Antoni, Prilozhenia*, p. 162, cf. pp. 161, 185).

61. Antoni, *Rechi*, pp. 246–7.

62. M. B., *Antoni*, pp. 246–54; V. A. Kerensky, *Mitropolit Antoni*, pp. 726–7.

III. The Soviet State and the Church

The Situation of the Russian Orthodox Church since the Revolution

The political situation of the Russian Orthodox Church and of all other religious groups in the Soviet Union is governed by two principles which are logically contradictory. On the one hand the Soviet Constitution of 5 December, 1936, Article 124, guarantees 'freedom to hold religious services'.[1] On the other hand the Communist Party has never made any secret of the fact, either before or after 1917, that it regards 'militant atheism' as an integral part of its ideology and will regard 'religion as by no means a private matter'.[2] It therefore uses 'the means of ideological influence to educate people in the spirit of scientific materialism and to overcome religious prejudices . . .'[3] Thus it is the goal of the C.P.S.U. and thereby also of the Soviet state, for which it is after all the 'guiding cell',[4] gradually to liquidate the religious communities. This goal is absolutely impossible to reconcile with freedom of belief and religion, which is guaranteed by the constitution, not merely as a temporary right for a transitional period. Thus the constitution guarantees something which it is an important domestic political aim of the state to destroy. Nevertheless, these two contradictory principles of freedom of belief and state obligation in respect of atheist education and the eventual defeat of all religions constitute one of those paradoxes which may easily be lived with and which permit a flexible, pragmatically orientated policy.

Thus from the beginning the Soviet authorities interpreted the right of free religious practice very narrowly. The basic decree of the Council of People's Commissars 'On the Separation of the Church from the State and of the School from the Church' of 23 January/5 February, 1918, lays down among other things that 'instruction in religious knowledge is not permitted' either in public or in private schools. 'Church and religious societies do not have the right to property. They do not have the legal rights of a person.'[5] Thus the victors of 1917 never thought of an equality of opportunity in the sense of a pluralism between atheistic Marxism and the religious outlook, even though the constitution of the R.S.F.S.R. (Russian Republic) of

10 July, 1918, and 11 May, 1925, guaranteed 'freedom of religious and anti-religious propaganda' (Art. 13 of 1918; Art. 4 of 1925).[6]

The first post-revolutionary years were in fact characterised by a sharp struggle against the Church, which hit the Russian Orthodox Church particularly hard, since it was regarded as the ally of the former ruling classes. In destroying the latter, the Soviet authorities thought they could also finally destroy the social-economic foundations of the Orthodox Church. However, this supposition proved to be false; the Orthodox Church was considerably weakened by the revolutionary reprisals of the Soviet power, but its existence even after the expropriation of the 'old exploiter classes' continued to be secure for the foreseeable future.

This, together with the hardening of the general domestic political climate and the establishment of Stalinism at the end of the 1920s, led to a new shrinkage in what the Soviet authorities understood by religious freedom. The legal basis for the Stalinist persecution of the Church, which by the beginning of the Second World War led to an almost complete devastation of the institutionalised Church, was the R.S.F.S.R. Law of 8 April, 1929.[7] It forbade the religious communities any kind of social, charitable or religious-educational activity. They were forbidden 'to organise special meetings for children, young people or women, for prayer or other purposes, likewise general Bible, literary or handwork meetings, gatherings for common work, religious instruction or other ends . . . also to arrange excursions and children's playgrounds, to open libraries and reading rooms, to organise sanatoria or medical assistance' (Art. 17c). The Churches were not allowed 'to give their members material aid' (Art. 17b). This catalogue of prohibitions gave very clear expression to a basic feature of Soviet religious policy that had been consistently applied since 1917, namely to limit the whole life of all religious groups largely to the worship meetings, in the narrowest sense, and thereby to restrict the influence of the Churches on society as far as possible. It may be said that domestic Soviet policy on the whole has achieved this aim, for the Churches in the Soviet Union today, despite their many millions of active members, are a fringe phenomenon in society and cannot assume any influence, on their own initiative, upon the solution of cultural, social or general political questions. It is probably to this limitation to the narrow internal Church sphere that they owe their survival in an atheist state – unwillingly tolerated, but legal.

The Law of 1929, however, not only set strict limits to the activity

of religious communities but at the same time it gave the state authorities comprehensive rights of control and intervention. Every congregation, its administrative organs and its ministers had to be registered
with the competent executive committee (*ispolkom*) of the Soviets
(Arts. 4–8); the registering authority could exclude individual members
from the administrative body (Church council) elected by the congregation (Art. 14). Congregational meetings, apart from the service of
worship, processions and religious open-air gatherings, had to receive
special permission in each individual case; likewise congresses and
conferences of religious societies at local or inter-regional level (Arts.
12, 59, 20). The law gave the regional executive committee and its
equivalent outside the region far-reaching powers for the liquidation
of churches which could be decreed if 'the building is required for state
or public purposes' (Art. 36). Alongside these individual provisions,
which made it possible at any time to interfere in or abolish Church
communities, and only the most important of which have been
mentioned here, the state authorities received in a very generally
formulated way 'oversight over the activity of religious societies as
well as over the condition of the buildings and cultic objects granted
to them on the basis of a contract of use' (Art. 64).

As a result of this Law, Art. 4 of the R.S.F.S.R. constitution of 1925
was altered and freedom of religious propaganda was removed; any
kind of internal mission was thus prohibited to the Church. The
constitution now spoke only of 'freedom of religious profession and
of anti-religious propaganda';[8] this formulation then went into the
Stalinist constitution of 1936 in a slightly emended form.

The extensive application of the laws on religion, massive atheist
propaganda and Stalinist terror in the 1930s had led by the eve of the
Second World War to the complete destruction of several denominations including the Baptists, the Evangelical Christians and the Evangelical-Lutheran Church. Even the Russian Orthodox Church as an
institution seemed in 1939 to be on the eve of disintegration. In the
whole of the Soviet Union there were only a few hundred clergy and
open churches left, only seven bishops were still in office and all
diocesan administrations, except those in Moscow and Leningrad,
had had to cease their activity.[9]

These apparent successes 'in the liberation of the working masses
from religious prejudices' did not, however, prevent Stalin at the
beginning of the war from making a complete about-turn in tactics
towards the religious communities and in particular the Orthodox

Church. During the years of the Second World War and immediately afterwards, the Russian Orthodox Church, tolerated and to some degree expressly protected by Stalinist Soviet patriotism, was able to build up a new Church administration which has secured the survival of the institutionalised Church up to today. The Russian Church owes this reversal of Stalinist tactics to her unconditional political loyalty to the Soviet regime since 1923 and especially since 1927, as well as to her sacrificial and selfless patriotism during the war. If one wants to understand Stalin's surprising change of attitude towards the Orthodox Church, it must also be remembered that in the integration of the Western lands of the Ukraine and Byelorussia, newly acquired in 1939, the Church found a not insignificant role which was recognised and exploited by Soviet policy. There was also Stalin's basic policy during the war of mobilising all forces to defend the country and in many cases of setting aside internal disputes. Besides that, the relaxation of the strong pressure against the Church must have had a favourable effect abroad; lastly, the Soviet ideologists (setting aside the Party programme) could this time appeal to the 'freedom of religious services' as guaranteed in the Constitution, when anti-Church propaganda was almost completely suspended after 1941.

For all these reasons Stalin was prepared to countenance the unconditional deployment of the Russian Orthodox Church in the war of propaganda and psychology. On 4 September, 1943, he received the three first hierarchs in the Kremlin, and four days later Metropolitan Sergi (Stragorodsky), for almost two decades patriarchal *locum tenens*, could be elected Patriarch by a hastily convened Synod of Bishops (*Sobor*).[11] In October of the same year there was called into existence a 'Council for Russian Orthodox Church Affairs with the Council of People's Commissars of the U.S.S.R.' With its lower branches down to regional level, this new body took over the position of mediator between state and Church. On the one hand it had the oversight of Church activity, while on the other hand it was to facilitate the reconstruction by the Orthodox Church of its administration – within certain limits. With this the state granted the Russian Orthodox Church an expressly privileged position which was retained when, in the summer of 1944, a corresponding 'Council' for all other confessions together was established.[12]

When the newly elected Patriarch Sergi died a few months after his enthronement in May 1944, the Russian Orthodox Church was able, with the active support of Soviet authorities, to hold a Local Council in Moscow from 31 January to 2 February, 1945. This time it was attended by representatives of the parochial clergy and the laity as well as guests, including the Patriarchs of Alexandria and Antioch. The Council unanimously elected as the new Patriarch the proposed candidate, Metropolitan Alexi (Simansky) of Leningrad; Alexi held this office for twenty-five years until his death on 17 April, 1970. The Council also approved without debate a 'Statute on the Administration of the Russian Orthodox Church', which had been worked out beforehand in consultation with the Council for Russian Orthodox Church Affairs. For the first time since the Revolution this statute established the Church administration with its organs and their competence in a canonically valid form.[13] The Soviet state thereby tolerated a Church organisation which it could in fact control at any time, but which, in order to be viable, claimed for itself powers of self-administration that went beyond the decrees of Soviet law. For in its statute the Orthodox Church established the hierarchical right of authority and appointment – this was clear in canon law – the duty of maintaining Church discipline, and the payment of parish offerings to the Church government and towards general Church needs (Arts. 24, 30, 36, 41); all these provisions are difficult to reconcile with the prohibition laid down in the 1918 Decree on 'compulsory measures' (Art. 11).[14]

Besides this, a decree of the Soviet government of 22 August, 1945, considerably improved the legal status of the Russian Orthodox Church by granting it 'legal rights . . . to obtain means of transport, to acquire Church equipment and cultic objects, to sell these objects to the communities of the faithful, to rent, build and acquire houses for Church needs with the permission of the Council [for Russian Orthodox Church Affairs]. . . .'[15]

All these liberal measures by the Soviet government, briefly sketched here, gave the Russian Orthodox Church more freedom of movement than it had ever had after 1917. At the same time, the considerably harsher religious laws of 1918 and 1929 were not repealed, although they were irreconcilable with the 1945 decree in a number of points (Art. 12 of the 1918 decree; Art. 11 of the 1929 Law). Thus the state always kept open the possibility of returning to the repressive statutes. Even at this time there could be no mention of a concordat between Church and state in the sense of a mutually binding agreement.

Nevertheless, by 1949 there were again seventy-four Orthodox bishops in office, administering seventy-three dioceses; but there were always many of these vacant, because in several important dioceses (as was the practice since the nineteenth century) assistant bishops were also in office. Between 1944 and 1947, the Church was able once again, for the first time since the end of the 1920s, to organise a systematic theological training for new priests, as well as to open two theological academies and eight seminaries. However, the state did not permit any further expansion of Orthodox teaching establishments.[16] But the Russian Church was able over a period of about fifteen years, with relative freedom, to reorganise its parishes, and when in 1961 it applied to join the World Council of Churches, it gave the number of parishes as 20,000, cared for by 30,000 priests.[17] There are no exact figures for the number of practising believers behind these statistics. One is reduced here to guesswork, which for the end of the 1950s varies between 20 and 40 million. Important considerations leading to these estimates, which are, under the circumstances, extraordinarily high, are on the one hand the overflowing churches even outside of Church festivals, and on the other the relatively free flow of money in the congregations, which must be maintained completely at the believers' expense.[18]

On balance it must be said that the Orthodox Church in the Soviet Union – protected by its unquestionable loyalty to the state – was able between the beginning of the Second World War and the end of the 1950s to build itself up; its existence was in principle always fragile but was relatively secure for the immediate future. This impression seemed all the more justified when Stalin's successors, even more than the dictator himself, drew the Church into their foreign policy, and it played an outstanding role in the international peace movement.

The Policy of Repression 1959–1964

The years when Khrushchev was at the height of his power are characterised by a renewed thrust of aggression by Party and state against the religious communities, which hit the Orthodox Church particularly hard. At first sight this may seem surprising, since Khrushchev's domestic policy is often characterised as a relaxation or even a de-ideologisation of the Soviet system of government. One speaks of 'new tendencies, reforming ideas in the various spheres of life', of a 'process of emancipation' for Soviet society, of 'modernisation'[19] and pragmatism as the guidelines of a Soviet development that was oriented towards the future and towards the problems of a modern industrial society. On the other hand, in a number of areas Khruschchev's policies were determined solely by doctrinaire ideological viewpoints,

and in general they aimed at strengthening the influence of the Party
on the state and society. Just as the educational reform and Khrushchev's agricultural policy are only properly to be understood when
their ideological motivation is borne in mind, so in Soviet religious
policy from the end of the 1950s the task of overcoming 'religious
survivals' again became the central point for all concrete measures.
This was all the more so, since the Church organisations that had
again been consolidated since the war must have been a particular
thorn in the flesh for the CPSU in the phase of 'the developed building
of Communism' declared by Khrushchev. The favours that Stalin
had granted the Church were now branded as 'departures from Leninist
legality',[20] that is, the struggle against the Church must be waged not
only with propaganda methods but also by the withdrawal of previous
concessions and by administrative pressure.

This renewed intensification of the struggle against the Church,
initiated by Khrushchev, did not however make itself felt in the years
immediately following Stalin's death, while his successors fought out
among themselves the battle for power. One might even have gained
the impression from a resolution of the C.P.S.U. Central Committee
of 10 November, 1954, announced by Khrushchev as First Secretary,
that the Soviet government had no immediate intentions of taking
new repressive measures against the Church. The resolution 'On
Errors in the Use of Scientific-atheist Propaganda among the People'[21]
reminded people once more that atheist propaganda must 'avoid any
injury to the feelings of believers', that it was not right 'to harbour
political suspicions against Soviet citizens on account of their religious
convictions', and that the 'servants of the Church', 'in the majority',
adopted 'likewise a loyal attitude towards the Soviet government'.
At the same time the Central Committee dissociated itself from 'cases
of administrative interference in the activity of religious societies',
and very correctly observed that 'administrative measures and offensive
words' only led to a 'hardening of religious prejudices'. In this observation by the Central Committee, not only must one see a reference to
Stalin's campaign of extermination against the Churches before the
Second World War, but it is essential to remember that a sharp control
was always exercised over the Church and police interference in
internal Church administration persisted even in the years of relative
freedom of movement after 1941. The Central Committee added to
its self-critical remarks the urgent observation that the social roots of
religion in the Soviet Union had been destroyed once and for all, and

that it was now more important than ever to wage a strengthened ideological struggle for the final eradication of religious survivals. The overcoming of the 'unscientific, religious outlook' by the 'scientific, materialist one' for the Central Committee thus implied only the establishment of a victory that had long since been won. The Party was exhorted to devote itself to this task with greater energy than before.

However, despite this Central Committee decision of November 1954, atheist activity in the years immediately following was not strengthened but rather further neglected.[22] Other more important problems stood at the forefront of Soviet domestic policy. But from 1958 to 1959 the Party and the state turned to religious policy again with renewed concern, and a broad-fronted atheist attack now began which took its chief bite from precisely those 'administrative methods' which the Central Committee had condemned in 1954.

The new phase opened with press campaigns against the Church and the clergy and a rapid increase in atheist publishing after 1958. The increasing number of cases of public apostasy by Orthodox clergy and lay people, under the pressure of individual agitation and communist enticements, were used here to great effect. Particular attention was aroused by the defection of A. A. Osipov, Professor of Old Testament at the Leningrad Theological Academy, which he announced in *Pravda* on 9 December, 1959.[23]

Surprisingly, the Moscow Patriarchate did not take this provocation lying down, but reacted – probably relying on the relatively wide freedom of action that it had been permitted in the previous years – with the excommunication of the apostates, of whom four (including Osipov) were mentioned by name. The Synod reached the decision to exclude the apostates who had 'publicly blasphemed the name of God' on 30 December, 1959; the Synod's decision was announced in the journal of the Patriarchate in February 1960. The Russian Church was thereby making a defence which, although weak, was still a public one; this had not happened for more than thirty years.[24]

A similar example of cautious opposition to the new state pressure was the address given by Patriarch Alexi on 16 February, 1960, to the conference of political and social organisations of the U.S.S.R. for disarmament. On the one hand he proclaimed the great achievements of the Orthodox Church in Russian history, but on the other he complained about the 'insults and attacks' of men to which the Church was exposed, and expressed his conviction that the gates of hell would never overcome the Church.[25]

The state reacted immediately to these concealed signs of Church opposition with decisive measures that were symptomatic of the more hostile attitude of state and Party towards the Church. The two men who on both sides had mediated the *modus vivendi* since 1943 were disposed of. G. G. Karpov, who had been President of the Council for Russian Orthodox Church Affairs since its inception, was replaced on 21 February by V. A. Kuroyedov, who transformed this Council from an instrument for the control of the Church into a tool of aggressive suppression.[26] On the Church side, the Patriarch's closest assistant, who represented the Russian Orthodox Church in political matters at home and abroad, was forced to retire. Nikolai (Yarushevich), Metropolitan of Krutitsy and Kolomna,[27] was in June 1960 relieved of the leadership of the Foreign Department of the Moscow Patriarchate and in September of the same year he lost the control of the Moscow diocese. Since the war he had become known to an international public through his political and patriotic activity in the service of the Church and Soviet foreign policy, but he probably stood out against the new reprisals demanded by Khrushchev's government. Metropolitan Nikolai was practically put under house arrest after his fall from power, and at the end of 1961, obviously against his will, he was placed in a Moscow hospital, where he died without witnesses on 13 December. Suspicions have never been silenced since then that he was forcibly done away with by the Soviet authorities, and today he is regarded by believers as a martyr.[28]

The successor to Nikolai as head of the Patriarchal Foreign Department, and thus international representative of the Church, was the young, ambitious and versatile Nikodim (Rotov), who in a very short time had made a striking career. Born in 1929, he became a monk in 1947 and a priest two years later; in 1956 he became a member of the Russian Mission in Jerusalem and in 1959 head of the Patriarchal chancellery. In June 1960, at the age of thirty-one, he took over the Foreign Department; at the end of 1960 he became a bishop, and in September 1963 he rose to be Metropolitan of Leningrad.[29] In his political statements, Nikodim has always followed the tradition of the Orthodox Church in the Soviet Union, and even during the time of Khrushchev's repressive measures, he maintained the outward appearance, claiming that there was no conflict between Church and state. After the unsuccessful attempts at concealed opposition, the Patriarchal Church sees in this meek tolerance the only hope of resistance.

In May 1972 Nikodim relinquished his office as head of the Church's Foreign Department for health reasons – according to the official announcement. He retained his post as Metropolitan of Leningrad. His successor in the Foreign Department was Metropolitan Yuvenali (Poyarkov), who had already been Nikodim's deputy in Moscow since 1965. Pending proof to the contrary, there is no reason to suppose that political difficulties and conflicts with state and Party were the cause of Nikodim's retirement. On the contrary, it is very likely that even in the future the basic decisions on the Patriarchate's foreign relations will remain his responsibility. For this purpose an expanded Commission of the Holy Synod on Questions of Christian Unity and Inter-Church Relations was created simultaneously in May 1972 under Nikodim's presidency. Obviously suffering from some ailment, the Metropolitan of Leningrad was thus freed from the considerable daily burden of his work as head of the Foreign Department.

The year 1960 brought not only new men to the most important offices in Church–state relations but also a new climax in the campaign, begun in 1959, to close down churches all over the Soviet Union. According to roughly corresponding figures from the atheist side and from unofficial circles of the Orthodox Church, about 10,000 Ortho- dox churches in the Soviet Union were closed by the state authorities between 1959 and 1964; in this way the number of churches open for worship was reduced by about a half.[30] Church closures were parti- cularly numerous in the Western lands of the Ukraine and Byelorussia, and in the republic of Moldavia. Having only been annexed to the Soviet Union in 1939–40 and 1943, they had not lived through Stalin's persecution of the Church; consequently, until the end of the 1950s, church activity was considerably better organised and more lively than in the rest of the Soviet Union.

There are no exact figures on church closures either from the official Church side or from the state. In this case we are reduced to various not always corresponding sources of information from the Soviet Union and consequent estimates. Thus, for example, in the diocese of Minsk the number of open churches fell from 750 to 420; in the Odessa diocese from 400 to ninety, and in the city of Odessa from nineteen to seven. In the city of Kiev, out of twenty-eight churches open in 1960 there were only seven in 1964, in Lvov the figures were respectively twenty-two and seven. But even the sees which only had a small number of places of worship anyway were not spared; thus in the diocese of Novgorod out of thirty-nine churches only thirteen remained, in the Kirov diocese thirty-three out of seventy-five.[31]

Although, as these figures show, the Church closures were carried out by the authorities with efficiency and enabled the competent regional executive committees and the officials of the Council for Russian Orthodox Affairs to report impressive successes, in most cases the attempt was made to preserve the appearance of legality. Thus in Western Russia appeal was made to a fifteen-year-old law annulling all measures of the German occupying forces. Since during the years of German occupation a large number of churches were reopened, it was possible for hundreds of churches in the Ukraine and Byelorussia to be closed in this way. On the basis of another statute limiting work to the place of habitation, and in connection with Article 19 of the 1929 Law which categorically forbade priests freedom of movement, clergy were prohibited from caring for other congregations. The churches in which no services could then be held were subsequently closed as being unused.[32] For the rest the Stalinist Law of 1929, to which a return was now made – ignoring the relaxations that had been in force after the Second World War – offered practically unlimited opportunity for arbitrary administrative action. For example, churches could be taken from congregations by being declared historic monuments, or church buildings could be pulled down under the pretext that they were a traffic hindrance. Often the detailed police, fire and building regulations of the 1929 Law provided the excuse to close and frequently also to destroy a church, for a building commission could at any time declare a church to be in a dangerous state of repair and demand its complete renovation. If the congregation lacked the necessary financial means or building materials, the church was closed.

Town planning demands also frequently offered an excuse to demolish churches. Another often-used method, which was not even legalised by the Soviet decrees on religion, was the manipulation of public opinion. The Party and the Komsomol would circulate a petition among the people demanding the closure of a certain church.[33]

It is obvious that in this anti-Church campaign no limits were set to the imagination of local authorities, and there were considerable local differences in methods and consistency of action in what was undoubtedly a centrally instigated process. One of the common features, however, was that the authorities completely ignored those few provisions in the Soviet laws on religion to protect believers against arbitrary administrative action. Thus for example the right of appeal to the Supreme Soviet granted to any community against a threatened church closure (Art. 37 of the 1929 Law) was nowhere enforced.[34] During these years in many cases the authorities were not satisfied merely with closing churches, but actually destroyed them. This mostly happened in great secrecy and at night so as to avoid if possible clashes with members of the congregation; this stratagem, however, did not always succeed. Thus in Kiev in March 1964 three churches were razed to the ground in one night. On the night of 15/16 July, 1964, suddenly and without the congregation having been informed, the church of the Metropolitan of Moscow, the Preobrazhensky Sobor, was pulled down, allegedly to make way for a metro shaft. The rumor subsequently persisted in Moscow for some time that even the Patriarchal church was to be removed for 'city planning reasons' – a plan which was then renounced.[35]

The closure or even destruction of a church does not automatically mean the dissolution of a congregation. But in fact the authorities – not least because of the weakness and complete passivity of most bishops – almost everywhere achieved both ends simultaneously. Either the priest was deprived of his registration for the congregation after the church had been closed and thus it was made impossible for him to exercise his office, or the withdrawal of registration preceded the closure of the church, which was then motivated by the assertion that the congregation could not function without a priest.[36]

One important method of exerting pressure on the clergy, which had also been used in the 1930s, was the rapid raising of income tax. Thus after the Church had already suffered severe financial losses through the closing down of many congregations, it was further put under pressure by the higher taxes. Because of the new financial burden many clergy were no longer in a position to exercise their office, or else if they continued nevertheless to care for their congregation, they were in continual danger of being prosecuted for tax evasion.[37]

The authorities also sought all kinds of other ways to act against the clergy. House visits were now interpreted as illegal religious propaganda. Priests were fined for winning young people for the Church, or they might suddenly be accused of collaboration with the Germans during the war.

Overall the total number of Orthodox parish priests was reduced between 1959 and 1964 by about half to 15,000. Some of these continued to exercise their duties illegally without registration, others went from place to place as migrant priests, and many – with difficulty – found simple jobs unrelated to their own calling.[38] Although the authorities, early in the 1960s, tried as far as possible to avoid creating martyrs, nevertheless a number of priests were sentenced, mostly for tax evasion. The same lot befell two bishops: Archbishop Iov (Kresovich) of Kazan and Archbishop Andrei (Sukhenko) of Chernigov were sentenced in 1960 and 1961 respectively to three and eight years' imprisonment; in both cases tax offences formed the main part of the accusation.[39]

After completing his term of imprisonment, Archbishop Iov lived under house arrest in Lvov, but in October 1967 he was reinstated as diocesan bishop of Ufa. Similarly, Andrei (Sukhenko) has recently been appointed Archbishop of Omsk and Tyumen. In the Soviet Union it is not unusual for Church leaders, despite slanderous attacks in the press, harsh reprisals and prison sentences, to be 'rehabilitated' after some years. But the requirement for this is their good behaviour and a certain *détente* in the Church's political situation.[40]

The Soviet pressures were directed not only against the churches and the clergy, but also against the Orthodox monasteries, of which the Moscow Patriarchate at the end of the 1950s again had almost seventy. The Patriarchate had taken over almost all of them in the western lands annexed by the Soviet Union, or else they had been built up during the German occupation. The only important monastery to be refounded by the Patriarchate itself was the Trinity Monastery at Zagorsk.

Between 1959 and 1962 the Soviet authorities closed forty monasteries, and since then the number has probably sunk still further. In 1966 A. E. Levitin-Krasnov, an extraordinarily well-informed Church writer living in the Soviet Union, spoke of no more than four monasteries for men being in existence.[41]

All monasteries in Moldavia and almost all in Carpathian Ukraine were forced to close; in both regions there had been a considerable number of them. Also one of the most famous Russian monasteries, in many ways part of Russian history, the Monastery of the Caves in Kiev, was closed in 1960-1, allegedly because of a landslide, which however the atheist museum that had been installed there managed to survive.

After 1958 it was almost impossible for the monasteries to accept novices. The authorities then forced many monasteries to close through the new high taxes – they had enjoyed tax exemption from 1945 to 1958 – by agitation and threats, and in the last resort often by pure open force.[42]

We know most about the pressure exerted by the authorities over a number of years on the famous Pochaev Lavra in Volhynia. This case, which is certainly a significant example, has become known to an international public by a number of statements and appeals written by believers and monks, and which have been partly published in the West.[43] The Western protests probably contributed to the Soviet authorities' final abandonment of their attempt to close this monastery. From 1961 they had tried to prevent pilgrimages to Pochaev, and by persuasion and threats to cause the monks to leave the monastery. Part of the monastic buildings were requisitioned. The monastery and the inhabitants of Pochaev were forbidden to lodge pilgrims, as a consequence of which the militia regularly searched the monastery at night for pilgrims – who, if found, were sometimes sentenced to prison as vagrants; more often they were simply transported away in lorries.[44]

The monks who were unwilling to leave the monastery voluntarily were deprived of their residence permits. If they refused to vacate the monastery even then, they were taken away by force either to their families or into old people's homes. There were even cases of forcible admissions to hospitals and nervous clinics. Thus out of the 140 monks living at the monastery in 1961, there were only thirty-six left by the autumn of 1962. Even most of these were living in the monastery illegally, for they had simply returned after being deported and were all living there without residence permits. Thus they were continually being fined for contravening passport regulations; many monks also received prison sentences – sometimes more than one.[45]

The police measures against the monastery several times took on the nature of a pogrom. Believers and monks were searched, beaten and robbed, and women were raped. The names of two women killed by the militia are known. The violence reached a new high point at the end of November 1964. The pilgrims were forcibly transported away from Pochaev and some were placed in a psychiatric clinic; several monks were imprisoned at the same time. The new head of the monastery, appointed by the Church leaders at the request of the authorities, remained totally passive.[46]

From the beginning of 1965 the situation in Pochaev seems gradually to have become more normal. Decisive here was the new direction in religious policy after the fall of Khrushchev; encouraged by this, even atheist officials such as the editor of *Nauka i Religia* ('Science and Religion'), B. T. Grigoryan, called for an end to the scandalous state of affairs (*bezobrazie*) in Pochaev. In 1966 about thirty monks were living in the monastery again.[47]

If the loss of many monasteries was painful for the Orthodox Church, the simultaneous reprisals against the theological schools represented an even more dangerous threat to the Church's future. From the end of the 1940s to the end of the 1950s the eight seminaries and two academies (both Leningrad and Zagorsk have one seminary and one academy as a joint institution) probably trained 1,500 priests. In view of the superannuation of the Orthodox clergy, that is a low figure, but it did make possible in the following years a significant rejuvenation among the higher clergy.

From 1960 the Soviet authorities have worked systematically to hinder the theological training of new priests. In that year the seminary buildings in Kiev, Stavropol, Saratov and Odessa were requisitioned. Except for the last-named, all of these seminaries, which by virtue of the number of their pupils ranked among the smaller institutions, were closed in the spring of 1961.[48] Only the seminary in Odessa was able to move out in time to the Assumption Monastery near the city, which is also the summer residence of the Patriarch; this may be the reason why it remained untouched in the following years. On the other hand the seminary in Zhirovitsy (Baranovichi Region) had to stop functioning in 1963, and the one at Lutsk held its last course in the academic year 1964–5.[49]

As usual the Soviet authorities achieved the closure by a combination of administrative and propaganda measures. Administrative methods were used to requisition buildings, to deprive students of their residence permits for their place of study, or to refuse a permit to candidates applying for acceptance at a theological school. From 1959 seminarists were no longer able, as they had been previously, to defer military service. Even students who had already been ordained as priests were now liable for call-up. This measure made it possible to empty the seminaries quite legally.

Furthermore, the number of students, which had grown steadily until the end of the 1950s, was reduced by massive individual agitation. Propagandists pressed students to leave the seminaries and tried above all to make new applicants retract their applications. Although in the 1950s there had constantly been more applicants than places in the seminaries and academies, the new repressive measures succeeded for example in reducing the first-year intake at the Leningrad seminary from thirty-seven in 1959 to sixteen in 1960 and eight in 1961.[50] In the autumn of 1965 the total number of students in Leningrad and Zagorsk combined was only about 600, half of whom were only correspondence students. Besides that there was only the Odessa seminary, where in 1964 no more than fifty students were able to prepare for the priesthood.[51]

Up to now discussion has been of those repressions which the state and Party used in order to exert pressure on the Church and its establishments mainly from outside. Beyond that attempts were also made to influence internal Church life and thus to limit freedom of activity among the congregations even further.

An important instrument here was the alteration of the Church statute of January 1945, carried through at the demand of the Council for Russian Orthodox Church Affairs. The Council demanded an alteration of the parish regulation (Chap. IV of the Statute), which gave the parish priest the presidency over the Church council, the executive organ of the Church community. In this demand the Soviet body appealed to the Law of April 1929, which had not made any provision for collaboration by the parish priest in the Church council and had limited his activity to the spiritual care of the community (Arts. 13, 19 of the Law of 8 April 1929). The Holy Synod complied immediately with the demand of the Council for Russian Orthodox Church Affairs to bring the Church statute into conformity with the 1929 Law; thus it was forced once again to acquiesce in Soviet recourse to the discriminatory religious Law of early Stalinist times. However, there was opposition among the clergy to the corresponding decree of the Synod of 18 April 1961, and the Patriarchate found it necessary to convene a Synod of Bishops which met on 18 July, 1961, in the Trinity Monastery, Zagorsk, and approved the decree of the Synod as well as a new parish regulation.[52] The new regulations provided for a considerable strengthening of the lay element in Church life, a point of view which possibly prevented many bishops from immediately seeing the danger threatening the parishes from a complete exclusion of the clergy from parish administration. The three-man Church council, elected by the parish meeting, with the elder (*starosta*) at its head, was now the only body competent to deal with the Soviet authorities; it alone managed the parish finances, paid the clergy, made work contracts and was responsible for the Church buildings and inventory. The priest was reduced to holding services and 'leading the congregation in the Christian life' (Art. 2:i) and in all secular matters he was completely dependent on the Church council, in which he had neither a seat nor a vote. It soon became clear that many of the new Church councils were helplessly exposed to the state authorities and to the representatives of the Council for Russian Orthodox Church Affairs in the individual dioceses, particularly since the authorities were always able to dismiss unco-operative members of the Church council and to make the congregation elect others who would be more compliant (Art. 14 of the Law of 8 April, 1929).

The new division of the congregations into Church council and clergy led to much internal tension, and numerous congregations were dissolved or broken up from within. The Soviet authorities undermined congregations not only through the choice of unclerical and unbelieving Church elders, who themselves helped to bring congregations to self-closure,[53] but also by supporting incompetent priests who caused moral offence to the congregation and were rejected by it. There were even priests who had infiltrated the Church, who collaborated enthusiastically with church closures, assisting atheist agitation in the congregation. As such obviously destructive elements were welcomed by the authorities, it was usually very difficult for the Church leadership to remove them.[54]

The unclear formulations of the new parish regulation of 1961 (Art. 2, c, d) made it possible for officials of the Council for Russian Orthodox Church Affairs to limit the parish meeting – the chief organ of every congregation, to which the church council was responsible – to twenty persons (*dvadtsatka*). This limitation, exceeding the demands of the 1929 Law, which had merely established twenty persons as the minimum number for a congregation, now excluded the great majority of congregation members from participation in the self-government of the parish. The authorities have also insisted on registering as members of the parish meeting only people who are prepared to fulfil to the letter the 'suggestions and commands' of the Soviet authorities, (the words are taken from an internal circular of the Council for Russian Orthodox Church Affairs). The Soviet administrative organs (*ispolkomy*) are here advised that it 'is desirable if they are present at the election of members of the executive organ (i.e. the Church council) and elect people who take our line'.[55] This circular could not be more explicit.

There is no doubt that this has been converted into practice. We have exact details of one case that may serve as an example. The believers of the parish of St. Nicholas-in-Kuznetsy in Moscow addressed the Premier, A. N. Kosygin, on 17 February, 1967, with an appeal signed by 170 persons protesting against the ruthless manipulation of parish life by the authorities. The opposition of the congregation was directed against its Church elder who was dependent on the administrative body and supported by it. The responsible organ of the Soviet therefore did not allow the congregation to elect a new Church elder. Instead, the rebellious council of twenty (which forms the core of every congregation) was declared deposed by the executive organ and a new council of twenty, consisting of completely unknown and doubtful individuals, was imposed on the congregation.

The Moscow parish of St. Nicholas is led by Archpriest Vsevolod Shpiller, an outstanding man, who has several times been entrusted with important tasks by the leaders of the Church, especially in connection with foreign visitors. Shpiller too has expressed himself sharply more than once in letters to Nikodim (Rotov) among others, against the decisions of the Synod of Bishops of 1961, which placed the clergy outside the canonical ordering of the congregation. The Church council, he said, as executive organ of the congregation, had been changed 'from an organ of Church power and Church government into an organ of non-Church government of the congregation'. Thus the danger of 'secularisation from within' was present in all congregations.[56]

We will now look more closely at the role of the Council for Russian Orthodox Church Affairs in the repressive policy against the Church. Its activity is conducted largely in secret; we know about it only fragmentarily through the testimony of Church circles in the Soviet Union, and any generalisation is bound to remain problematical. Nevertheless it does seem certain that under Kuroyedov's guidance from 1960, the Council changed from an institution to mediate between state and Church bodies 'into an organ of unofficial and illegal direction of the Moscow Patriarchate'. The Council interfered constantly in the internal administration of the Church and could not be checked. 'Telephone orders, oral instructions, unwritten, unofficial agreements – such is the atmosphere of unhealthy secrecy surrounding the relations between the Moscow Patriarchate and the Council like a thick fog.'[57]

Thus the Council and its branches in the dioceses from about 1961 achieved the registration of official Church acts, particularly baptisms, in almost all parishes on the basis of secret instructions; before baptism the written permission of both parents also has to be produced. A list of all official Church acts, which actually represents a veiled form of registration of religious affiliation, which is forbidden in the Soviet Union, is supplied by the Church council to the state authorities, and has led to the mocking of Christians, to well-directed atheist propaganda, and to discrimination against believers in factories and schools, going as far as dismissal.

The Patriarch, who felt unable to resist the demands of the Council, expressly made the registration of such Church acts obligatory in a circular of 22 December, 1964. In order to make evasion of this regulation more difficult, the giving of the sacrament outside churches in private houses was forbidden.[58] Even the last-named regulation of the circular was no more than a sanctioning of a state of affairs which officials of the Council had widely brought into effect from 1961 on the basis of secret instructions. First of all, at the beginning of the 1960s all baptismal chapels independent of the churches were closed. Then the officials of the Council demanded of the priests that official Church acts in private houses and masses for the dead in cemeteries should only be held after permission had been obtained from the local Soviet bodies, although even the Soviet legislation of 1929 had not demanded any special permission for either of these. Since such permission was 'almost never given' by the local Soviets in the tense atmosphere of the fight against the Church in the first half of the 1960s, this meant in practice a prohibition on official Church acts outside the church buildings.

This was a very painful measure for the congregations, and a very important one for atheist officials at a time when churches were being closed all over the country and the atheist administration was thereby paralysing all parish life, but also trying as far as possible to prevent any move into an underground Church.

The officials of the Council found appropriate means to lend weight to their instructions in this matter. Thus in 1961–2 the official of the Council for the Moscow region, Trushin, made the routine renewal of registration of priests dependent on the priests making a previous written undertaking that they would in future seek permission from the authorities for official Church acts in families and masses for the dead in cemeteries. Although not yet published, this restriction of Church life, which surpasses the 1929 limitations, has meanwhile entered Soviet administrative law.[59]

As the object of atheist propaganda has always been the youth, so too officials of the Council for Russian Orthodox Church Affairs were concerned from the beginning of the 1960s to limit by administrative methods the influence of the Church on children and young people. Any Church-organised instruction of young people under eighteen is in any case forbidden by law. But here, too, practice went beyond the 1929 regulations: the officials of the Council in many dioceses managed to stop young people between three and eighteen from taking any active part whatsoever in services, and they were not even allowed to come to communion. Often the bishops had to confirm this order of the Council officials themselves, and occasionally the order was even implemented by the police who prevented young people from entering churches at the times of important Church festivals.[60]

In the course of its constant repressive interference in the internal affairs of the Church from about 1960, the Council assumed a decisive influence on Church appointments policy at all levels. The legal handle for this was provided by the obligatory registration of the clergy with the Soviet authorities, whereby in practice local officials of the Council availed themselves of the right to be heard by Church bodies before all cases of appointment, transfer and dismissal of deacons, priests and bishops, and then to give or to withhold their oral agreement. But the duty of registration of the clergy was exploited by the Council not merely as a practical right of veto in all Church appointment decisions, but the officials of the Council themselves took the initiative and demanded of the Church certain changes of appointment. In some of the frequent translations of bishops from one diocese to another – an unhealthy phenomenon of Church life dating from the nineteenth century – complaints by the authorities formed the spur to which the Synod promptly reacted. Even the fall of Metropolitan Nikolai (Yarushevich) in 1960 was engineered by the Council for Russian Orthodox Church Affairs; likewise Archbishop Yermogen (Golubev) of Kaluga declared that his enforced retirement was effected by the Synod in November 1965 on Kuroyedov's instruction.[61]

To support the authorities and the officials of the Council for Russian Orthodox Church Affairs, the 'Commissions on Observation of the Legislation on Cults' (*Kommissii po Kontrolyu za Soblyudeniem Zakonodatelstva o Kultakh*), which existed alongside the administrative authorities, were activated. These commissions have no administrative power, but are supposed to spy on Church congregations and groups as efficiently as possible and make continual reports to the relevant organs. In a decree in the first half of the 1960s it was stated that the commission should take care that children were not being baptised without the permission of both parents, and that priests were not conducting ceremonies in private houses or avoiding tax on the money thus received. The commissions are to report on young people who are particularly close to the Church and generally keep an eye on the most active congregational members, reporting on them to the authorities. The most exalted task of the commissions was described by the decree as the 'working out of concrete proposals to limit and weaken the activity of religious communities and servants of cult (within the framework of the law)'.[62]

In summary, it may be said that while the repressions of various kinds against the Orthodox Church and the other religious denominations during the years of Khrushchev's sole rule led to a loss to the institutionalised Church of half its constituency in 1959, bloodshed was avoided as far as possible, in contrast to the 1930s, and the Soviet authorities in most cases tried to preserve the appearance of legality.

These tactics were improved by one added refinement. During the more recent offensive against the Church, in contrast to the ruthless frontal attack in Stalin's time, the higher clergy and Church leaders were – with some exceptions – left untouched. It is true that from 1959 the bishops were in many cases hindered in the ecclesiastical direction of their dioceses, and were practically speaking limited to celebrating services; the authorities also requisitioned a number of episcopal residences, probably because the Church could not afford the newly imposed high taxes. But on the other hand it was precisely during these years that the Patriarchate was able to carry through the above-mentioned generation change and rejuvenation of the episcopate. The total number of bishops in active service under Patriarch Alexi rose from fifty-three in the summer of 1961 to seventy-one in the spring of 1965. Most prominent among the younger bishops are Nikodim (Rotov), consecrated in 1960, and Alexi (Ridiger), consecrated in 1961, who were both born in 1929; of the eight bishops called to office in 1965–6, three were only in their thirtieth year.[63]

The fact that on the whole the authorities spared the higher clergy has had significant consequences for the Church. In this way a certain external grandeur was preserved in Church life which frequently deceived the numerous foreign visitors to the Orthodox Church as to the true situation. False assessments were further promoted by the fact that the Russian Orthodox Church decisively extended its own collaboration in international Church organisations in just these years of severe internal pressures. This growing international role became evident when the Russian Orthodox Church joined the World

Council of Churches in 1961 and in the same year, by taking part in the first pan-Orthodox conference in Rhodes, expressed its intention of actively collaborating in the preparation of an all-Orthodox Council. Since the opening of the Second Vatican Council in 1962, these international relations were paralleled by a swift rapprochement with Rome.

The paradox of these two things happening simultaneously – danger threatening internally and an increasing international importance – explains why the wider public outside the Soviet Union did not become aware of the new wave of church persecution until about 1964.[64] A more serious feature of the internal Church situation, however, was the fact that although the bishops did remain unharmed, the Council for Russian Orthodox Church Affairs in most cases demanded their assent to the reprisals. Dismissal of priests, the dissolution of congregations and the obligation of registering official Church acts had to be confirmed by the responsible bishop or the Patriarchal leadership, who by virtue of the basic loyalty of the Orthodox Church towards the Soviet power, only rarely made any attempt to resist.

This submissiveness, which was also interpreted as opportunism, led in many congregations to a growing opposition to the Church leadership, who seemed to the individual congregations to have left them unprotected. Thus since about 1963, the compromised Church leadership has been exposed to oppositional movements in its own Church; and these do not exclude the danger of a schism, a *raskol*. As far as is known, admittedly, the opposition in the Church has not yet coalesced into an organisation, and the priests and congregations involved have not abdicated from the patriarchal Church, but the oppositional attitude towards the Church leadership is undoubtedly shared by a large number of believers in all parts of the Soviet Union. We know this from a succession of testimonies.[65]

The reproaches and accusations against the Patriarch and bishops are mostly made in very sharp language; they are accused of having become 'an obedient tool in the hands of the atheists in power'.[66] Fathers Eshliman and Yakunin compared the submissiveness of the Church leadership with conditions before 1917, when the imperial Oberprokuror stood at the head of the state Church; only the freedom of the Church was much more seriously endangered now, 'for in place of a Christian official standing at the head of the Holy Synod, now in practice atheist officials are coming to the helm of the Church.'[67]

Indignation and scorn are expressed in a letter written by parishioners of Pochaev to their bishop Damian in Lvov, in which they complained that he had done nothing to save the Pochaev Lavra. 'Why are you afraid of death and prefer to live on earth serving the Communists? If you do not wish to be our shepherd, then give up your position and we need no successor. . . . You close our monastery, you tread the whole Gospel underfoot with your Church leadership. And how will you stand at the Last Judgment? . . . Go, leave us.'[68]

At least one prelate, Yermogen (Golubev) of Kaluga, has joined the critics who reproach the official Church with its unresisting surrender to the new Soviet attacks. This greatly increased the danger of a schism because, even in the case of a split from the patriarchal Church, the apostolic succession could have been maintained. In the summer of 1965, Archbishop Yermogen made a declaration (which he had written with seven other bishops) to the Patriarch in which the most important concrete demands of the ecclesiastical opposition were expressed. They demanded that the decisions of the 1961 Synod of Bishops be revoked and that a Local Council be convened to consider the whole Church situation and seek a solution. Besides this, opposition circles without exception demanded that the interference of state authorities in internal Church matters should cease. They appealed here to the 1918 decree on the separation of Church and state as well as to the Soviet constitution, but any accession to such a demand would imply a decisive change in Soviet reality.

Archbishop Yermogen, who refused before the Synod to revoke the declaration of the eight bishops, was in November 1965 retired against his will to the monastery of Zhirovitsy near Minsk, where he still lives today. Meanwhile, on 25 November, 1967, he wrote again to Patriarch Alexi and reminded him that in November 1965 he had been retired – apparently voluntarily but in fact on the orders of Kuroyedov, head of the Council for Russian Orthodox Church Affairs. Yermogen therefore categorically demanded his reinstatement, since he had been removed from his see against all canon law. He complained about the uncontrolled interference of the state authorities in Church life, and demanded, appealing to Lenin, that in future Church–state relations should once again be limited to the legal sector. In particular he demanded that the Council for Religious Affairs should only intervene in the appointment or removal of a bishop when the transgression of the bishop in question against Soviet laws has been proved in court. The head of the patriarchal office, Archbishop Alexi (Ridiger), answered this letter on behalf of the Patriarch on 22 December, 1967, and told Yermogen that the Church would not entrust him with any new

diocese. Before 1965, the letter declared, in every diocese that Yermogen had administered (Tashkent, Omsk, Kaluga) 'complications had
always arisen', and 'we [i.e. the Patriarch] had then in each case to
smooth them over and arrange a translation to another diocese'.

These remarks confirm that part of the inordinately frequent
episcopal translations in the Soviet Union may be ascribed to 'complications' with the Soviet authorities; in such a case the patriarchal
leadership orders a translation in order to avoid a crisis in whatever
troubles have arisen, or else the authorities themselves demand the
removal of a certain bishop.

Yermogen's reply to the Patriarch of 20 February, 1968, shows clearly
that he did in fact stand up to the state authorities much more firmly
than most bishops. He had resisted unjustified demands by the officials
of the Council for Russian Orthodox Church Affairs, and refused
to 'assist' in the closure of churches in the Tashkent diocese; during
his period of office there (1953 to September 1960), not a single church
had been closed. Yermogen names the building of the cathedral in
Tashkent under his direction as one further cause of the 'complications'
with the authorities; this was the largest new church building in the
Soviet Union for fifty years.

In Kaluga (May 1963–November 1965) he had then had clashes with
the Council officials over appointments to the parishes. It was well
known, he declared, that the officials sometimes made such appointments themselves, 'without even taking the position of the bishop into
consideration; the latter's role often consists of establishing and formu-
lating with his own decrees changes which have been made or demanded
by the Council officials.' Since the official registration of the clergy
served as an instrument of these arbitrary measures, Yermogen demanded its abolition in the present legal form.

Yermogen also strongly criticised the Church leadership and its
submissiveness towards the state repressions in an article on the
fiftieth anniversary of the restoration of the Moscow Patriarchate,
which has also been published in the West.

Yermogen repeatedly called for the convening of a Russian Local
Council to correct the decisions of the 1961 Synod of Bishops, which
he described as uncanonical. In the opposition circles of the Church
there is a constantly recurring appeal to the canons, which are said to
have been broken by arbitrary interference from the state in the internal
order of the Church and by the servility of the Church leadership
towards the state organs. Thus the reformers, as before 1917, demand

D

the restoration of canonical Church self-government; however they frequently assume that they can call upon the Soviet constitution and Lenin as authority for this. The opposition has not realised that a self-ruling Church in a Communist state is completely alien to Lenin's total concept, even though individual formulations may suggest the contrary.

The Synod found it necessary to confer about Yermogen once more on 30 July, 1968, because he had 'sent letters that caused a snare in Church life...' and his activity 'is damaging Church unity and peace in the Church'. This decision of the Synod was announced very late, in the April 1969 number of the Patriarchate journal. It is an unambiguous confirmation of the authenticity of Yermogen's letters, which have only been published in the West, and indicates that the bishop's exile to the monastery near Minsk must for the time being be considered absolute.[69]

It has not, however, come to a Church split, and the critics have frequently emphasised that they do not want any schism: '. . . unity is possible even where there are differences of opinion' (Levitin); rather they demand the freedom to criticise.[70] Moreover, it appears out of the question that the opposition, after seceding from the patriarchal Church, could put into effect its programme for an actual separation of the domains of Church and state. That would presuppose the Soviet leadership tolerating pluralism. While the Orthodox Church, with its much stronger clerical orientation, was able to preserve its unity, the same causes behind the tensions in Russian Orthodoxy led at the beginning of the 1960s to the split of the so-called Action Group from the Evangelical Christians and Baptists.

The Relaxation of Administrative Pressure after the Fall of Khrushchev

Since 1965 a certain *détente* has been evident in the Church political situation in the Soviet Union. At least the worst consequences of state pressure have ceased; there is no longer any mass closure of churches, nor are priests deprived of their registration. There are many reports to the effect that the number of those attending church has significantly grown, and among these young people are again appearing in large numbers. Overflowing churches are a normal phenomenon in the Soviet Union today. Some of the churches closed in the previous years have been reopened for services since 1965 – the figure of one per cent is quoted.

The situation in the theological schools has also been normalised.

The state authorities still maintain a strict and extraordinarily low *numerus clausus* for the two academies and three seminaries, but the students once accepted seem to remain unmolested. Reports of the reopening of the seminary in Zhirovitsy (Byelorussia), however, have not been confirmed.[71]

With the general *détente* in Church–state relations it naturally follows that the number of baptisms and Church weddings has again risen. Again and again cases are cited in the Soviet press where even members of the *Komsomol* and the Party are making use of the Church sacraments. Although in principle the two are irreconcilable, in practice there is a broad range of Party reaction, from a tolerant winking at simultaneous membership of Party and Church, to expulsion and public scandal.[72]

Although state and Party since 1965 have to some extent been seeking new methods in their controversy with the Church, nevertheless the repressive restrictions on internal Church life from the early 1960s are mostly still in force today. Both parents must still give permission for the baptism of a child, and official Church acts must be registered, and are prohibited outside Church buildings. Also the prohibition on young people under eighteen coming to communion, which is very grievous for the Church, still exists. But in the more relaxed climate it is easier to evade such prohibitions.

If one seeks the reasons why the Soviet power has altered its course towards the Church, a number of motives come into view. One important factor has undoubtedly been the insight expressed as follows by one atheist propagandist: 'It is true that over a great part of the territory of the Soviet Union there are no more churches or ministers, but that there are believers. . . . The closure of a parish does not make the believers into atheists. On the contrary it increases people's inclination towards religion and also hardens their hearts.'[73] Thus the administrative suppression of Church life had not brought about the success that the Party had envisaged; it also increased the danger of some of the dissolved congregations going underground – a development which the Soviet authorities fear and try as far as possible to prevent.

Another reason for the relaxation of pressure is probably that the state repression had by now hit a 'hard core' in the Church which could not be destroyed even by means of the methods previously used. Finally, it is also possible that Western protests against Church persecution, which were precisely recorded in the Soviet Union – Orthodox bishops occasionally had to give them the lie[74] – helped to alter this course. On the other hand, it seems even more important that within the Soviet Union itself the internal Church opposition, which turned against the atheist state and its own Church leadership and was a topic of discussion at a high level, took on large proportions. This opposition element is accurately registered by the state authorities and must be very unwelcome to them,[75] since it endangers the control of one realm in the Soviet state which already stands outside the 'totalitatian' order. There was also a surge of indignation against the campaign of church closures, which had been going on for years, and against the related atheist propaganda which was considered excessively abusive, even by the non-ecclesiastical Soviet public, particularly by some professional atheists. This displeasure was linked with the criticism – expressed all over the Soviet Union after the autumn of 1964 – of Khrushchev's *'administrirovanie'* (arbitrary rule), of which the Church had been a particular victim.

The Council for Russian Orthodox Church Affairs soon adapted itself to the new development. Perhaps its head, V. A. Kuroyedov, had even been aiming at a change in its tactics; in any case he defended a certain relaxation with the same vehemence with which he had previously carried through the reprisals. In 1965 a number of local officials of the Council were summoned from the provinces to Moscow, where they were reprimanded for their arbitrary actions against the Church; in future socialist legality was to be maintained over the closure of churches. It appears that congregations were again given the right, among other things, of appealing to the Supreme Soviet over church closures.[76]

Kuroyedov himself, as a sign of the new course, attested that 'the majority' of the clergy were loyal 'towards all measures of the Soviet government'; and he declared in an astonishing piece of self-contradiction: 'It has long been known that any kind of prohibition or administrative pressure are unsuitable means in the struggle with religious ideology. . . . Atheist convictions . . . cannot be forced on anyone by violence, decrees or other administrative measures.'[77]

Kuroyedov was able to strengthen his position still further through the reorganisation of the state authorities for control of the religious communities at the end of 1965. The two Councils, respectively for Russian Orthodox Church Affairs and for other religious communities, which had existed since the war, were combined and renamed 'Council for Religious Affairs with the Council of Ministers of the U.S.S.R.', in which the chief posts were filled by officials of the former Council for Russian Orthodox Church Affairs. At the same time the competence of the new Council was much widened. This should be interpreted not so much as a strengthening of pressure against the religious communities as simply an administrative simplification. The two former Councils had probably assumed most of the new areas of competence before 1965 anyway. The officials of the new Council now officially received many rights which had formerly belonged to the executive committees of the Soviet authorities (*ispolkomy*). In the exercise of its controlling function over the religious communities, the Council today can on its own initiative adopt administrative measures which before were reserved, at least formally, for the general administrative bodies. The Council is empowered in cases of offence against the Soviet laws on religion to deprive the religious communities and their clergy of their registration and to close their places of worship; it also checks the congregational accounts. In this the local Council officials are always obliged to work closely together with the state administrative bodies.[78]

On the other hand it has been one of the tasks of the Council from the very beginning to assure the religious communities of their right to free religious practice and to protect them against unjust state interference. It is true this has remained only a verbal obligation; nevertheless, as a sign of the new orientation in the struggle with the 'religious survivals', the legislature in March 1966 passed a statute prepared by the Council in which it is expressly stated that discrimination against believers is a criminal offence. The statute 'On the Application of Art. 142 of the Penal Code of the R.S.F.S.R.', which lays down the penalties for transgressing the laws on the separation of Church and state, defines as offences in the sense of Art. 142 as, for example, 'refusal to accept citizens for work or in an educational institution, breaking of a work contract or exclusion from an educational institution . . . on the basis of their religious affiliation'. The statute as a whole, as well as the simultaneous *ukaz* 'On Administrative Responsibility for Transgressing the Laws on Religious Cults' and an expansion of Art. 142 of the R.S.F.S.R. Penal Code, are, moreover, primarily directed against the '*Initsiativniki*', a schismatic group of the Evangelical Christians and Baptists, which openly opposes the limitations on religious freedom in the Soviet Union, and has therefore been persecuted as an illegal sect since the mid-1960s with administrative and legal procedures.[79]

Personal discrimination against believers, condemned by the legislature in March 1966, had been a frequent phenomenon in the Soviet Union in the previous years; it had ranged from slanderous attacks in the press, through the non-allocation of earned rewards and promotions, to the general refusal of work places in a whole area; the exclusion of students from places of education was a frequently practised form of such discrimination.[80] Even today the new regulations have not led to an integration and equal rights for believers in Soviet society. As before, they have to put up with personal disadvantages, and a professional career is, as a general rule, incompatible with open participation in Church life. However, as long as Christians keep to the officially tolerated denominations and do not join dissident groups, they do not need today to be afraid for life and limb.[81]

To obtain a true picture of the Church situation after 1964, it is imperative to remember that atheist propaganda since the fall of Khrushchev has lost little in intensity, and has even been strengthened in many areas. In 1959, together with the administrative measures against the Church, a large-scale atheist propaganda campaign was launched. The flood of atheist books and brochures rose in 1962 to 355 new publications, which were spread over the Soviet Union in 5.4 million copies; in 1964 the number of copies reached more than 6 million; also in this year seventy anti-religious films were shown in the Soviet Union.[82] These provided the material for hundreds of thousands of atheist congresses, seminars, lectures, discussion evenings, film shows, radio and television broadcasts, which have been mounted every year in the Soviet Union since then. In the Moldavian Republic alone in 1967, several thousand atheist lectures were held, as were more than 2,000 atheist conferences, discussion evenings and other mass meetings; 20,000 Komsomol members carried on individual propaganda among believers.[83] The atheist work is directed by appropriate sectors in the Party organisations. Lecturers and propaganda material are frequently provided by the 'All-Union Society for the Spreading of Political and Scientific Knowledge', renamed in 1963 'Knowledge' (Znanie).

In spite of the tremendous outlay, criticism of atheist work in the past years has frequently been exercised in the Soviet Union itself. Even the President of the Ideological Commission with the Central Committee of the C.P.S.U., L. F. Ilichev, in a paper to this body in November 1963, emphasised the 'serious shortcomings in atheist propaganda'. 'In atheist work up to the present day there is much formalism, it is frequently without reference to life, it does not penetrate to people's minds and hearts and has very little influence on believers.'[84] In order quantitatively, but above all qualitatively, to improve the atheist education of the 'new man' in the 'stage of the developed construction of Communism', the C.P.S.U. Central Committee made a resolution in January 1964 'On Measures to Strengthen Atheist Education of the People'.[85] The measures projected here and realised during 1964 survived the fall of Khrushchev.

For the organisation and co-ordination of all atheist research, to which the Party attributes a great deal of weight, an Institute of Scientific Atheism was founded within the Academy of Social Sciences of the C.P.S.U. Central Committee.[86] Instruction on questions of atheism was, moreover, extended from 1964 at all school levels. Chairs of Scientific Atheism were created at a number of universities and pedagogical institutes. And for all students at universities and medical agricultural and pedagogical colleges, 'Principles of Scientific Atheism' became obligatory as from the academic year 1964–5. Alongside the traditional forms of atheist propaganda via lectures, films, exhibitions, etc., more intensive individual propaganda work with believers has come to the fore in recent years; these had mostly remained unreached by the traditional propaganda methods.

The intensification of atheist research and education has fortunately not prevented some reflection on the atheist position itself; up to now, however, strict ideological frontiers have been set to such reflection. If at the beginning of the 1960s there were already complaints about the flatness and primitive quality of atheist brochures, this critique has become much stronger since 1965 and has brought in some basic questions. The Soviet press attacked not only the superficiality and intellectual poverty of atheist textbooks, but also the mockery and slander of clergy and believers in atheist propaganda.[87]

In this connection a controversy between atheist propagandists of various tendencies which comes to light in a 'Letter from the Editors' of the journal *Nauka i Religia* ('Science and Religion') and the ensuing discussion are of symptomatic importance.[88] The three authors of the letter (B. Maryanov, G. Ulyanov, A. Shamaro) make sharp attacks on A. Ya. Trubnikova, the well-known author of atheist articles and brochures which have been published in the Soviet Union in large editions. Trubnikova is charged with directing her attacks not against religious ideology, but against believers, who in her writings appear solely as scoundrels, deceivers, vagrants, and mental and physical cripples. Instead of religiosity being regarded as a misfortune for the people concerned, it appeared in Trubnikova's writings as a crime for which they were personally responsible. The writers of the letter emphasise that it is anachronistic to represent believers as politically unreliable individuals and enemies of Soviet society. On the basis of many quotations from her writings, they reproach Trubnikova with a 'scornful, mocking attitude to believers', saying that she lacked journalistic taste as well as a feeling for moderation. The only way to success in atheist work, they said, lay in entering into dialogue with believers; instead of this, Trubnikova was erecting additional barriers. Her writings were well-adapted 'to encourage the lovers of crude administrative measures'.

The editors of *Nanka: Religia* received many favourable reactions to their 'letter', in which of course the debate concerned not only Trubnikova, but 'the direction . . . of atheist propaganda in general'; but there were also a number of sharply negative reactions, particularly from Trubnikova herself, who accused the editors of taking religion and believers under their protection and stabbing atheist propaganda in the back. Nevertheless, the editors, in their closing word on the discussion, defended the view that it was a question 'in the first place of the humanitarian character of our atheist movement' and they now included even *Izvestia* in their criticism; in the editorial board there, they said, there were obviously some comrades who believed 'that it was in order to carry on the struggle against religion chiefly within the framework of the Penal Code, and who forget that religion is an ideology'.

It is true that the insights of *Nanka: Religia* have not remained unchallenged and there are still the 'hawks' who in the interests of 'militant' atheism, do not take time to reflect on the methods of this struggle. Nevertheless, it is remarkable that in the same journal a writer could appear in print who even advocated that all administrative prohibitions be abandoned in the struggle against religious convictions.[89]

Even if Soviet religious laws and poltical practice are still far from such principles, still the view has largely prevailed among atheist officials in recent years that the previous, purely negative alignment of atheism is insufficient. Extensive religio-sociological research has promoted the realisation that religion has powers of attraction against which Communist ideology has little to offer. Among these powers are, besides the religious answers to man's last questions about the meaning of life and about death, the application of the Christian religion to the 'humble and oppressed', the outcasts of modern production society. In one article it states that these unfortunate and sick people are 'somehow not envisaged in our optimistic framework'; the article also calls on atheist propaganda to 'compete' with 'Church consolation' on behalf of these people.[90]

These new tones in the language of Soviet atheism should not, however, deceive us as to the fact that the ideological formula of the irreconcilability of Communism and religion is still adhered to with undiminished vigour. Or does the continual pounding of these formulae indicate that people are no longer so certain of them? It has become difficult to defend them even before a Communist audience.[91]

Anyway, the Russian Orthodox Church and almost all other religious communities in the Soviet Union start in their own self-understanding from the unspoken premise that religion is quite compatible with the present Soviet social order and with any future one; but they avoid any open confrontation with atheism.

REFERENCES

1. *Istoria sovetskoi konstitutsii (V dokumentakh) 1917-1956*, Moscow 1957, p. 744.
2. V. I. Lenin, *Polnoe sobranie sochinenii*, 5th ed., Vol. XII, p. 143.
3. Programme of the CPSU of 1961 (B. Meissner, *Das Parteiprogramm der KPdSU 1903-1961*, Cologne 1962, p. 229.
4. Art. 126 of the 1936 Soviet Constitution (*Istoria sovetskoi konstitutsii*, p. 744).
5. Arts. 9 and 12 of the Decree of 23 January/5 February 1918 (*Kirche und Staat in der Sowjetunion. Gesetze und Verordnungen*, R. Stupperich (ed.) Witten 1962, pp. 5-6).
6. *Istoria sovetskoi konstitutsii*, pp. 145, 530.
7. *Kirche und Staat in der Sowjetunion*, pp. 13-28.
8. Law of 18 May 1929 altering the Constitution (*Syezdy Sovetov*, Vol. IV, I, 1962, p. 140.
9. J. Chrysostomus, *Kleine Kirchengeschichte Russlands nach 1917*, Freiburg 1968, p. 126; N. Struve, *Christians in Contemporary Russia*, p. 57.
10. From the programme of the CPR(B) of 1919 (*Kirche und Staat in der Sowjetunion*, p. 12).
11. Struve, op. cit., p. 66.
12. W. Kolarz, *Religion in the Soviet Union*, London-New York 1961, pp. 53-5. The competence of the Councils has never been given in a codified form. They succeeded the 'Standing Commission with the Presidium of the Central Executive Committee of the U.S.S.R. for Religious Affairs' (cf. D. Loeber, 'Die Rechtstellung der Kirche in der Sowjetunuin', in *WCO*, VIII, 1966, p. 268, Note 85).

D*

13. Struve, op. cit., pp. 81 ff.; Stupperich (ed.), Die Russische Orthodoxe Kirche in Lehre und Leben, Witten 1966, pp. 57-8. The Statute is printed in Kirche und Staat in der Sowjetunion, pp. 35-41.

14. Loeber, op. cit., p. 271, section 4.

15. The decree of 22 August 1945 has not been published; its content is seen in a letter from the President of the Council for the Affairs of the Russian Orthodox Church, G. G. Karpov, to Patriarch Alexi of 28 August 1945, from which this quotation is also made (pub. in Loeber, op. cit., pp. 272-3). Despite the awarding of these 'legal rights', Churches in the Soviet Union – according to Soviet legal terminology – still do not count as persons at law (Loeber, op. cit., p. 268; A. E. Luneva (ed.), Administrativnoe pravo, Moscow 1967, p. 506; also R. Maurach, Handbuch der Sowjetverfassung, Munich 1955, p. 358, and K.-H. Ruffman, Sowjetrussland, Munich 1967, p. 177).

16. Struve, op. cit., pp. 123 ff.

17. KIO, V, 1962, p. 140.

18. Struve, op. cit., pp. 186 ff.

19. E. Boettcher et al. (ed.), Bilanz der Ära Chruščev, Stuttgart 1966, pp. 8, 12, 15.

20. L. Ilichev in a speech before the Ideological Commission of the CC of the CPSU on 25 November 1963 (Kommunist, 1/1964, p. 29).

21. The resolution is printed in Kirche und Staat in der Sowjetunion, pp. 29-34; the following quotations pp. 29, 30, 31, 32.

22. Struve, op. cit. p. 269; L. Pistrak, 'Moskau verschärft den Kampf gegen die Religion', in Aussenpolitik, XII, 1961, p. 824.

23. The names of about thirty former priests are given in Struve, op. cit., p. 294, 319-20, 453. Note 114. Their apostasies have been published on the atheist side in several collections: Pochemu my porvali s religiei, Moscow 1958; My porvali s religiei, Moscow 1963, 2nd ed.; My porvali s religiei, Moscow 1964.

24. JMP, 2/1960, p. 27.

25. The Patriarch's address is published in German in Struve, Die Christen in der UdSSR, Mainz 1965, pp. 412-14; the quotation, ibid., p. 414.

26. A. Kischkowsky, Die sowjetische Religionspolitik und die Russische Orthodoxe Kirche, Munich 1960, 2nd ed., p. 161; G. Stokl, 'Todeskampf der russischen Kirche?', in Zeitwende. Die neue Furche, XXXVII, 1966, p. 26.

27. This title is held by the patriarchal deputy, who also governs the diocese of Moscow.

28. W. C. Fletcher, Nikolai: Portrait of a Dilemma, New York–London 1968.

29. Struve, op. cit., pp. 166-8; KIO V, 1962, p. 136; Who's who in the U.S.S.R. 1965/66, 1966 2nd ed., pp. 594-5.

30. Struve, op. cit. p. 300 (taken from N. Yudin, Pravda o Peterburgskikh 'svyatynyakh', Leningrad 1963, p. 8); Letter of the priests Eshliman and Yakunin of 21 November 1965 (Grani, 61/1966, p. 132); Informationen aus der Orthodoxen Kirche, 2/1967, p. 27.

31. KIO, VIII, 1965, p. 146; XI, 1968, Struve, op. cit., pp. 180-4, 300; Posev, 23 September, 1966, p. 3.

32. Struve, op. cit., p. 296.

33. Ibid., p. 298. The most colourful and at the same time most depressing description of the arbitrary action of the Soviet authorities in church closures is given in the open letter by B. V. Talantov of Kirov, 10 November 1966 (*VRSKhD*, 1/1967, pp. 29–64; English extracts in M. Bourdeaux, *Patriarch and Prophets: Persecution of the Russian Orthodox Church Today*, London 1969, pp. 125–52).

34. Letter of the priests Eshliman and Yakunin to Patriarch Alexi (*Grani*, 61, 1966, pp. 130–1, cf. p. 179); letter from B. V. Talantov, see Note 33.

35. Struve, op. cit., pp. 301–2.

36. Letters of the priests Eshliman and Yakunin (*Grani*, 61, 1966, pp. 169, 180); letter by B. V. Talantov, see Note 33.

37. Struve, op. cit., pp. 297–8; *Neues Forum*, XIV, 1967, p. 354 (Interview with the Deputy Head of the Council for Religious Affairs, P. V. Makartsev).

38. Struve, op. cit., p. 317; *Informationen aus der Orthodoxen Kirche*, 2/1967, p. 27; *KIO*, IX, 1966, p. 121.

39. *KIO*, VI, 1963, pp. 128–9; IX, 1966, p. 119. Note 13; Struve, p. 312. On the other hand the tightening up of Art. 227 of the Penal Code of the RSFSR of 25 July, 1962 (*Vedomosti Verkhovnogo Soveta RSFSR*, 1962, p. 452) is aimed primarily against the sects and in particular the radical group of *Initsiativniki* among the Evangelical Christians and Baptists.

40. *JMP*, 11/1967, p. 10.

41. Struve, op. cit., p. 303; *KIO*, X, 1967, pp. 127–8 (Levitin); *Salzburger Nachrichten* of 22 April, 1968.

42. *Neues Forum*, XIV, 1967, pp. 351, 353 (interview with Makartsev); Loeber, p. 262.

43. The large number of documents permits us to gain a detailed picture of reprisals against the monasteries. Documents up to 1964 are largely collected in: *Situation des Chrétiens en Union Soviétique: Documents*, Paris 1965, and in: (A. E. Levitin-Krasnov, *Zashchita Very v SSSR*, Paris 1966, pp. 63–87 (partial German translation in *Kampf des Glaubens: Dokumente aus der Sowjetunion*, Bern 1967, pp. 108–19). The following documents, which are passed from hand to hand in the Soviet Union, have become known in the West in recent years: (1) Appeal 'from parishioners and pilgrims of the Pochaev Lavra' of 5 December, 1964 'to the U.N., the heads of all world governments, the presidents of all Christian Churches and bodies, Christians of the whole world' (*Posev*, 20 August, 1965); (2) Appeal from 'Orthodox believers from all over Russia' of 9 December, 1964 to the Gen. Sec. of the U.N., U Thant (*Posev*, 13 August, 1965); (3) Appeal from 'parishioners and pilgrims of the Pochaev Lavra' to the Gen.-Secretary of the U.N. (of December 1964) (*Posev*, 13 August, 1965); (4) Complaint 'to the United Nations, to all world governments, to the presidents of all Christian Churches, to the Christians of the whole world' by priest-monk Apelli (Stankevich) of 10 February 1966 (Bourdeaux, *Patriarch and Prophets*, pp. 80–4); (5) 'Description of the events in Pochaev monastery in our times' (second half of 1966) (*VRSKhD*, 2/1967, pp. 39–69; partial English translation in Bourdeaux, *Patriarch and Prophets*, pp. 98–115; (6) Appeal of priest-deacon Pavel (Batanov) of Pochaev monastery to Patriarch Alexi, 14 October,

1966 (*Posev*, 7 January, 1967); (7) Appeal of priest-monk Amvrosi (Dovgan) of Pochaev monastery to Patriarch Alexi of January 1967 (*Posev*, 5/1968, pp. 8–9); (8) Appeal of priest-monks Sergi (Solomko) and Apelli (Stankevich) of Pochaev monastery to Patriarch Athenagoras of Constantinople, August 1967 (*VRSKhD*, 3–4/1968, pp. 46–8). Cf. the extensive bibliographical collection of underground documents by E. Voss in *Osteuropa*, XIX, 1969, pp. 534–7.

44. Letter from the Pochaev monks to Prime Minister Khrushchev of September 1962 (*Frankfurter Allgemeine Zeitung*, 12 December 1962; Extracts in Struve, op. cit., pp. 304–8, 322–3).

45. Petitions by various monks for the restoration of their residence permits are printed in *Zashchita very v SSSR*, Paris 1966, pp. 63–74; a list, put together by the leaders of the monastery on 31 October, 1964, of nineteen monks who had been deprived of their residence permits between 1961 and 1963 and who were living at the Lavra without permits, is published in *Posev*, 20 August 1965.

46. Cf. in particular documents Nos. 1, 2 and 5 in Note 43.

47. *Zashchita very v SSSR*, p. 93; *KIO*, X, 1967, p. 127.

48. *KIO*, VI, 1963, pp. 122–3; a group photograph of students and teachers of the Stavropol seminary at the end of the 1950s shows eighty-eight people (*Die Russische Orthodoxe Kirche*, Moscow 1958, p. 118).

49. *KIO*, VIII, 1965, p. 147; IX, 1966, p. 126.

50. Struve, op. cit., pp. 310–11; E. T. Muravev – Yu.V. Dmitriev, 'O konkretnosti v izuchenii i preodolenii religioznykh perezhitkov', in *Voprosy Filosofii*, XV, 3/1961, p. 68.

51. *KIO*, VIII, 1964, p. 153; IX, 1966, p. 126; X, 1967, p. 128. Cf. the documentary reports from the Soviet Union in Bourdeaux, *Patriarch and Prophets*, pp. 117–18, 139–40.

52. The decisions of the Synod of Bishops of 18 July, 1961, are printed in *Kirche und Staat in der Sowjetunion*, pp. 41–5.

53. Letter of the priests Eshliman and Yakunin to Patriarch Alexi (*Grani*, 61, 1966, pp. 143–6); A. E. Levitin (pseudonym Krasnov), 'Slushaya radio...' in *Posev*, 1 October, 1966, pp. 3–4; R. Stupperich, 'Die Russisch-Orthodoxe Kirche Fünfzig Jahre nach der Oktoberrevolution', in *Osteuropa*, XVII, 1967, pp. 892–3; also 'Zwischen staatlichem Druck und Kirchlicher Opposition', in *Osteurpoa*, XVII, 1967, p. 210.

54. Eshliman and Yakunin, ibid., pp. 169–70, 185; the circular from the time between 1961 and 1966 in: *VRSKhD*, 1/1967, pp. 4–6.

55. Eshliman and Yakunin, ibid., p. 149; *Posev*, 30 April, 1967, pp. 3–4; Struve, op. cit., pp. 319–20.

56. The documents known in the West about Archpriest Shpiller and his parish are partially available in English in Bourdeaux, *Patriarch and Prophets*, pp. 304–29. The quotations from a letter from Shpiller to Archbishop Vasili (Krivoshein) of 2 January, 1967, in *Mess* 58, 1967, p. 108.

57. Letter of the priests Eshliman and Yakunin to Patriarch Alexi (*Grani*, 61, 1966, p. 126).

58. Eshliman and Yakunin, ibid., pp. 127–8, 182; Struve, op. cit., pp. 327–8.

59. Eshliman and Yakunin, ibid., pp. 132–3 (quotation p. 133), 135; Loeber.

Die Rechtstellung der Kirche in der Sowjetunion, op. cit., pp. 264, 267; A. E. Luneva (ed.), *Administrativnoe pravo*, Moscow 1967, p. 508.

60. Eshliman and Yakunin, ibid., pp. 134–5; *KIO*, IX, 1966, p. 122; X, 1967, p. 145.

61. Eshliman and Yakunin, ibid., pp. 137, 177; *Posev*, 1 October, 1966, p. 3; Struve, op. cit., p. 142; letter of Archbishop Yermogen to Patriarch Alexi of 25 November, 1967 (*VRSKhD*), 4/1967, pp. 61–65).

62. *VRSKhD*, 1/1967, pp. 3–4. The decree printed here I consider to be an independent document from the following one. Both pieces up to now have usually been treated as one whole.

63. Struve, op. cit. pp. 311–12; *Die Russische Kirche in Lehre und Leben*, pp. 284–5; *KIO*, VI, 1963, pp. 119–20; X, 1967, p. 122. A general suspicion of the younger bishops as expressed by Chrysostomus, *Kleine Kirchengeschichte Russlands*, p. 180, is unfounded.

64. This is revealed by the otherwise extraordinarily informative chronicles of Church life in *KIO*, cf. *KIO*, VIII, 1965, pp. 145–6; J. Lawrence, *Soviet Policy towards the Russian Churches*, p. 276.

65. The documents from the Soviet Union published in the West, giving us information about the state of opposition in the Church, have appeared in very scattered places, partly in little-known Russian newspapers. They have been collected and translated into English by Bourdeaux, *Patriarch and Prophets*. The most important testimonies are the open letters of the priests Nikolai Eshliman from Moscow and Gleb Yakunin from Dmitrov of 1965, the various open letters by B. V. Talantov of Kirov, the articles of the religious writer A. E. Levitin-Krasnov from Moscow, which circulate in the Soviet Union in manuscript form, the letters and articles of Bishop Yermogen (Golubev) from Zhirovitsy monastery near Minsk and the significantly more restrained open letters of Archpriest Vsevolod Shpiller from Moscow. On this see pp. 125 ff.

66. Letter of twelve believers from Kirov diocese, *VRSKhD*, 4/1966, p. 5.

67. *Grani*, 61, 1966, p. 160.

68. The letter was probably written at the end of 1964, *Posev*, 20 August, 1965.

69. The exchange of letters between Yermogen and the Patriarchate in: *VRSKhD*, 4/1967, pp. 61–5, and 1–2/1968, pp. 8–14; Yermogen's article on the 50th anniversary of the restoration of the Patriarchate: ibid, 4/1967, pp. 66–80. English version of the documents in Bourdeaux, *Patriarch and Prophets*, pp. 239–54. The decision of the Synod of 30 July 1968 in *JMP*, 4/1967, pp. 2–3.

70. Bourdeaux, *Patriarch and Prophets*, p. 288. The picture given of the Church opposition by D. Konstantinov in *Ostprobleme*, XVIII, 1966, pp. 386 ff., and in his book *Religioznoe dvizhenie soprotivlenia v SSSR*, London (Canada) 1967, is, in the author's opinion, exaggerated.

71. *KIO*, VIII, 1965, p. 146; IX, 1966, p. 123, Note 33a; *Posev*, 27 August, 1965; 30 April, 1967; May 1968, p. 7.

72. *Ostprobleme*, XX, 1968, pp. 156–8; W. C. Fletcher, 'Russian Orthodoxy: The Church and the Communist State', in *Studies on the Soviet Union* N.S., VII, 2/1967, pp. 78–9.

73. G. Kelt, 'Svyataya Svyatykh-chelovek!' in *Komsomolskaya pravda*, 15

August, 1965, p. 3. Such a public statement at this time undoubtedly confirms a political change of course; however the fact that published statements in the Soviet Union do not necessarily mirror a political change of direction is shown by the essay by A. Valentinov, 'Azbuka materializma', in *Kom. pravda*, 14 June, 1963, which contains the same arguments as the above-mentioned article and – at the climax of the repressions against the Church – expressly warns against 'administrative methods in the struggle with religion'.

74. *KIO*, VIII, 1965, pp. 145–6; IX, 1966, p. 122.

75. Cf. in particular *Zashchita very v SSSR*, pp. 88 ff.; V. Kuroyedov, *Leninskie printsipy svobody sovesti v SSSR*, London (Canada), 1967, p. 49.

76. *Posev*, 27 August, 1965; D. Konstantinov, *Religioznoe dvizhenie soprotivlenia v SSSR*, London (Canada) 1967, p. 49.

77. *Izv*, 30 August, 1966, p. 4.

78. Ibid.; *Administrativnoe pravo*, pp. 509–10. No corresponding alteration of the 1929 Law on religion has so far been published.

79. The three decrees of 18 March, 1966, have been published in *Vedomosti Verkhovnogo Soveta RSFSR*, 1966, pp. 219–20.

80. Struve, op. cit., pp. 321 ff.; *Ostprobleme*, XVIII, 1966, p. 59; *Posev*, 7 January, 1967, p. 5.

81. G. Matetsky, "Voina s Bogami", in *Trud*, 12 May, 1968; cf. G. Simon's documentation in *Osteuropa*, XIX, 1969, pp. A 51 ff.

82. Struve, op. cit., pp. 276–8; *Posev*, 29 April, 1966.

83. *Nauka i Religia*, IX, 3/1968, p. 61.

84. Speech by Ilichev at the session of the Ideological Commission of the C.C. of the C.P.S.U. on 25 November 1963 in *Kommunist*, 1/1964, pp. 23–46 (the quotations p. 34).

85. *Partiinaya zhizn*, 2/1964, pp. 22–6.

86. Since 1966 the Institute publishes regularly, *inter alia*, collections under the title *Voprosy nauchnogo ateizma*, amounting to twelve volumes up to the present. On the other hand the two periodicals *Voprosy istorii religii i ateizma* and *Yezhegodnik Muzeya istorii religii i ateizma* ceased publication in 1964. The number of copies printed decreased from 25,000 on the first volume to 16,700 on Vol. 12.

87. Similar data is assembled in *Nauka i religia*, VII, 10/1965, p. 12; *Posev*, 10 April 1966, pp. 3, 7; May 1968, p. 10. Cf. G. Simon's documentation in *Osteuropa*, XIX, 1969, pp. A 55 ff.

88. *Nauka i religia*, VII, 3/1965, pp. 23–6. Excerpts from readers' letters and opinions, ibid., 9/1965, pp. 14–15; 10/1965, pp. 12–14; final editorial comment: 10/1965, pp. 5–8. The following quotations: 3/1965, pp. 24, 26; 10/1965, pp. 5, 6, 8.

89. D. Balashov, 'Traditsionnoe i sovremennoe', in *Nauka i religia*, VII, 12/1965, p. 28. This article was however provided with a critical preface by the editor.

90. L. Korobkov, 'V teni i na solntse', in *Komsomolskaya pravda*, 6 July, 1968.

91. I. P. Tsameryan, *Kommunizm i religia*, Moscow 1967, p. 3; V. Drugov, 'Ateisticheskaya propaganda i ee deystvennost', in *Pravda*, 18 April, 1968; cf. the Ilichev speech (Note 84), p. 35.

IV. The Churches in the Soviet Union Today

In a communist-ruled state, according to pure doctrine, religious communities should not exist, especially when the state has been boasting of its 'achievements' for half a century already. But the decades that have passed since the October Revolution have shown that pure doctrine, while it can certainly change political reality to a great extent, cannot replace it. The constant adaptation of a supposedly total ideology to the socio-economic and cultural environment is one of the leitmotifs of Soviet history.

In China and Albania, where Church institutions were dissolved in 1966–7 by terrorist police action, we see the violent triumph of totalitarian rule over the religious communities, as that rule claims fully to implement the total demands of doctrine. Albania thus arrogated to itself the title of 'the first atheist state in the world'.[1] The Soviet Union went through this phase in the latter half of the 1930s, and today, while the Churches are subject to the most severe repressions, they are tolerated as a fringe phenomenon in society. They are the only institutions that are able to express publicly their rejection of large parts of Marxism–Leninism, and they thereby represent an intellectual and cultural opposition which offers no political alternative, but rather an ideological one. This sums up one of the main attractions of the religious Communities in communist-ruled countries. Nevertheless, after persecution and thanks to atheist education among the people, the Churches have only been able to retain a fraction of their size and influence; however, the squeezing of the Church out of public life and public consciousness is equally a consequence of the overall process of secularisation in European culture. For even the social-political weight of the Churches, which is still considerable in many Western European countries, is basically difficult to justify now on principle. It is quite possible that the number of believers in the Soviet Union is not much less than in western and northern Europe. One particularly well-informed Soviet Church writer, who tends if anything to make conservative estimates, puts the number of religious believers (not only Christians) in the Soviet Union at 30 million, which is about 12 per cent of the population.[2]

The present religio-political situation is determined by the state of affairs existing since the fall of Khrushchev in October 1964. The terrorist administrative measures, especially the mass closure of churches, have ceased; however, many of the restrictions on Church life which were newly introduced at the beginning of the 1960s are still in force and place great limitations on the freedom of movement of religious communities. The contacts of the Church leaders with international Church organisations and the Churches throughout the world remain relatively undisturbed and not infrequently are actually promoted by the state. International Church gatherings have their fixed place in the calculations of Soviet foreign policy. The relatively large freedom of action of the Church leaders often deceives foreign visitors concerning the fact that the repression today is directed chiefly against the grass-roots of the Churches. The aim of Soviet religious policy is the destruction of the believing communities from the bottom up, so that finally the facade collapses of its own accord.

The post-Khrushchev situation is characterised by one further feature. The opposition groups within several religious communities have brought about considerable crises and attack the continual interference by state bodies in the life of the Church – and, at the same time, the over-submissive attitude of the Church leaders. This has led to a certain softening of state and Party towards the Church leaderships. A few church-political concessions are supposed to make the Church leadership more acceptable again in the eyes of the opposition, and prevent these forces from going underground. At the same time the opposition itself is severely persecuted by the police and the courts, with the aim of wholly obliterating it.

Atheist propaganda, which reached an all-time high point at the beginning of the 1960s, has subsided somewhat since then. But every year there are still millions of atheist lectures, discussion evenings, exhibitions, film shows and other manifestations. There is argument over their effectiveness, even among professional atheists. There is open criticism both of the defamation of religiously inclined citizens, especially in the provincial press, and also of the primitive nature of official atheism, particularly as represented in central professional publications. *Pravda* has given numerous warnings against neglect of the atheist struggle, and thus probably described the actual state of affairs.

Not only are there no published statistics on the large denominations in the Soviet Union, but we do not even have reliable data on which confessions exist or are officially tolerated. In July 1969, in Zagorsk near Moscow, a conference of 'all religions in the U.S.S.R. for co-operation and peace between nations' was held; the published list of participants probably contains the names of all accepted religious institutions. According to this supposition, they are: the Russian Orthodox Church; the Georgian Orthodox Church; the Armenian-Gregorian Church; the Old Believer Archdiocese of Moscow and all Russia; the Old Believer Archdiocese of Old Orthodox Christians of Novozybkov, Moscow and All Russia; the Supreme Old Believer Council in Lithuania; the Moscow community of Old Believers-Pomortsy; the Moscow Preobrazhensky Old Believer community; the Riga Grebenshchikov Old Believer community; the Roman Catholic Church of Latvia; the Roman Catholic Church of Lithuania; the Evangelical-Lutheran Church of Latvia; the Evangelical-Lutheran Church of Estonia; the Evangelical-Lutheran Church of Lithuania; the Reformed Church of Carpathian Ukraine; the Evangelical-Reformed Church of Lithuania; the All-Union Council of Evangelical Christians and Baptists; the Seventh-Day Adventists; the Methodist Church of Estonia; the Jewish communities; the Spiritual Government of the Muslims of Central Asia and Kazakhstan; the Spiritual Government of the Muslims of Transcaucasia; the Spiritual Government of the Muslims of North Caucasus and the Central Spiritual Government of Buddhists in the U.S.S.R.[3]

This list indirectly confirms that a number of religious communities are operating illegally. These include the Jehovah's Witnesses, who have spread in the Soviet Union only since the Second World War and who form there a small but effectively organised group, as well as the Catholics, united with Rome but of the Slavic rite, in West Ukraine, who in 1946 were officially joined to the Moscow Patriarchate by administrative pressure. Also prohibited in the Soviet Union are the True Orthodox Christians and the True Orthodox Church, which do not recognise the communist state and have preserved the heritage of the struggle against the Church in the first years after the October Revolution. Also illegal are the remains of the Russian sects of the eighteenth and nineteenth centuries: the Dukhobors, Khlysty and Skoptsy. The Molokan sect, which exists mainly in the Caucasus, is not actually prohibited and was still represented at the first Zagorsk peace conference in 1952, but seems to be undergoing absorbtion by the Baptists. The Evangelical Christians and Baptists have in fact become a sort of all-Protestant movement, into which have come even the German Evangelical Christians, who during the war were deported from the Volga and Southern Ukraine to Central Asia and Siberia. No Evangelical-Lutheran Church organisation outside the Baltic Soviet republics is permitted. The most recent and at the present time undoubtedly the most important underground group is the 'Council of Churches of Evangelical Christians and Baptists', which left the officially recognised All-Union Council of Evangelical Christians and Baptists during the 1960s.

The above list of recognised religious communities makes it clear, too, that a number of denominations have not been allowed to build up any central administration, and can only operate in certain Soviet republics. That applies to the Lutheran and the Catholic Churches, but above all to the Jewish communities, who are forbidden any regional union. The splintering of the Old Believers, on the other hand, corresponds to their historical development and is independent of Soviet religio-political measures.

Scarcely any details of some smaller denominations penetrate to the outside world, especially as most of them did not join international Church organisations until later; the Evangelical-Lutheran Church of Lithuania, for example, did not join the Lutheran World Alliance until 1967.[4] The following section therefore is limited to the larger Christian denominations which are more in the public eye in the Soviet Union and in international Church circles, and of which detailed analyses are possible. However, many of the general remarks and conclusions are relevant also to the smaller Church communities. Among the Churches in the Soviet Union, Russian Orthodoxy undoubtedly occupies a special position.

1. *The Russian Orthodox Church*

The Russian Orthodox Church is by far the largest Christian denomination and is considered the most important even by the Communist Party. In all important ecumenical and political questions, the other Christian denominations and to some extent also the non-Christian religions move today in the wake of the Russian Orthodox Church. Absolute political loyalty to state and Party is mandatory for all of them. In this respect just as in international Church relations, the Russian Orthodox Church sets the tone. It actually seems that the state authorities handle all Church-political questions with the Russian Orthodox Church as if it represented all the denominations, and give their permission or refusal accordingly.

The special position of Orthodoxy, however, is not explained merely by its size. More than any other denomination it is linked with the history of the 'fatherland' and with its 'heroic' episodes; it is ethnically rooted in the East Slav peoples, and its Russian patriotism and nationalism are never questioned. In a country with such a living and unbroken sense of history as the Soviet Union, such values are very important, even today. Orthodoxy has not been spared persecutions on this account, and it continues as before to be exposed to various kinds of discrimination and defamation. But a climate in which the 'Society for the Preservation of Historical and Cultural Monuments', founded in 1966, is appealing to the intellectual youth to protect churches and monasteries and to collect old icons, at least guarantees the Orthodox Church against further destruction.

The Congregations

The last chapter already spoke of the fact that the approximately 7,000 existing Orthodox congregations are almost exclusively limited in their activity to the celebration of the liturgy. Any other activity, even carrying out official Church acts – not to mention any secular activities, from the sale of church candles to the calling of a parish meeting – is severely hampered. In spite of the necessity for written permission from both parents, it is probable that half the children in the European part of the U.S.S.R. are still baptised. Grandmothers often have an influence over baptism, as they are frequently responsible for the care of children while their mothers are working. However, baptism in many cases is more of a custom than a religious matter and it is thus apparent that official Church acts in the Soviet Union have undergone a development similar to that in Western Europe. A. Okulov, Director of the Institute of Scientific Atheism of the Academy of Social Sciences with the C.P.S.U. Central Committee, in 1967 estimated the number of believers (of all Christian denominations) at 15 per cent in the towns and 30 per cent in some rural areas. Church life, he said, was particularly active in the Baltic lands, the western parts of the Ukraine and of Byelorussia as well as in Moldavia.[5] On the other hand there are very few Orthodox churches open in Siberia. Thus Okulov's statistics are higher than those of the Church writer Levitin quoted previously.

Many of the churches which are open are constantly overfilled, and the lack of space in churches and prayer houses is a central problem for all denominations. Travellers in the Soviet Union are impressed again and again by the number of people attending churches, who can be counted in thousands, and by the whole-hearted participation of the believers in the services. On the other hand, this impression is decidedly put in perspective by the small number of churches that are open, particularly in the cities. In the cities of Central Russia and the Ukraine there is only one open church to 200,000–300,000 people. Thus in Minsk (600,000 inhabitants) there are two Orthodox churches, in Kalinin (300,000 inhabitants) one, and in Kiev, with 1·3 million inhabitants, ten churches and two convents. In Moscow about forty Orthodox churches are open, and in Leningrad the number is thirteen. In the small towns, however, the proportion is supposed to be much more favourable. According to one Western estimate, the number of regular worshippers in the cities is 0·3 per cent of the population.[6] Comparison with the above-cited figures for religiously inclined people shows that only a small percentage of them participate regularly in Church life. Many are afraid of discrimination at work and in society if they declare their affiliation openly, and prefer to remain secret Christians while supporting the Church financially, with the result that the congregations in the Soviet Union, although not rich, do not, so far as we know, suffer serious financial difficulties. The income of most clergy is considerably above the Soviet average.

Some of those who call themselves believers may also stand apart from the Church because it does not have enough to offer them. The liturgy, which is still celebrated in Church Slavonic, is no longer understood by many people. Church sermons are frequently in a frozen, stereotyped style and without relevance to the daily problems of the hearers, and theological discussion is limited almost completely to the narrow circles around the theological schools. All these unsolved problems weigh heavily on the Orthodox Church and intensify the inner crises which will be discussed again later in connection with the internal Church opposition. Even the Church leadership appears resolved to find answers to some of these questions and to try a limited reform. Metropolitan Nikodim (Rotov) of Leningrad and Novgorod, on the occasion of the 1,100th anniversary of the death of Kirill, apostle to the Slavs, said at Sofia in May 1969 that by holding on to a Church language that was no longer understood by the believers, 'the work of our holy Slavic apostles is not being glorified'.[7] Such thoughts of reform on the part of Nikodim and other churchmen, have probably been inspired by the experiences and results of Vatican II.

As for numbers, so also for the sociological composition of the congregations, it is only possible to give approximate data – which, however, are valid with some reservations for all denominations. Seventy to eighty per cent of regular churchgoers are women, and most of these are middle-aged or older. On the other hand, more recent eye-witness accounts again and again underline the fact that today, in contrast to the Khrushchev era, many young people are again to be seen in the Orthodox churches. At Easter 1970 half the worshippers in the patriarchal cathedral in Moscow are said to have been under thirty.[8] At the same time it must be added that in the most recent decades, the Easter services have in many cases become a centre of attraction for sightseers.

The active participants in Church life come overwhelmingly from lower classes. However, in recent years there has been an increasing interest among some young intellectuals in religious questions; this, of course, is stimulated by disillusionment with official ideology which is unable to give any answer to man's ultimate questions and does not even seriously consider them. While the average young person in the Soviet Union knows scarcely anything about Christianity and regards religion and Church with a 'mixed feeling of interest and distrust', there is a small group experiencing a 'regular religious revival'.[9] These young people are often led to the Church by committed laymen and not by priests. It is well known that the Church is forbidden any kind of catechistic work, and even hampered over participation in services by young people, who may only be present as hearers; any co-operation for example in the choir or as acolytes is not allowed.

In the Soviet Union as in the West, participation in Church life is not identical with interest in religious questions and commitment to the Christian revelation; but there seem to be more and more groups in the Soviet Union, particularly among young people and intellectuals, who have an affinity to Christian thought and are at least potential helpers in Church life.

Because of the existence of these individuals with an interest in religion, and because of the traditional Christians, Party and state are labouring to keep the numbers of churches and priests artificially low through repression. Nevertheless, in recent years, as a sign of a certain Church-political *détente*, a number of churches have been renovated and then reconsecrated. In Odessa in 1968 the cemetery church of St. Dmitri was repaired and in September 1969 the Church of the

Immaculate Conception was reconsecrated after a thorough restoration. In the last two years there have also been reports of church renovations from Morzhansk, Tambov diocese, Zavidovo, Kalinin diocese, Chernovtsy, Bukovina, and a number of villages.[10]

On the other hand, the opening of new churches – although legally permitted – is not possible in practice. In this case, as in others, believers are prevented from exercising the rights granted them in law. This is clearly revealed in letters from Orthodox Christians of Gorky in autumn 1968 to the Secretary-General of the World Council of Churches, E. C. Blake, and to the then Secretary-General of the United Nations, U Thant; these letters show once again that arbitrary administration is an essential instrument of government in the Soviet Union, by which legal norms may be set aside at any time in many spheres. The believers here had tried in vain for more than a year – with numerous petitions to the most varied authorities, some bearing as many as 1,500 signatures – to open new churches in this city of a million inhabitants. The administrative authorities were not even prepared to give a properly argued refusal, probably because this would have contradicted all too obviously the right, guaranteed by the 1929 Law, to open new church buildings.[11]

However, the most prominent Russian bishop, Nikodim (Rotov), was responsible for a kind of diocesan meeting of representatives of clergy, laity and the Theological Academy taking place twice at Leningrad in 1968, with reports and discussions on the ecumenical relations of the Russian Orthodox Church.[12] Such an activisation of the congregations from the grass-roots is extremely unusual.

The Hierarchy

In contrast to the parish life in the Soviet Union, which is precarious and constantly in danger, there is a fairly complete network of Orthodox dioceses. In 1972 under Patriarch Pimen there were sixty-nine bishops (nine metropolitans, thirty archbishops and thirty bishops) in the active service of the Russian Orthodox Church.[13] This figure has varied only slightly since the end of the 1940s. Besides the active bishops, there are about thirty-five other hierarchs who have been retired by the Synod for reasons of age or because they have come in conflict with the Soviet authorities. After a number of years those in retirement are occasionally put over a diocese again.

The number of bishops working abroad is strikingly large. This reveals the concern of the Moscow Patriarchate for its small émigré communities; and indeed the intensive life of these communities is well adapted to deceive Western public opinion as to the real situation in the Soviet Union. In 1969 in the patriarchal Exarchates and in the Spiritual Mission in Japan there were one metropolitan, four archbishops, four bishops and four assistant bishops. While the number of those working abroad has increased in recent years, a number of the bishoprics in the Soviet Union are vacant – which to some extent has been the case for some time. Out of the list of dioceses published by the Russian Orthodox Church in 1958, the sees of Chelyabinsk, Khabarovsk, Dnepropetrovsk, Grondo, Izhevsk, Krasnoyarsk, Lugansk, Olonets, Pinsk, Semipalatinsk, Stanislav, Sumy, Ulyanovsk and Velikie Luki were unoccupied in 1972.[14]

Between autumn 1967 and autumn 1969 five new bishops were consecrated in the Moscow Patriarchate; the youngest of them, German (Timofeyev) was only thirty-one at the time of his consecration.[15] Thus he joins the group of quite young bishops around Metropolitan Nikodim (Rotov), himself born in 1929, who will determine the future of the Church. However the two rather older bishops Gedeon (Dokukin) of Smolensk (born 1919) and Savva (Babinets) of Pereyaslav-Khmelnitsky (born 1926) also belong to the generation of theologians who received their theological training after the war at the reopened academies and who can orient themselves without difficulty in a Communist environment.

Bishop Gedeon, born near Krasnodar, completed his studies at the seminary in Stavropol (which has meanwhile been closed again) and from 1955 to 1960 he studied with the Leningrad Academy by correspondence. At the same time from 1953 he was parish priest in various congregations of Stavropol and Olonets dioceses; in 1960 he took his monastic vows.[16] Bishop Savva, who as assistant bishop stands alongside Metropolitan Filaret in the direction of the Kiev diocese, comes from Carpathian Ukraine and took monastic vows in 1947. He completed his studies at the Zagorsk Theological Academy in 1961 and was parish priest in various places after that.[17] The other two newly consecrated bishops Nikolai (Sayama) and Mark (Shavykin) were designated to represent Russian Orthodoxy respectively in Japan and the U.S.A.[18]

The congregations and the bishops are directed by the Holy Synod with the Patriarch at the head. The position of the central Church government is very strong; in all important questions of personnel it makes the final decision, and it represents the whole Church before the state. The Local Council, which is canonically superior to the Synod and the Patriarch, has only been convoked three times so far in the Soviet period (1943, 1945 and 1971) and, in keeping with the Soviet pattern, it has largely exercised a rubber-stamping function; the Church-political decisions had already been taken.

Since 1961 the College of the Holy Synod has had eight members. Standing members are the Metropolitan of Krutitsy, who represents the Patriarch and administers the Moscow diocese, and the Metropolitans of Leningrad and Kiev. Then there are the heads of the two most important offices of the Patriarchate, who belong to the Synod *ex officio*: these are the Department of Foreign Relations and the Patriarchal Office. Besides the above-mentioned hierarchs, three bishops from the provinces are summoned as temporary members of the Synod for six months at a time.

Besides the two offices already mentioned, the Church leadership has departments for theological training, economy, publications and pensions as executive organs.[19] The editorial department co-ordinates all the publications of the Patriarchate, which like all Church activity is controlled and limited by the state, particularly since the Church has no printing works of its own and has to give its printing orders to state presses. The central organ of the Church is *Zhurnal Moskovskoi Patriarkhii* ('Journal of the Moscow Patriarchate'), which is not available through normal magazine distribution either in the Soviet Union or abroad. Then the Ukrainian *Pravoslavny Visnyk* ('Orthodox Messenger') has been able to appear again since September 1968 after a long interruption. While these are the only periodical publications inside the Soviet Union, each of the three exarchates abroad brings out its own journal for a mere handful of congregations, often re-printing articles from the 'Journal of the Moscow Patriarchate' in the national language. In Berlin-Karlshorst appears *Stimme der Orthodoxie* ('Voice of Orthodoxy'); in Paris the *Messager de l'Exarchat du Patriarche Russe en Europe Occidentale* and in New York *One Church*. It goes without saying that such a false distribution of weight is not determined by the Church.

Besides the journals, the Patriarchate has published since the end of the war a number of service books, prayer books and calendars and twice an edition of the Bible (1956 and 1967). All these editions appear in limited numbers. There have also been editions of speeches and essays by Metropolitan Nikolai (Yarushevich) and Patriarch Alexi with a strong political content. The *Bogoslovskie Trudy* ('Theological

Works'), which were supposed to appear annually after 1959, have not exceeded five volumes so far. On the other hand in 1968, to celebrate the fiftieth anniversary of the restoration of the Patriarchate, several recordings of choral music of the Eastern Church appeared.[20]

The restoration of the Patriarchate and the concentration of comprehensive powers in the person of the Patriarch – allowing for the conditions of Soviet rule – has certainly worked out favourably for the Russian Church. It is doubtful if Orthodoxy could otherwise have ever reconsolidated its organisation after the Church splits of the 1920s and the Stalinist terror of the 1930s. The third occupant of the patriarchal throne, Alexi (Simansky), died on 17 April, 1970, at the age of ninety-three and was buried four days later in the Uspensky Cathedral of the Trinity Monastery, Zagorsk, in the presence of Church delegations from all over the world.[21]

Alexi was one of the last hierarchs firmly linked through tradition and education with pre-revolutionary Russia. Born in Moscow in 1877 in an aristocratic family, he graduated in law at Moscow University in 1900 and then entered the Theological Academy – a highly unusual step at a time when many educated theologians were taking refuge in secular professions. Two years later he took his monastic vows, and in 1913 was consecrated bishop. After the Revolution, unlike many bishops, he had no connection with the 'Living Church'. At the beginning of the 1920s, Alexi was imprisoned for a short time by the revolutionary authorities, but he immediately aligned himself with Patriarch Tikhon's declarations of loyalty to the Soviet state. A certain legalistic resignation towards those in power was always characteristic of his Church policy. In 1926 he became Archbishop of Novgorod and in 1933 came to Leningrad as Metropolitan. During the three-year siege by the Germans in the Second World War he refused to leave the city and the congregations which were springing up as a result of famine and patriotism.

The Local Council elected Alexi on 2 February, 1945, to succeed Patriarch Sergi on the latter's death, and the post-war history of the Russian Orthodox Church is thus closely linked with him. He led the rebuilding of the Church in the years up to 1948; in his name the Russian Church praised the 'wise leader' Stalin in hymn-like words and lent all its diplomatic strength to supporting Soviet foreign policy. But Alexi also had to undergo the severe wave of persecution against the Church in the years from 1959 to 1964 without being able to offer resistance.[22]

In the following years, scarcely any further initiatives originated from him, and it was now Nikodim (Rotov), entrusted with the Foreign Department in 1960, who came clearly to the fore in all Church-political action and decision-making. Nikodim, younger than Alexi by two generations, is a man of extraordinary energy and great ability – a fact admitted even by his opponents. He is obviously prepared for moderate reforms, yet his political loyalty to state and Party is beyond all doubt.

Nikodim thus seemed at first to have a good chance of securing the patriarchal succession. However, there were a number of factors against him: his youth, and the fact that his ecumenical activity was considered by many Church circles as too precipitate. Nor was he the senior bishop according to rank; finally, his extraordinary ability, energy and independence may have told against him in the eyes of state and Party. In May 1972 Nikodim resigned his position as head of the Church Foreign Department for health reasons.

The Local Council which met in Zagorsk from 30 May to 2 June, 1971, elected Metropolitan Pimen (Izvekov) – who had been the *locum tenens* since Alexi's death – as the new Patriarch. Pimen had previously been very little in the limelight, so that we know very little apart from a few dates in the life of this man marked by his monastic career. He was born in 1910 in the Moscow district and at the age of seventeen he entered the Trinity Monastery at Zagorsk. He did not receive a systematic theological training, because at that time the Soviet authorities had closed all the seminaries and academies. Pimen was ordained a priest in 1931, after which he probably spent about ten years in Stalin's concentration camps. In 1957 he was consecrated a bishop and in 1960 he took over the leadership of the patriarchal chancellory. He reached the highest rung in the hierarchical ladder with his appointment in 1961 as Metropolitan of Leningrad, and in 1963, with his translation to Moscow as Metropolitan of Krutitsy and Kolomna, he became deputy to the Patriarch.[23]

Needless to say, his election by the Local Council was previously agreed with the Soviet authorities, and it proceeded unanimously.

The Theological Schools

Since the Church persecutions at the beginning of the 1960s, the Russian Orthodox Church has had only two theological academies – in Zagorsk and Leningrad – and three seminaries offering an intermediate theological education. Two of the seminaries are organisationally linked with the academies, the third being in the Monastery of the Assumption near Odessa. Seminary and academy both offer a four-year course and take applicants who are over eighteen and who have completed a Soviet secondary school education. All students receive a Church scholarship and are resident.[24]

For some years there have been more applicants to the theological schools than the Church has places to give. Every year about forty applicants are accepted for the first year at the Zagorsk seminary; on average, half of those who graduate from the seminary continue their studies at the academy, the other half going immediately into parish work. Thus at the theological schools in Zarogsk there are at present about 240 theology students registered; about 150 candidates are studying in Leningrad.[25] A group photograph of the seminarists in Odessa for the academic year 1967–8 shows twenty-one students.[26] The Orthodox Church is of course unable to meet its own need for parish priests with the small number of those graduating from the seminaries and academies; hence there are regular ordinations of priests and deacons who have had no formal theological education. Since 1963–4 there have been correspondence courses for them at Zagorsk – these had previously been connected with the schools at Leningrad – and they give priests the opportunity, while they are carrying out their parish responsibilities, to complete their theological training. In 1972 there were more than 400 priests taking part in correspondence courses.[11]

Theological study is on the whole deeply conservative in orientation, being directed towards practical church preparation rather than academic theological training. Since the students are quite unprepared in theological study, seminary teaching has to begin with very elementary things, upon which the new teaching courses introduced in 1967–8 have laid great stress.[28] Limits are set to the controversy with the secular environment at academy and seminary, since up to now a confrontation with the official atheism of the Soviet Union is just as impossible as a Christian–Marxist dialogue. Nevertheless, the academies have tried in recent years to broaden the scope of topics for written theological works, and to include the development of Western theology as well as their own recent history – particularly the 'Living Church'.

In his lecture 'The Tasks of Theology Today', given at the Leningrad Academy in October 1968, Metropolitan Nikodim stressed the need for 'a thoroughgoing relation of theology to life'. In today's 'pluralistic religious world' it was important 'to put the eternal truth of the Gospel in new and convincing categories that are understandable to modern man'. This, however, must occur, according to the conviction of the Russian Orthodox Church, 'in the light of Church tradition' and the 'great heritage of the ancient Christian Church'.[29]

On 14 June, 1969, the theological schools in Zagorsk celebrated the twenty-fifth anniversary of their reopening. Between 1944 and 1969 the academy had given eleven doctor's and thirty-one master's degrees; 451 candidates had received the diploma of graduate in theology. Since almost all students finished with a degree, the last-quoted figure gives the approximate number of all those who had passed through the academy.[30] In recent years the theological doctorate has been granted among others to the professor of homiletics, Archpriest A. A. Vetelev, who for his dissertation presented a five-volume course on sermon instruction and pastoral care with about 200 sample sermons.[31] This work, written as a practical introduction for students and preachers, adds to the considerable fund of type-written manuscripts which are the basis for study at the theological school. The Church is unable to consider printing the numerous theological manuscript collections in Zagorsk and Leningrad.

In the academic year 1968–9 Professor M. A. Starokadomsky (born 1889) received a doctorate at Zagorsk for a work on the speculative foundation of theism in Russian theology. The work considered among other things speculative theology from Solovyov to Florensky. Starokadomsky is also a learned geographer and a holder of the Order of Lenin.[32]

For the furthering of theology, there has been for a short time at Zagorsk (probably since 1967) a three-year research course (*aspirantura*). Here some theologians have the chance, after completing their studies, of continuing in research and preparing themselves for future teaching work.[33] This innovation will certainly contribute to raising the level of theological teaching and research in the Soviet Union.

In 1966 a 'Faculty of Afro-Asian Christian Youth' was established at the Leningrad Academy, which was obviously supposed to give some kind of development aid, and acquaints African young people with the Orthodox Church and the 'struggle for peace' of the Churches in the Soviet Union. In the academic year 1968–9 seven Africans completed the three-year course at the 'faculty'.[34] This institution is well adapted to give the Russian Church a certain resonance in the developing countries and to remind the Soviet authorities of the importance of Church work in the international sphere.

In December 1968 the Leningrad Academy received as its new rector the young Bishop German (Timofeyev). Born on 11 November, 1937, in Tashkent, German had completed his studies at the Academy in 1966 and become a monk in 1965. He had already exercised the rectorate provisionally since August 1968, after the unexpected transfer of the previous rector, Bishop Mikhail (Mudyugin) to Astrakhan. It is easy to imagine that Mikhail, who was very frank, had had conflicts within the hierarchy and with the Soviet authorities.[35] The appointment of the inexperienced and unknown German is an example of Metropolitan Nikodim's undoctrinaire decisions; however, German may temporarily be bound to him in obligation. In June 1970 German was transferred to Vienna as Bishop of the West European Exarchate; Bishop Meliton (Solovyov), born in 1897, took over responsibility for the Leningrad theological schools. The new rector had no academic experience; his background was pastoral work in the Leningrad diocese, and he was only made a bishop in July 1970.

On the whole the intellectual climate in Leningrad, both generally and in Church and theological respects, is considered more liberal, less dogmatic and less tradition-bound.

Monasteries and Convents

Until the end of the 1950s there were sixty-seven monasteries and convents in the Soviet Union; their number was drastically reduced by Khrushchev's terror measures and today amounts probably to about fifteen. There is no complete list.

The Trinity Monastery in Zagorsk is particularly important because it is at the centre of Church life and there are always students entering as novices from the seminary and academy. They represent the next generation of the episcopate, which of course comes exclusively from the monastic clergy. There are about ninety monks in Zagorsk today, of whom more than half are ordained as priests.[36] On the Trinity Monastery's great festival days, tens of thousands of believers pour in there, some having covered long distances to make the pilgrimage.

Another nationally important place of pilgrimage is the Monastery of the Caves near Pskov. Visitors report that on Church high days as many as 30,000 pilgrims arrive there to celebrate the service with the monks, who number approximately sixty.[37] Many of the monks are advanced in years, but here too for some years it has been possible to accept a few novices. In many cases in the Soviet Union it is men well on in life who, after a long career in the world, decide to enter a monastery. Between 1960 and 1968 widespread repairs and restorations could be made to the buildings of the Pskov Monastery and the Church of St. Nicholas, so that today foreign visitors are again taken there regularly.[38]

A focus for Church piety in the south of Russia is still to be found in the Monastery of the Assumption in Pochaev, which the authorities tried in vain to close at the beginning of the 1960s. However, many monks, some of whom spent several years in camps, have not been permitted to return there. Thus priest-monk Amvrosi (Dovgan), who had lived in the Lavra from 1950 to 1962, appealed to the Patriarch at Christmas 1967 to help him return to Pochaev. Amvrosi had spent a total of three years in prison for refusing to leave Pochaev.[39] Also priest-monks Sergi (Solomenko) and Apelli (Stankevich) in August 1967 wrote to Patriarch Athenagoras of Constantinople, asking him to accept them in one of the monasteries on Mount Athos, since after years of vexations and imprisonments they were not allowed to return to Pochaev.[40]

Besides those already named, there are also the Monastery of the Assumption near Odessa, which is at the same time the Patriarch's summer residence; the monastery of the same name in Zhirovitsy, Minsk diocese; and the small Holy Ghost Monastery in Vilnius, Lithuania.

Because of the dissolution of many monasteries and because of the urgent need for parish priests, some monks are also active today as parish priests and live outside the monasteries.

The largest convent belonging to the Patriarchate is the Convent of the Protection of Mary in Kiev, which houses 200 nuns; in Kiev there is also the smaller Frolov convent.[41] A focal point of Orthodoxy and of Russian life in Estonia since the end of the last century has been the convent in Pyukhtitsa (Püchtitz), which received a new abbess in January 1968, Varvara (Trofimova).[42] Apart from Pyukhtitsa, there are in the Soviet Baltic republics also small Orthodox convents in Riga and Vilnius.

Of a few other convents, little more than the name is known. This is true for example of the Nikolai convent in Mukachevo or the Convent of the Immaculate Conception in Alexandrovka village, Odessa diocese, in which over thirty nuns live together. The church belonging to this convent community, also called the Convent of the

Archangel Michael, was reconsecrated in September 1969 after restoration. The journals of the Patriarchate reported briefly that the convent maintained itself by the sale of candles and icons and by the manufacture of *prosphoras* (consecrated bread). Many of the nuns also work in the fields and vineyards of the neighbouring kolkhozes.[43] The nuns of the Trinity Convent in Korets, Volhynia diocese, are active in Church work on the one hand, as they make liturgical vestments, while on the other hand they too work on the land.[44]

Ecumenical Relations

Since the thaw in the middle of the 1950s and particularly since 1961, much of the activity of the Church leadership has been directed towards ecumenical relations. The public, who learn almost nothing about internal Church life, receive running reports with extremely detailed information about external relations, which would of course be unthinkable without the approval of state and Party. International Church contacts have four centres of gravity. The Russian Orthodox Church's collaboration in the Prague Christian Peace Conference is its most important contribution to the Soviet-inspired struggle of the Churches for peace in the world. Then the second centre of gravity is the activity arising from membership of the World Council of Churches, which Russian Orthodoxy joined in 1961.

Through the World Council of Churches it comes into contact with the Protestant Churches, with which the Church's Foreign Department in Moscow is also seeking links in the developing countries. An important place in international Church life then goes to the *rapprochement* between Moscow and Rome, which since the beginning of Vatican II has made unexpected progress. A fourth centre of gravity consists of inter-Orthodox relations and the preparations for a pan-Orthodox Council.

The Christian Peace Conference hit a grave crisis in 1968, for which the Russian Orthodox Church bears much of the responsibility. At the Third Prague Christian Peace Conference (31 March to 5 April, 1968) participants were still united in the demand that all lands must be freed 'from the control of foreign powers over their political, economic and cultural life', and of course the U.S.A. was named as the sole example of imperialist exploitation.[45] Not many months later, the invasion of Czechoslovakia by the Russians forced the Prague leaders of the movement, in an unprecedented moment of clarity, to realise the one-sidedness of such an attitude.

For the rest, the Third Peace Conference had occupied itself with the social and political responsibility of Christians for the world, and thus touched on questions that are at present of burning importance for all Churches in East and West. The Churches are becoming conscious of their responsibility for hunger in the world, for global social injustice and the consequent danger to world peace. Charity, whether motivated by Christianity or humanism, is powerless against these threats, and the Prague Congress declared social revolution in the Third World to be necessary, even from the Christian point of view. The revolutionary process can be accompanied by the use of violence . . .' At the same time, however, the Congress left it in no doubt that socialism had no need of such revolutionary changes.[46]

However, the events in Czechoslovakia in 1968 caused these maxims, formerly considered unshakeable, to totter. Professor J. Hromadka, the President and Founder of the C.P.C. in a striking letter of 22 August, 1968, to the Soviet ambassador in Prague, Chervonenko, described the Soviet invasion as 'the greatest tragedy' of his life.[47] Similarly the World Council of Churches, after pressure from many member Churches, especially from Czechoslovakia, made a declaration on 28 August demanding the immediate withdrawal of the Warsaw Pact troops from Czechoslovakia and announced its solidarity 'with the Churches and people of Czechoslovakia'.[48]

Patriarch Alexi, in a letter to the World Council of Churches of 14 September and in a declaration of 28 September, dissociated himself from the position taken by the World Council and described the invasion as 'the manifestation of solidarity – even though expressed in unusual form – of peoples linked in brotherhood. . . .'[49] The other member Churches of the W.C.C. in the Soviet Union (the Georgian Orthodox Church, the Evangelical-Lutheran Churches of Latvia and Estonia, the Council of Evangelical Christians and Baptists) also (in contrast to the Churches in Czecholsovakia and Rumania) aligned themselves with the official Soviet attitude.[50] This episode illustrates the dependence of the Churches on the prevailing political situation in their country.

The differing judgments on the events of 1968 in Czechoslovakia have led to a deep rift in the otherwise united front of the C.P.C.; and the East European Churches, with Russian Orthodoxy at the head, have up to now tried in vain, under political direction, to silence the critical voices. In November 1969 Hromadka's closest collaborator, and General Secretary of the C.P.C., J. Ondra, was forced by political intrigue to resign. Hromadka, against whose statements of August 1968 the action against Ondra was really directed, drew his own conclusions and likewise resigned as president of the C.P.C. on 14 November, 1968.[51] Shortly afterwards, on 26 December, 1969, he died in Prague, at the age of eighty.

However, this ruthless action of the Churches of the Warsaw Pact countries against the critics within the C.P.C. of the Soviet invasion has not led to the restoration of unity. On the contrary, in March 1970, nine Western Regional Committees, whose co-operation was especially valued by the East European countries, separated themselves from the C.P.C. and formed their own group.[52] The Regional Committee for West Germany has split, and the majority, under the former President, Oberkirchenrat H. Kloppenburg, has likewise left the C.P.C. Thus the aim of the organisation – co-operation of Churches in East and West on an East European socialist basis – is placed in jeopardy. At the Fourth Christian Peace Conference from 30 September to 3 October, 1971, Nikodim was elected as the new President and successor to Hromadka. These events have made it abundantly clear that in future there can be no conflicts of loyalty within the C.P.C. and that in this respect the organisation wholly follows the Soviet line.

Another forum of the Russian Orthodox Church in the struggle for peace, which at the same time is a struggle for Soviet foreign policy goals, was the Zagorsk 'Conference of Members of all Religions in the U.S.S.R. for Co-operation and Peace among the Nations' on 1–4 July, 1969, in which 176 delegates of the Soviet religious bodies and more than 130 guests from forty-four countries took part. The guiding body at this, as at the previous conference in the spring of 1952, was the Moscow Patriarchate.

The communiqué and the various declarations on political questions 'on the basis of religious responsibility' contained the usual 'realistic' attitudes to the world situation. West Germany was accused of 'militaristic politics', and the 'removal of the dictatorships in Greece, Spain and Portugal' was demanded. The Churches of the Soviet Union called for the unconditional withdrawal of the Americans from Southeast Asia and condemned the 'aggression of Israel' with the same candour with which they supported the 'just struggle of the Arab peoples'.[53]

In his main speech, Nikodim suggested a strongly dualistic, rather naïve social ethic of the 'permanent struggle . . . between the forces of good and evil'. Political evaluation by reference to this framework

E

is then not very difficult, for the 'manifestations of ill will' are found in 'racism, colonialism, neo-colonialism and imperialism', which of course only exist in the 'West', because in the socialist society through the 'social ownership of the means of production', 'the possibility of man exploiting man is removed'. Nevertheless, Nikodim evoked 'peaceful coexistence' as a 'sacred legacy for all religious persons' and in a few formulations he almost appeared as a secret theorist of convergence.[54] The mixture of patriotic admiration for heroes and appeal to the longing of man for peace, which is characteristic of the Russian Church's political position, received particular expression in the speech of Bishop Pimen (Khmelevskoi).[55]

In spite of the one-sided political colouring of such occasions, their non-political value for the Churches in the Soviet Union cannot be ignored. This consists on the one hand in the relatively public effect – even the Soviet government paid the Zagorsk Conference its respects with a greetings communication – and on the other in private conversations of Church leaders behind the scenes, for which there is otherwise no opportunity in such a large circle.

The religious bodies in the U.S.S.R. can also appear publicly on a few other occasions, all in connection with patriotic political action. Thus they are members of the Soviet Committee for the Defence of Peace and the Soviet Peace Fund, founded in 1961. At the meeting of the Peace Fund on 1 April, 1969, in Moscow, Metropolitan Alexi (Ridiger) made a speech in which he announced that the Patriarchate had contributed 200,000 roubles to the Peace Fund in both 1967 and 1968. The dioceses gave respectively 903,760 and 876,774 roubles. Besides that, the congregations also made direct contributions to the Peace Fund, the congregations in fourteen dioceses alone giving 2,240,150 roubles in 1968.[56] These figures prompt the suspicion that such generosity is the result of some pressure, but they also show the considerable financial resources of the Russian Orthodox Church.

The international relations of the Moscow Patriarchate within the framework of the World Council of Churches ran especially high with the participation of a thirty-five-man delegation at the Plenary Assembly of the Council in Uppsala from 4 to 19 July, 1968. Although the Orthodox Churches have meanwhile obtained a decisive weight in the W.C.C. – the entry of the Russian Church caused other Orthodox Churches of Eastern Europe to follow suit – nevertheless the initiative continues to come mainly from the Protestant member Churches. However, the Eastern Church represents an important, theologically conservative factor, and in accordance with its high self-esteem it regards itself among the Protestants as being primarily at the giving end. But Russian Orthodoxy and other member Churches from the Eastern European countries have not succeeded in aligning the World Council wholly with the political line of the Prague Peace Conference, although they did attempt during the preparations for Uppsala to impose their position on the Vietnam question and the situation in the Middle East.[57]

The co-operation of the Russian Church in the W.C.C. does not by any means have agitation as its a primary object; out of elementary self-interest, it is concerned with the promotion of Christian unity and the involvement of the Churches in the world. This factor came to the fore in a meeting of the W.C.C. in March 1968 at Zagorsk, where the preparations for Uppsala figured on the agenda. (This was the third large W.C.C. meeting in the Soviet Union, after the Executive Committee session in Odessa in 1964 and that of the Working Committee on Faith and Order in Zagorsk in 1966.[58]) In a public lecture devoted to the then forthcoming Plenary Assembly in Uppsala, Metropolitan Nikodim spoke on the position and limits of ecumenical co-operation in the Orthodox view. He warned against the occasional Protestant attempts to see in the World Council a 'new ecclesiological reality'. Church unity would only be achieved 'when all member-Churches of the World Council believed in common with the ancient, undivided Church. . . .' On the basis of this as yet unyielding theological conservatism, Nikodim took issue against the 'heretical theological modernism', to which the member-Churches of the World Council had to set limits. Orthodoxy also regarded the 'revolutionary changes' in the life of the Church, often advocated from the Protestant side, as being of little importance.[59]

There is a striking contrast between this conservative, protectionist attitude and the more and more outspoken support of the Russian Orthodox Church in recent years for the so-called 'theology of revolution'. Nikodim calls upon Christians 'to take part in the revolutionary reconstruction of the world . . .', [60]and the Russian Church emphasises 'the right and duty of Christians . . . to support progressive social movements', even when they 'follow revolutionary paths'.[61] The Russian Church leadership here agrees with tendencies in the Western Churches which for the first time received emphatic official endorsement at the Beirut Conference on development questions (April 1968). This conference, arranged jointly by the World Council and by the papal commission Justitia et Pax, had concluded that in extreme situations men could be led 'to involvement in violent revolution'.[62]

Both inside and outside the World Council of Churches, the Russian Church has made a large number of contacts with Protestant Churches throughout the world, and the programme of visits and return visits is almost too great to survey. In the Moscow Patriarchate some foreign Church delegation or other is being received almost the whole year round. Relations with the developing countries have intensified in recent years. In September 1967 a delegation of the Malabar Church of India made a visit to the Soviet Union, which the Patriarchate returned in January and February 1969.[63] In 1967 and 1968 the Russian Church sent three official delegations on extended visits to Africa, chiefly West Africa.[64]

In contrast to their relations with many Churches, contacts with the Evangelical Church in West Germany have a more academic theological character. In September 1969 theologians on both sides met in Leningrad for their fourth discussion, this time on the subject 'Baptism and the Ministry of the Baptised in the World'.[65] These discussions began in 1959 in Arnoldshain/Taunus. On the Evangelical side they are carried on in an attempt to establish common ground theologically; there is evident fear of a confrontation between Orthodoxy and modern Protestant theology.

The third centre of gravity of Moscow's international Church relations is the *rapprochement* with Rome, which was instigated in connection with Khrushchev's maxims on coexistence at the beginning of the 1960s. The Moscow Patriarchate was the only Orthodox Church to send official observers to Vatican II in 1962, since which it has tried through a lively diplomacy of visits and conversations to bring down prejudices and barriers. Moscow has repeatedly emphasised that in dogmatic questions of faith the Catholic Church is nearest to Orthodoxy. On the other hand the Russian Church gains access through Rome to internal Church reform movements, which are more acceptable to it than left-wing Protestant 'heresies'. Besides this, a closer link with Rome could strengthen the position of the Church against the Soviet government, for the Vatican carries a certain prestige in the calculations of diplomacy.

On the Russian side the conversations are led by Metropolitan Nikodim and his former deputy and now head of the Foreign Department, Bishop Yuvenali (Poyarkov). On the Roman side leadership is in the hands of Cardinal Jan Willebrands, who in November 1968 succeeded Cardinal Bea as President of the Secretariat for Christian Unity. On the death of Patriarch Alexi in April 1970, Cardinal Willebrands visited the Soviet Union for the fourth time. But the *rapprochement* is not limited to the highest Church level; it tries as far as possible to penetrate the lower ranks. Thus in 1968 for the first time two Orthodox theologians came to study at the Papal University in Rome, and in the same year two monks, including the Abbot of the Trinity Monastery in Zagorsk, visited Catholic monasteries in France.[66]

The good relations reached a new high level on 16 December, 1969, when the Synod decided to admit Roman Catholic Christians in the diaspora to the Orthodox sacraments. The announcement of the *communicatio in sacris* came without consultation with the other Orthodox Churches and led to a sharp reaction from the Greek Orthodox Church as well as to new tensions with Constantinople.[67] The Greek hierarchy sees in Moscow's unilateral step a break of trust and an injury to pan-Orthodox unity. It cannot be ignored that the Russian Church's action is connected with its attempt, noticeable in other ways also, to contest the primacy of Constantinople among the Orthodox Churches. Perhaps Rome can act as a balancing factor here.

Pan-Orthodox links, which come in here as the last focus of international Church activity, have not been undisturbed in other areas. Since 1967 the Russian Church has made repeated protests – this too in harmony with Soviet foreign policy – against the suppression of 'freedom and democracy' in Greece and against the interference of the government in internal Church affairs. It has thereby aroused considerable tensions with Greek Orthodoxy which has identified itself more and more with the military dictatorship.[68]

Renewed friction with the Patriarchate of Constantinople was caused by the events concerning the largest Russian émigré Church, that in the U.S.A. The American Metropolia (as this Church called itself) has renamed itself the Orthodox Greek-Catholic Church in America, so as to express its having taken root in a new homeland and its claim to unite all Orthodox Churches in North America. The Moscow Patriarchate, from which this Church had virtually become separated after 1946, recognised the autocephaly of the Orthodox Church in America in May 1970.[69] At the same time it took up canonical relations with this Church, which had previously been considered schismatic, without first consulting with Constantinople; the latter is now afraid for the obedience of its Greek communities in the U.S.A., which could be drawn into the wake of the new independent Orthodox

Church in America. The Moscow Patriarchate simultaneously dissolved its American Exarchate in its previous form.

It is easily understood that such tensions do not help in the preparations for the pan-Orthodox Council, for which planning has been in progress for ten years. Although the Council was expected to gather in 1968, its realisation now seems to be even further postponed. The initiative for a great work of Orthodox unification had come from the late Patriarch Athenagoras of Constantinople, and the Russian Church had always supported it in principle without at the same time losing sight of its own expansionist aims as the largest Orthodox Local Church. The fourth inter-Orthodox conference in Chambésy near Geneva in June 1968 decided on a complicated method for the coming work of preparation; thus there will undoubtedly be more preconciliar conferences before a Council can really meet, by which time it is clearly desired that all controversial points should have been dealt with.[70]

The above details have shown how far the Church is dependent on Party and state, but also how strongly it identifies itself with them. In this it is often impossible to distinguish genuine feelings of loyalty from conscious camouflage and manipulation of political conditions in order to purchase continuing legality in such a state.

The fiftieth anniversary of the October Revolution in autumn 1967 was an occasion for special declarations of loyalty by the Church towards the Soviet state. Patriarch and Synod formulated their good wishes to the leaders of the Soviet Union, 'the bearers of the hopes of the whole people', in a circular to all believers dated 10 October, 1967. The actions of Soviet policy in the last fifty years, it said, were 'in agreement with the ideals of the Gospel'.[71] Metropolitan Nikodim, too, at a ceremonial session of the Soviet Committee for the Defence of Peace on 25 October, 1967, emphatically welcomed the achievements of the Revolution 'which Christianity had not realised with its own strength'.[72]

Nevertheless, the identification of the Orthodox Church with the state has its limitations. These were visible in the circular for the October Revolution, for the Patriarchate leadership emphasised here 'the possibility for a fruitful social work by the Church within socialist society'. Precisely such a combination of socialism and Christianity is rejected by the state ideology and condemned as a relapse into bourgeois pluralistic thinking.

The interweaving by the Church of its international relations and propaganda statements with Soviet policy is moreover of use to both sides and should not be evaluated solely as servility on the part of the Church. State and Church are equally involved when leading representatives of the Church are regularly invited to state receptions at the Kremlin, or when, for example, the French and Belgian Foreign Ministers, Maurice Schumann and Paul Harmel, make an official visit to Zagorsk Monastery.[73]

Through the activity of the Church in the international arena, Soviet policy reaches areas of the foreign public which had previously been closed to it, and it tries – with partial success – to create the impression in ecclesiastical and political circles abroad of unhindered freedom of belief and conscience in its own land. The Church, for its part, has the chance of winning support and friends abroad who might one day exert their moral and political weight in its favour. Until now, admittedly, the international Church organisations have largely had their hands tied, because the Russian Church leadership has never been prepared to admit any conflict with state and Party and has always preserved the outward appearance of complete harmony and security of existence. It is against this falsification of the true situation that the opposition movements in the Church are protesting.

The Opposition Movements: 1. Literary Activity

The strong opposition movements against the Church leadership and the arbitrary actions of the Soviet authorities were activated by the Khrushchev church persecutions, and have brought the Russian Church to the verge of schism; this has already been discussed in the previous chapter.[74] In the following years, too, the voices expressing solidarity with the first spokesmen of this opposition, Fathers Nikolai Eshliman and Gleb Yakunin, became ever more numerous. 'They expressed the general feeling and the general pain . . . their voice is the voice of the Church,' says the letter of one Russian priest.[75]

The medium of this opposition, as with the anti-Stalinist political-literary intelligentsia, consists of a large number of typewritten copies of letters, petitions, articles and historical essays, which are passed from hand to hand in the Soviet Union and which increasingly reach the West. The quantity and quality of this illegal press, which is the expression of a non-conforming public opinion and shows an increasing awareness among the Soviet intelligentsia, grow continually. Even frequent police raids in recent years have failed to master this underground press. But, despite the ruthlessness of police action, the K.G.B. does not work today with the methods of the 1930s, when the goal was simply the physical liquidation of all possible opponents. Opposition Church writers who have been known in East and West for years are still at liberty, although others have recently been imprisoned. The opposition's very existence would be unthinkable, despite all 're-Stalinisation tendencies', without the internal liberalisation that has gone on in the Soviet Union since the middle of the 1950s.

The Church authors do not form any organised group, but come from various parts of the country and from different generations, and represent different opinions over many questions of detail; nevertheless, they agree over basic demands and intellectual starting-points. Just like the anti-Stalinist, liberal intelligentsia in general, they demand the opportunity to exercise the rights due them under Soviet laws. In their protests against the continual and arbitrary interference of the authorities in internal Church affairs, the Church authors appeal again and again to the 1918 law on the separation of Church and state and thereby to Lenin, who is held up as a shining counterpart against contemporary Stalinist practice. The human rights proclaimed by the United Nations and the Soviet Constitution are contrasted with day-to-day practice in administration and law. The protesters show not only civil courage in standing up against the ecclesiastical and secular authorities in a Communist-ruled country, but they are also prepared to suffer public and private discrimination for their convictions and to accept long prison sentences.

In the illegal Church press there is a constant demand for the retraction of the decisions of the 1961 Synod of Bishops, which excluded priests from the secular control of the congregations. All related questions are to be discussed at a Local Council. The Church authors also make more or less clear demands for a revision of the 1929 Law which, through the obligation of registration and other repressive regulations, has legalised many of the continual inroads into internal Church spheres. However, in this the Orthodox do not go as far as the breakaway free Baptists, who uncompromisingly demand the abolition of the 1929 Law and of many of the regulations of the 1918 Leninist decree. One of the most outspoken Orthodox spokesmen, A. E. Levitin-Krasnov, expressly rejected any claim to private (*sic*) religious instruction for children. 'We [only] want guarantees against any kind of arbitrary administrative action or violence against religious individuals.'[76]

One centre of internal independent Church movements – one about which we have knowledge – rose around Boris Vladimirovich Talantov in Kirov. Talantov, a mathematician born in 1901, was until 1958 a teacher at the Kirov Polytechnic, but in that year he lost his job because of his sharp protests against the injustices of Stalinist rule, under which his father, a priest, and his brother had died in camps.[77] Since the 1950s Talantov has written a large number of petitions and open letters; he became known in wider Church circles through the letter of the twelve believers from Kirov to Patriarch Alexi in June 1966 and through his open letter in November of the same year.[78] In them he described in great detail the methods of mass church closures and the persecutions of the Khrushchev era. A petition to the U.S.S.R. Attorney-General dated 26 April, 1968, confirmed the authenticity of Talantov's letters.[79] Here he reported how the state security police had tried to make him and the other signatories of the 'Letter of the Twelve' retract their signatures after this letter had been broadcast by the B.B.C. on 8 December, 1966; in February 1967 Metropolitan Nikodim made a false statement to the London press that the Kirov letter was anonymous and could therefore be disregarded. A slander campaign in the local press accompanied the action of the K.G.B., and the Patriarchate expelled one of the signatories of the letter, the theology student N. N. Kamenskikh, from the Odessa seminary.[80]

The opposition movements in the Church have involved the theological schools in other ways too. Talantov and the other opposition spokesmen obviously have personal relations with a fairly large circle of students and influence them both theologically and politically. On the whole Talantov went beyond other writers in his criticism of state and Church. He accused the Patriarchate of appearing 'on the international platform as a secret agent for the fight against World Christendom', and believers must therefore 'cleanse the Church of false brethren and false shepherds'.[81] Such formulations, which nearly amount to a call for separation from the patriarchal Church, are linked in Talantov's writings with a fundamental critique of Communist ideology, which, he wrote, had revealed itself as an illusion and so lost its seductive power over the masses.[82]

It is characteristic of the tactics and style of the Church leadership that the Patriarchate journals in the spring of 1969 carried an interview with the acting Bishop of Kirov, Mstislav (Volonshevich), in which he stated that in Kirov as in the Soviet Union generally 'there had never been any suppression of freedom of belief.' However, the K.G.B. decided at this point that a method other than interviews was needed, and it imprisoned Talantov on 12 June, 1969. On 3 September, 1969, at the age of sixty-eight, although seriously ill, he was sentenced to two years in a labour camp.[84] The basis of the charge was Article 190/1 of the R.S.F.S.R. Penal Code, which was also used at the writers' trials and had only been introduced in 1966; this made 'deliberately false statements slandering the Soviet state and social order' a criminal offence.[85] Talantov died in Kirov prison in January 1971.

In recent years the literature teacher A. E. Levitin-Krasnov, a writer with considerable theological as well as historical erudition, has become more and more the centre of internal Church criticism in Moscow. Born in 1915, Levitin spent the years from 1949 to 1956 in Stalin's camps, and in 1959 he lost his post as a teacher of literature. Since then he has written a large number of articles and historical essays and distributed them in typed copies; at times he employed several private secretaries. Levitin has levelled severe accusations at the episcopate, describing Metropolitan Nikodim as a 'hated person' and charging Patriarch Alexi with 'betraying the Church to unbelievers'.[86] Nevertheless, he agrees with the Church leadership on a number of basic points. He, too, sees the task of Christianity in the world not in terms of humility and submission, but as a militant co-operation in building earthly existence. The kingdom of God does not only begin in us, but also in 'external conditions, in social life, in society. . . .'[87]

Levitin has always emphasised that he regards himself as a socialist and opponent of capitalism, and he is for a 'socialist democracy', which should doubtless be seen as inclining towards the Czechoslovak 'socialism with a human face'.[88] It is normal for the great majority of the opposition intelligentsia to consider themselves socialists or Communists; they understand their critique of today's Soviet reality as a return to the true sources and intentions of socialism. Talantov's fundamental rejection of Communist ideology is rather the exception.

Levitin also agrees with the Church leaders in his unbroken national consciousness: 'to sacrifice oneself for the people' is for him one of the highest callings.[89] In the progressive, non-conforming intelligentsia there is certainly something of the impetus of a latter-day 'going to the people' (narodnichestvo); and Levitin is closely connected with these critical, independent intellectual circles in Moscow. He was a signatory of a number of protest resolutions against the writers' trials, and appeared as a witness in one of them. He was also a member of the 'Action Group for the Defence of Human Rights in the U.S.S.R.' which was much reduced by arrests in 1969.[90] Levitin's close connection with the literary-political intelligentsia may have been one added reason why the security police arrested him in Moscow on 12 September, 1969. So that as little commotion as possible would be caused in the capital, he was removed in October to the prison in Krasnodar[91] – a tactic frequently used by the K.G.B. after the undesired public repercussions of the writers' trials.

Only a few days after Levitin's arrest, thirty-two Soviet intellectuals wrote an appeal *To Public Opinion in the Soviet Union and Abroad*, in which they protested against this violent act and declared their solidarity with Levitin as a fighter for the 'liberation of our people from its accursed Stalinist past'. Also, still in September 1969, a number of Moscow Orthodox Christians addressed an urgent appeal to the World Council of Churches to intervene with the Soviet authorities 'for the liberation of Talantov and Levitin as well as for the normalisation of religious life in the U.S.S.R.'[92] However, these appeals did not prevent Levitin being sentenced in May 1971 to three years in a labour camp.

The link between the critical voices in the Church and the anti-Stalinist intelligentsia has become ever more evident in recent years, even if we overlook in this context the Christian overtones, motifs and questions in the writings of a number of leading intellectuals and if we omit Gorbanevskaya, Dorosh and others, because we are limiting our discussion to controversies within the Church. The letters of Fr. Sergi Zheludkov of Pskov show how strongly the internal Church opposition feels itself to be linked with the liberal intelligentsia.

Zheludkov obviously has a strong affinity with modern Western theology and he considers as vitally important not only the reform of the liturgy and Christian teaching, but also an adaptation of dogma to our times. If there is not a thoroughgoing reformation of the Church, he has doubts about its continued existence.[93] This deep sense of crisis, conditioned by external political suppression and the consequent inability to make timely and effective reforms, is obviously more widespread in many Russian Orthodox circles than we are aware.

In letters to the spokesmen of the anti-Stalinist intelligentsia, P. M. Litvinov, A. D. Sakharov and A. I. Solzhenitsyn, Zheludkov has spoken of 'our practical unity' to create a 'socialist society' which must be 'a viable combination of organised structure and creative freedom'. However, said Zheludkov, present-day Soviet reality was not socialist but a 'discrediting of socialism'.[94] Zheludkov draws a sombre picture of contemporary Soviet society, as being characterised by fear, pretence, self-deception and compromising with one's conscience.

Young people were sinking into intellectual apathy, petty bourgeois ideas and a craving for consumer goods. These were the fruits of Stalinism, for which no one person but the whole of society bore the guilt. Today it was necessary to regain internal and external freedom; but the problem of freedom for Zheludkov is a religious one, in so far as 'freedom is an absolute, divine right of man and his sacred duty'.[95] He therefore addresses the Soviet intellectuals fighting for freedom as unconscious Christians, who unknowingly belong to the 'church of good will'. His argument here recalls the discussions of the Religious-Philosophical Meetings at the turn of the century.[96]

No one, of course, can determine the exact extent of free criticism and of the new self-awareness among the theologians and laity of the Orthodox Church. But hundreds of signatures under petitions testify to the involvement of many congregations. This internal divide will remain for the foreseeable future one of the most urgent problems to be faced by the Church leaders and the Soviet authorities. Levitin has defined the goal of the movement as the 'struggle for the freedom of religion, for the freedom of atheism and for complete freedom of conscience'. For, he said, even atheism in the Soviet Union was not free but enforced, like Orthodoxy in pre-Revolutionary Russia.[97]

Such a goal must appear illusory in the present state of Soviet society. But even if the opposition does not achieve its goals, that still does not mean that it has achieved nothing. A certain *détente* in the Church-political situation since 1965 and certain relaxations in recent years are due partly to the harsh criticism and radical demands of the internal Church opposition. The opposition can probably also exercise pressure on the Church leaders to use greater firmness in their relations with the state authorities. On the other hand it cannot be overlooked that the Orthodox Church is still exposed to the danger of an attempt at schism as a result of the new self-awareness of many clergy and laity. At any rate the inner life forces of the Church have become more apparent in the last decade.

2. *The Old Believers*

The Old Believers separated from the state Church in the seventeenth century because they were not prepared to accept the Church reform introduced by Patriarch Nikon. In the course of their history they have splintered into a multitude of groups over theological and ritualistic disputes. The number of their members in the Soviet Union today is still reckoned at several millions, although even their Church organisations were not spared by the violent administrative measures at the beginning of the 1960s.[98]

While the largest Old Believer Church, the Old Believer Archbishopric of Moscow and All Russia – the Belaya Krinitsa Concord (see above p. 32ff.) – still had 300 congregations and 200 priests in five dioceses at the end of the 1950s, in 1968 the number of congregations was only 100, looked after by about the same number of priests. Since 1961 this group, which established an episcopal hierarchy in the middle of the last century at Belaya Krinitsa (Bukovina), has been headed by Archbishop Iosif (Morzhakov), a sick man; of the three other working bishops, one has had his registration removed by the authorities because he protested against state interference in internal Church matters. The protodeacon G. A. Ustinov is supposed to be the key figure where relations with the authorities and the political position of the Archbishopric are concerned.[99] Archbishop Iosif died on 3 November, 1970, and was succeeded by his former deputy, Archbishop Nikodim.

Since the last century the centre of this Old Believer denomination has been the Rogozhsky Cemetery in Moscow, where they have at their disposal what is actually one of the largest churches in the capital, with room for 10,000 worshippers. Most members of this the largest Old Believer group, which before the Revolution was fiercely attacked by the state Church, live outside the city and region of Moscow, around Gorky, where there are still villages which take their entire character from their Old Believer inhabitants. The Old Believer Archbishopric, which in 1956 was able to issue a volume of icons, is today only able to print a Church calendar in an edition limited to 4,000 copies.

Since 1923 there has been in the Soviet Union a second Old Believer episcopal hierarchy, recognised by the former *Beglopopovtsy* (an Old Believer Group). Previously these had been cared for by runaway priests from the state Church. Since 1963 this Archbishopric of Old Orthodox Christians of Novozybkov, Moscow and All Russia has its seat in Novozybkov, and the area of influence of this denomination is mainly the central and lower Volga and Siberia. The Old Believers of Novozybkov, likewise the Belaya Krinitsa Concord and four priestless Old Believer groups, were represented at the Conference of All Religions in July 1969 at Zagorsk.

Some of the priestless groups, which do not recognise any clergy at all, have maintained an astonishing organisational strength and group consciousness. In fact all Churches against which discrimination or persecution had been practised before 1917 were at first better adapted to Soviet reality than the former state Church. The priestless Old Believers today have a large body of adherents and a working organisation, particularly in Latvia, Lithuania and Moscow.

The *Fedoseevtsy* (named after Feodosi Vasilevich who lived at the beginning of the eighteenth century) sent delegations to Zagorsk in July 1969 from both their main branches, which were represented by the Moscow Preobrazhensky congregation and the Riga Grebenshchikov congregation. These two congregations are the focus for a large number of other dependent groups respectively in Central Russia and Latvia. The two branches differ in their attitude to marriage; while the Riga Old Believers have a kind of church wedding carried out by their congregational leaders, the Moscow *Fedoseevtsy*, with their centre at the Preobrazhensky Cemetery, reject a church wedding as devoid of grace. In the 1960s the *Fedoseevtsy* too were able, together with the Pomortsy, to issue a Church calendar for priestless Old Believers.

The second main group of priestless Old Believers, the *Pomortsy* (named after their region of origin, the Pomorye between the White Sea coast and Lake Ladoga) are found today chiefly in Lithuania where they are led by the Supreme Old Believer Council in the Lithuanian S.S.R., and have formed a few dozen congregations. At Zagorsk in 1969 the Moscow *Pomortsy* congregation was also represented; it had sent no representation to the first conference in 1952.

The most radical priestless group, the *Filippovtsy* (named after Filipp, living in the early eighteenth century) lives completely withdrawn in a kind of internal emigration and has never yet made any public appearance in the Soviet Union.

Old Ritualist piety – as in all religious groups in the Soviet Union – is chiefly handed on within the family, the area furthest removed from the influence of state ideology. Nevertheless, the Old Believers are not in opposition to Soviet society and their Russian national consciousness was probably the reason for most of them to participate in the patriotic Zagorsk Conferences.

The relationship of the Russian Orthodox Church to the Old Believers has entered a decisively new phase since 1969. Efforts are being made on both sides to overcome an enmity dating back centuries and to reach a new *modus vivendi*. The new ecumenical spirit within Russian Orthodoxy found its most daring manifestation to date in the annulment of the anathema pronounced against the Old Believers by the Local Councils of 1666 and 1667. The 1971 Zagorsk Council declared these curses null and void.

3. *The Georgian Orthodox Church*

The Orthodox Church of Georgia is 'one of the oldest and one of the least fortunate Churches' in the Soviet Union.[100] The baptism of the Georgians (Iberians) took place in A.D. 330, six and a half centuries before that of the Russians, and the Georgian Catholicosate dates back to the fifth century.

After centuries of foreign rule by an Islamic power, Georgia was conquered at the beginning of the nineteenth century by the largest Orthodox country in the world and thus at the same time lost its ecclesiastical independence. From 1811 to 1917, a Russian Exarch, appointed by the Synod in St. Petersburg, ruled in Tiflis instead of an autocephalous Catholicos-Patriarch, and this official often became a tool of Russification policies in Georgia. Attempts to denationalise the Georgian Church led to outbursts of hatred by the clergy and the Georgian nobility against Russian Orthodoxy and Russia generally.

With the Revolution and Georgia's state independence, the national Church also declared itself autocephalous. After the annexation of Georgia to the Soviet Union, because of its Georgian separatist attitude, it had to suffer particularly from atheist terror and propaganda measures, which decimated the Church.

There was no relaxation until the Second World War; however, in 1943 full ecclesiastical communion was restored with Russian Orthodoxy, which recognised the autocephaly of the Georgian Church after more than twenty-five years. Since then the Russian congregations in the Georgian Republic have been under the jurisdiction of the Catholicos. Still, the Georgian Orthodox Church has not been able to regenerate itself after the Second World War to the same degree as many Churches in the Soviet Union. According to its application for membership of the World Council of Churches in 1962 it had eighty congregations looked after by seven bishops and 105 priests, with four monasteries and about 100 open churches. At the beginning of the 1960s it succeeded in establishing a theological seminary in Mtskheta, the old Georgian capital.[101]

Since 1960 Efrem II (Sidamonidze), born in 1896, has held the office of Catholicos-Patriarch; he died in 1972. The eleventh assembly of the Georgian Orthodox Church in July 1972 elected David (Devdariani), born in 1903, as his successor. Efrem II worked closely with the Moscow Patriarchate, and the Georgian Church has played a significant role for some years in the political-patriotic struggle for peace. In 1962 Efrem II undertook his first trip to the West, to the World Council of Churches.

4. *The Armenian–Gregorian Church*

In contrast to the Georgian Orthodox Church, the Armenian Church is regarded today as an active and living community. It owes its relatively privileged position within the Soviet Union above all to two factors. On the one hand a large number of Armenians, who come under the jurisdiction of the Catholicos-Patriarch of Echmiadzin, live in the West; and on the other, the present Catholicos Vazgen I (Baldzhian) has very cleverly exploited this fact for the consolidation of the Armenian Church within the Soviet Union too, without at the same time ever putting his loyalty to the Soviet state in question.

The Armenian Church is labelled monophysite, because it rejected the Christological decisions on the 'dual nature of Jesus' doctrine made at the Council of Chalcedon in 451. It does not therefore have sacramental communion either with the Orthodox Churches or with Rome, although since the Second World War the Armenian Church has worked in extreme closeness to the Moscow Patriarchate and is now also making moves towards a rapprochement with Rome. Of the approximately 4 million Armenian Christians, 1½ million live in Armenia and about the same number in the other Soviet republics. Half a million live in the Near Eastern countries, and 200,000 live in the U.S.A., 150,000 in France, and 150,000 in South America.[102] All Armenian bishops cede a primacy of honour to the Catholicos of Echmiadzin, although there have been recurring tensions with the anti-Communist Catholicos of Cilicia whose seat is in Beirut. On the other hand, the two other remaining patriarchates of Jerusalem and Constantinople feel firmly linked with Echmiadzin. In 1965 there were twenty-six bishoprics under the immediate jurisdiction of this Christian centre of Armenia, of which only six were in the Soviet Union.[103] In 1962 the number of open Armenian churches in the Soviet Union was given as 200.

Catholicos Vazgen, on a tour abroad at the time of his visit to Cardinal Koenig in Vienna, emphasised the interest of Armenian youth in religious questions, and that the 'government in Yerevan exercised particular tolerance towards the Church'.[104] The Soviet government

is concerned through the medium of the Catholicosate of Echmiadzin
to maintain and strengthen ties with influential Armenian circles in the
West; Echmiadzin has always been ready to support the campaign
to bring Armenians abroad back to the Soviet Union.

The energetic personality of Catholicos Vazgen, who was born in
1908, has played an important part in achieving the present notable
position of the Armenian Church within the Soviet Union. After his
election as Catholicos in 1955 by the Armenian Church assembly,
in which lay representatives also have considerable weight, Vazgen
succeeded in obtaining important concessions from the Soviet authorities. A number of churches and monasteries were restored and reopened; the residence of the Catholicos was renovated, and the
Academy, which had existed since 1945, was extended; there are from
fifty to 100 students registered there today. The Armenian Church
also received permission to accept financial help from Armenians
abroad, and it is the only Church besides the Moscow Patriarchate
and the Evangelical Christians and Baptists that publishes its own
journal.[105]

The close connection of the Church with the national self-conscious-
ness of the Armenians found clear expression on the occasion of Vazgen
I's sixtieth birthday in September 1968. The President of the Presidium
of the Armenian Supreme Soviet, N. Arutyunyan, bestowed a high
decoration on the Catholicos, and in his speech said that the activity of
the Church leader 'always served the Armenian people and our fatherland, Soviet Armenia, that ancient land, which thinks of the heroic
and tragic past and where the present blossoms gladly'.[106] Vazgen
linked the Church celebration of his birthday with the great ecumenical
event of September–October 1969, for which twenty-five Armenian
bishops and representatives of friendly Churches (including the
Vatican and the World Council of Churches) came to Echmiadzin.
The blessing of the holy oil, celebrated every seven years by the
Catholicos-Patriarch of all Armenians, took place on this occasion.
The Catholicos of Cilicia, Khoren I, was also invited but did not come
to Echmiadzin – nor did the seven bishops under him; this made it
clear how sharp the tensions are still between the two Catholicosates.[107]

The Armenian Church maintains close relations with the Georgian
Orthodox and the Russian Orthodox Churches; the Armenians joined
the World Council of Churches in 1962. For some years they have
also sought contacts with the Roman Catholic Church, and a climax
was reached recently with the visit of Vazgen I to Rome in May 1970.

Pope Paul and the Catholicos made it clear on that occasion that they were striving to overcome the 'inherited misunderstandings' (the Pope's words). Joint theological studies are to be the medium for *rapprochement* for the meantime.[108]

5. *The Roman Catholic Church*

The centres of Catholicism in pre-Revolutionary Russia (the western parts of the Ukraine and Byelorussia, Lithuania and the southern part of Latvia) were not annexed by the Soviet Union until 1939–40. The Stalinist terror in the years after 1945 largely destroyed Catholic organisation in these areas. Catholicism, which was very closely linked with Poland, was considered – as it even was before 1917 – a hindrance to the integration of the newly-won territories into the Soviet federation of states, and the persecution of the Catholic Church was an integral part of Soviet nationalities policy. The Roman Catholic Church was unable later to build up any central organisation again, and only in Lithuania and Latvia is there today any regular division into dioceses. But even here the bishoprics are administered by only a few Apostolic Administrators. In Lithuania there are nominally six dioceses: Vilnius, Vilkaviškis, Panevėžys, Kaišiadorys, Kaunas and Telšiai, and the Apostolic Prelacy Klaipeda. In 1967 the number of Catholics in Lithuania was given as 2 million, cared for by about 800 priests. In Latvia there remain 150 congregations for the 350,000 faithful.[109]

There are four episcopal administrators in office in Lithuania today. The Administrator of the Archdiocese of Kaunas and of the diocese of Vilkaviškis is Juosapas Matulaitis-Labukas, who was consecrated bishop at the end of the Vatican Council in December 1965. Matulaitis, who is over seventy, received permission to consecrate seventy-two-year-old Luosapas Pletkus Bishop of Telšiai in February 1968, and at the beginning of 1970 to consecrate two suffragan bishops, fifty-nine-year-old Lindas Povilonis and thirty-nine-year-old Romualdas Krikcinnas.[110] These were the first episcopal ordinations that could be carried out in the Soviet Union for more than ten years. Besides this, there are in Lithuania two titular bishops who have been living under house arrest in distant parishes for many years. Vincentas Sladkevičius and Julijonas Steponavičius have been prevented by the authorities from exercising their office respectively since 1958 and 1960. Neither has been judicially sentenced.

The Latvian bishoprics, Riga and Libau, are managed by Apostolic Administrator Julijans Vaivods, who was consecrated bishop in Rome in November 1964 .Suffragan Bishop Kazimirs Dulbinskis, who lives in Latvia, is also unable to exercise his office.

Forty priests of the archdiocese of Vilnius protested at discrimination against the Catholic Church in Lithuania in a letter to Premier Kosygin in August 1969.[111] The seminary for priests in Kaunas, which is the only one – there is a second for Latvia in Riga – is only able, according to the forty priests, to take thirty seminarists in its five grades, so that in one year no more than five or six priests can be ordained. This limitation to one priestly ordination per diocese per year is also familiar in Latvia. In general the priests' complaints show that the Catholic Church is discriminated against in the same way as other denominations. Priests may not look after vacant neighbouring parishes, and even priests of the same deanery are unable to meet formally. There is a shortage of the most elementary religious books and the authorities will not give permission for confirmations to be held in the smaller towns. Preparation of children for first communion and any active participation by children and young people in services, in the choir or processions, or as acolytes, are forbidden. Priests and lay people who protest against the repression or disregard it lose their registration or their job. Several priests in recent years have been sentenced to fines and imprisonment because they gave religious instruction or allowed children to help in services. Teachers who openly show their allegiance to the Church are dismissed.

Since 1969 the troubles in Lithuania have steadily increased in intensity and scope, so much so that today this Baltic Soviet republic is a definite crisis spot within the Soviet Union. The revolts against Soviet rule are motivated by a mixture of national and anti-Russian feelings and religious convictions. In mid-May 1972 there was a violent revolt in Kaunas. After the self-immolation of twenty-year-old Roman Kalanta, there were demonstrations and street fighting. Thousands of young people demanded 'Freedom for Lithuania'; the army had to be brought in to quell the disorder. There were several more attempted self-immolations in June. The Catholic Church has not come out in favour of the violence, nevertheless national and religious resistance to Soviet repression are clearly linked.

Protest against the restrictions on Church life found its most comprehensive expression so far in a petition to Brezhnev and the Secretary-General of the United Nations, Kurt Waldheim, signed by more than 17,000 Lithuanians. This became known in the West in March 1972.[111a]

In spite of these depressing conditions, there have been a few glimmers of light in recent years, and the Vatican hopes that the *rapprochement* between the Soviet government and the Russian Orthodox Church, introduced since Khrushchev, will also gradually work out in favour of the Catholic Church. In 1968 it was possible to publish a Lithuanian missal, and the bishops nowadays receive visas to travel to Rome.

In the Baltic lands, where in the last century the different denominations were thrown against one another by the passions of the nationalities struggle, an increasing ecumenical awareness has grown in recent years. Discrimination against all denominations in common has undoubtedly contributed to this. The participation of Orthodox, Catholic or Lutheran clergy or bishops at the services of denominations other than their own at Christmas, Easter and other festivals is today a firm custom. The ecumenical spirit seems to be particularly developed in Riga, as was clearly demonstrated when the fiftieth anniversary of Bishop Vaivods's priesthood was celebrated in April 1968.[112]

Alongside the officially tolerated Catholic Church, there is in the West Ukraine a Catholic underground of the Slavic rite. The Union with Rome was dissolved after the Second World War, but it continues to exist illegally, and experienced a new wave of persecution in 1968-9. At the end of 1968 two Uniate priests who travelled from congregation to congregation were imprisoned in Kolomyya and Lvov, and at the beginning of 1969 the Greek-Catholic bishop Velychkovsky, who is about seventy years old, was captured in Lvov. After serving a three-year sentence, Velychkovsky was released at the beginning of 1972 and permitted to go to Rome. The action against the Uniate Church was accompanied by a slander campaign in the Ukrainian press, in which the Uniates were accused of Ukrainian nationalism; they were said to have 'betrayed the [Ukrainian] nation for 350 years'.[113] This shows again how closely the suppression of Catholicism is bound up with the struggle against separatist tendencies.

6. *The Evangelical–Lutheran Church*

The Evangelical-Lutheran Church is able to work legally only in Latvia and Estonia, where traditionally the population is mainly Protestant. The Lutheran communities in the rest of Russia, particularly among the German settlers along the Volga and in Southern Ukraine, were destroyed in the Stalinist terror of the 1930s. Even after the war the Germans who were deported to Kazakhstan and Siberia were never again allowed to build up any church organisation of their own, and some of them have joined the Evangelical Christians and Baptists. Pastor E. Bachmann was known to be the only Lutheran minister, working with some lay preachers in Kazakhstan.[114] Unable to continue his work because of age and ill health, he went to live in West Germany early in 1972.

The Lutheran Churches in Estonia and Latvia suffered in the same way as the Orthodox and Catholic Churches under the campaign of church closures at the beginning of the 1960s. For about 500,000 Lutheran Christians in Latvia there are today only eighty-six congregations and about ninety pastors; in Estonia the percentage is a little better, where there are about 120 congregations for 350,000 believers.[115]

Both in Latvia and Estonia the Archbishops have recently been newly elected. Seventy-eight-year-old Gustavs Turs retired as leader of the Lutheran Church in Latvia after twenty years, and the General Synod elected his deputy, Peter Kleperis, as the new Archbishop. However, sixty-four-year-old Kleperis died suddenly on a journey to Budapest. So the Eleventh General Synod of the Latvian Church met in February 1969 and declared Jan Matulis Archbishop. Matulis was born in 1911 in Kaluga, and studied mathematics and science at the Latvian University in Riga from 1931 to 1936. Only then did he turn to theology, being ordained pastor in 1943. Finally he was a lecturer at the theological school in Riga.

Archbishop Jan Matulis was ceremonially inducted by the Swedish bishop Sven Danell with the laying on of hands in St. John's Church, Riga, on 14 September, 1969. There were present on this occasion representatives of the Orthodox and Catholic bishops of Riga and, for the first time, a member of the Old Believer Grebenshchikov congregation. The Swedish bishop made his ceremonial speech in German.[116] As a sign of ecumenical co-operation the Latvian and Estonian Churches have made close links with the Scandinavian Churches, which is politically easier and less suspect than it would be, for example, to have relations with West Germany, as would be natural for the Baltic lands.

The theological courses in Riga, which have been continued after a break of several years, received a new head when Dr. Albert Freijs died in November 1968; the new director is Provost R. Prijede.[117] There are also courses for the training of new theologians in the Estonian Church in Tallinn (Reval), and these are obviously very well organised, even though only about twenty students are allowed to take the correspondence courses at any one time. The young theologians received typed textbooks by the lecturers in their own languages, and are regularly gathered for lectures and examinations lasting several days. They usually receive grants from particular congregations where they are already working as assistant preachers.

The Evangelical-Lutheran Church of Estonia also elected a new Archbishop in October 1967. The previous incumbent, Jaan Kiivit, retired for health reasons at the age of only sixty-one. Although he had suffered a severe illness, the supposition remains that his retirement was preceded by considerable political difficulties. Kiivit had maintained a greater independence *vis-à-vis* the authorities than his Latvian opposite number Turs, and it is probably not least thanks to his efforts that the Lutheran Church in Estonia today is more firmly based than in Latvia.

The Church assembly elected as his successor Alfred Tooming, who was only one year younger; Tooming was inducted in June 1968 in Tallinn cathedral. At the ceremony there were, apart from the Russian Orthodox bishop, two Finnish bishops and representatives of the Lutheran World Council and of the Archbishop of Uppsala. While the Latvian Church has particular relations with Sweden, the Estonian Church orientates itself more strongly towards its near neighbour Finland with its language affinity.

7. *The Evangelical Christians and Baptists*

The most lively Christian Church in the Soviet Union is that formed by the Evangelical Christians and Baptists. They are probably the only denomination which is still growing in numbers today. Although the Evangelical Christians and Baptists are subject to the same repressive Soviet legislation as the other Churches and suffer equally through the arbitrary action of local officials, congregational life is still amazingly lively and through strong pressure from the grass-roots, they have been able to secure concessions which are not given to other Churches.

The biblical revival movements have played a large role in the religious and Church life of Russia since the second half of the nineteenth century; the Evangelical Christians and the Baptists emerged as the most important streams, and joined together for the first time in October 1944, after numerous previous attempts.

In contemporary Soviet society, just as in pre-Revolutionary society, the Evangelical Christians and Baptists exercise strong powers of attraction which are conceded and taken seriously even by the atheist ideologues.[118] Atheist researchers see the most important social cause for the liveliness of Baptist 'collectives' in the large number of those who feel humiliated and deceived by life and victims of fate, who are outside socialist society and are not provided for in it. It is true that such people form a virtually inexhaustible reservoir for all denominations; but they are undoubtedly not the only ones.

Soviet religio-sociological investigations of recent years have actually shown that the Evangelical Christians and Baptists are not only loyal Soviet citizens, but in many cases are the best workers, exemplary artisans and collective farm labourers. The Baptists are not by any means only people who are unfit for the productive society. The conclusion that suggests itself is that the Evangelical movement is particularly adapted to meet men's religious needs and is best suited to answer their religious questions in Soviet society. The congregational meetings are simple and unpretentious, free from the complicated tradition of the Orthodox liturgy. There are no icons, and neither veneration of the saints nor ceremonial processions are practised, but only Bible readings, very emotional anthems and a biblically and morally orientated exposition. The service usually lasts two hours with two or three readings, songs and sermons, in which pietistic and eschatological motifs are prominent. There are no less than three weekly services in any congregation; in the big Moscow congregation with 5,000 members there are six, each with an average attendance of 2,000. In these meetings not only the elected presbyters, deacons and preachers but also other members of the congregation can speak.

However, services are not the only manifestation of the congregational life; also important is the human feeling of belonging together, the private fellowship of members among themselves and with the presbyter, and mutual support, both moral and material. Private gatherings on the occasion of family celebrations frequently assume a missionary character. Alongside the official congregational services there are also unorganised discussion circles and Bible studies. The omnipresent church choirs also have an important missionary and catechistic task. All these forms of religious life exist in the Soviet Union on the fringes of legality, but they seem to be tolerated at the moment as long as they remain within the framework of the congregations of the official Union.

Private and semi-private gatherings are naturally harder to control and to suppress than services in a registered church; thus the Evangeli-

cal movement is much better equipped to avoid administrative measures, and has been able to go on functioning even in times when
there has been an almost complete destruction of Church apparatus.
Lay preachers and presbyters of the Evangelical Christians and Baptists
are not dependent either on a theological education or a Church
hierarchy, or ordination, church buildings or the prescribed celebration of the liturgy or mass; all of them have civil professions and can
at any time disappear or re-emerge.

This capacity to adapt to Soviet reality, together with the sincere
human bonds in many communities, have made the Evangelical
Christians and Baptists of particular importance in Church life in the
Soviet Union. Even though atheist sociologists of religion comfort
themselves with the statement that in most congregations, as in other
denominations, women, old people and unskilled labourers are over-
represented, nevertheless they themselves again and again publish
astonishing facts to the contrary. Thus in Kazakhstan 43 per cent of the
members in registered congregations are under fifty, and in the unregistered congregations the averge age is even lower. The percentage
of young people (eighteen to thirty) in registered congregations in the
Soviet Union is 10 to 15 per cent, but in many areas in recent years
it has increased. In the Ukraine during the last few years a third of all
new members were young people. In the unregistered congregations
and among the dissident free Baptists (*Initsiativniki*), more young
people are involved than in the officially tolerated Union.[119]

Although there are very exact individual statistics, in assessing the
total number of Evangelical Christians and Baptists we can only rely
on approximate data. There are about 500,000 members of the officially
recognised Union, those who have gone through adult baptism. The
Union has more than 5,000 – to a large extent independent – congregations not all of which, however, have been able to obtain their
registration from the state authorities. Although in recent years a
number of congregations have been registered – in the environs of
Moscow alone twelve congregations obtained legalisation between
1966 and 1968 – today probably still only just over half of the baptised
members are in registered congregations, which are less subject to
arbitrary administrative action than the illegal Baptist groups.[120]

In every congregation there is an outer ring of sympathisers and
interested persons around the inner circle of the baptised, frequently
relatives and friends; it is therefore reckoned that the Evangelical
Christians and Baptists actually exercise an influence on 3 million

Soviet citizens. A large part of these belong to the non-Slav peoples of the Soviet Union. Important centres of the movement are the western border lands, which only fell to the Soviet Union during the Second World War, the Southern Ukraine and the Northern Caucasus, but there are also numerous congregations in the new industrial towns, in the cities of Western Siberia and Central Asia, and in the Far East. The Evangelical Christians and Baptists are relatively weak in Central Russia and in the Volga region. In the Byelorussian Republic about 40 per cent of all Christians consider themselves Evangelical Christians and Baptists.[121]

About 5,000 people are baptised per year, and certain congregations are expanding in this respect particularly; every year in the large Moscow congregation there are 130 to 150 baptisms for every 100 deaths. While the authorities up to now have not permitted any further congregations to be opened in Moscow, in Kiev for example there are four and in Tiflis there are three: one Russian, one Georgian and one Armenian.[122]

The congregations of the Union are led and represented by the All-Union Council of Evangelical Christians and Baptists. The Plenum of the All-Union Council, which meets at least once a year, consists of twenty-five persons, since its enlargement in 1966; these are complemented by candidates for the All-Union Council and members of the Revision Commission. The real leadership of the Union lies in the hands of a nine-man Presidium of the All-Union Council with the President and General Secretary at its head; this administers current business as executive organ of the Council and of the triennial All-Union Congress. The last All-Union Congresses took place in October 1966 and at the end of 1969; at present there is one delegate to every 500 congregational members. Formally, the Congress is the supreme decision-making body.[123]

The congregations of the Union are cared for by 300 full-time and about 30,000 part-time presbyters, deacons and preachers, who are elected by the congregations themselves and ordained by the Senior Presbyters; however, these ordinations are not yet carried out everywhere strictly according to the rules. The Senior Presbyters – in 1969 there were fifty-three of them in office and eleven assistants – lead the congregations of one region, the size of which is determined by the density of the congregations in an area.

The new Union statute approved by the 1966 Congress has brought about a considerable democratisation at this level. The Senior Presbyters are now elected by the presbyters and Church workers of their region and then appointed by the All-Union Council. They also have an elected Council of presbyters on hand. Strict demands by the congregations and particularly by the *Initsiativniki* have brought about these decentralising measures, which again show to what extent Church organisation is thought of from the congregational aspect and not in terms of a Church hierarchy. This makes more difficult control by the state authorities, who are therefore trying to encourage the tendency to strengthen the central administration.

Communication between the congregations and with the All-Union Council in Moscow is extremely lively and takes place at the most varied levels. Members of the All-Union Council or special envoys are constantly travelling around the congregations, and the correspondence of the Council with the congregations in recent years has 'reached record proportions'.[124] Congregational representatives also frequently visit the Moscow headquarters.

The All-Union Council employs forty workers in the organisational and spiritual care of the congregations. The money for the activity of the central headquarters is raised by collections in all the congregations at the five chief festivals (Christmas, Easter, Whitsun, Harvest and Unity Day). Although the whole organisation at all levels is dependent exclusively on the freewill offerings of the congregational members, the General Secretary A. V. Karev, in his report to the Plenum of the All-Union Council in March 1969, described the financial situation as good.[125] Karev died in November 1971; A. M. Bychkov was elected as the new General Secretary in December.

Communication at local level is served by the Senior Presbyters travelling to visit the congregations in their care, and by the meetings of presbyters and active congregational workers in an area. Such meetings of workers have taken place almost everywhere since 1966 – sometimes more than once – first because, according to the 1966 Statute, the Senior Presbyters had to be re-elected or confirmed in office, and again because in 1969 delegates to the Congress had to be appointed. A further link among presbyters is the Presbyters' Councils which assist the Senior Presbyters.

No other Church in the Soviet Union has such a many-tiered system of communication. In 1968 there were seventeen local presbyters' meetings; there were probably even more the following year. Particularly well-attended were the meeting of presbyters and congregational workers of Byelorussia in March 1969, at which 106 people participated, and the gathering for the Don region in Makeevka on 28 June, 1969, where 165 people met.[126]

Since the Second World War several groups have joined the Union of Evangelical Christians and Baptists, and today it draws in people from the remains of the old Russian sects as well as the Russian Orthodox Church; most of all it is probably believers from those congregations closed at the beginning of the 1960s who are joining the Baptists.

During and after the Second World War several hundred Pentecostal congregations joined the Union of Evangelical Christians and Baptists under the pressure of the authorities. Soviet religious policy is interested in a centralisation of sectarian tendencies, which are otherwise difficult to control. However, up to now the Evangelical Christians and Baptists have been unable to obtain a complete integration of the Pentecostals into the Union, and consideration of this problem is permanently on the agenda of the All-Union Council. The Pentecostals are separated from the Baptists by considerable theological differences, and it is not surprising that the dogmatic groups, for whom the coming of the Holy Spirit in 'speaking in tongues' is the central point of their theology, will not join the Union.

After a number of trials of Pentecostals had already been held at the beginning of the 1960s on account of their 'anti-state and anti-social' attitude, in May 1969 the two leaders of a German Pentecostal group in Angren, Uzbekistan, were sentenced to five years' imprisonment each, and six other defendants were sentenced to between two and three years. Their religious ceremonies were described by the court as 'harmful to health'.[127]

In contrast to the Pentecostals, the incorporation of the Mennonite Brethren into the Union of Evangelical Christians and Baptists makes steady progress. These so-called New Mennonites have been in contact with the Union since 1963, and by 1967 18,600 Mennonites had already joined it.[128]

But to say that the Evangelical Christians and Baptists have become a melting-pot for various Protestant groups is not to tell the whole story; internally they are constantly threatened by disputes and splits. The greatest concern of the All-Union Council at present is to win back the so-called *Initsiativniki* group, who broke away at the beginning of the 1960s. This problem will be dealt with at length in the next chapter. The Council for Religious Affairs, the supreme organ of Soviet religious policy, supports the efforts of the All-Union Council to this end, because it is concerned that the free Baptists, at present illegally active, should again be incorporated into a central apparatus that can be controlled. It is one of the tasks of the Council for Religious Affairs to prevent if possible the formation of any underground groups. This is why in recent years some concessions have been made to the legal Baptist Union, in order to meet the *Initsiativniki's* demands for more freedom of movement for the religious groups and thus to make it easier for them to return to the Union.

It is particularly significant that in the summer of 1968 the theological correspondence courses, which had been announced for some time, were able to begin. The Evangelical Christians and Baptists now have the opportunity again, after a break of forty years, to train their preachers properly. This is especially important for this biblically oriented denomination, which moreover, has constantly to fight against sectarian tendencies. These courses will contribute not only to an internal theological strengthening for the Union, but they will also raise the theological level and the general education of the preachers, some of whom today do not have a complete secondary education. However, the number of participants in the courses was limited by the authorities to 100, although there were 500 applications for the first course.

The participants are put forward by their congregations, and when they have passed the entrance examination in Moscow, they receive the prepared teaching materials by post. The candidates are called to Moscow twice a year for lectures and examinations. The head of the courses is A. I. Mitskevich, member of the Presidium of the All-Union Council. As well as these, the Union has the chance to send some theologians to study at Baptist seminaries in the West.[129]

The teaching is oriented towards practical preparation for future preachers and is extremely conservative theologically. The Presidium of the All-Union Council 'is watchful that not a milligram of the modern poison, that is, the poison of the so-called "new theology" is contained [in the lessons of the courses]'.[130] Karev, the General Secretary, had already stated at the 1966 Congress: 'The names of the modernist theologians Adolf Harnack, Rudolf Bultmann, Walter Hartmann and others are completely unknown in our brotherhood.' Karev warned against the snares of modern Western theology, for 'it destroys faith with its speculative criticism'.[131] Thus the Evangelical Christians and Baptists, like the Russian Orthodox Church, have still to experience the confrontation with historical-critical theology.

As well as establishing the correspondence courses, the All-Union

Council was also given permission in 1969 to publish 26,000 new song-books and 20,000 Bibles, which however only satisfied a fraction of the demand. The Union magazine, (*Bratsky Vestnik*) ('Fraternal Herald'), was also able to increase its circulation, which now stands at six to seven thousand.[132] In recent years the *Fraternal Herald* has given regular reports on the opening of a few new churches. Thus in 1968 six churches were dedicated in Vilnius, Vinnitsa, Tselinograd (Kazakhstan), Kislovodsk, Dzhetysai (Syr-Darya Region) and Grimma (Oryol Region). The congregations usually request houses which can then be converted and renovated by the members themselves as opportunity arises.[133]

The ordination of new presbyters and the registration of new congregations causes less difficulty today than at the beginning of the 1960s, when both were practically impossible. In 1967 in Estonia five presbyters, two of them with higher education, and twenty-four deacons were appointed; in the Don region it was three presbyters and four deacons. In the same year it was possible to establish five new congregations in northern Russia.[134]

The Union of Evangelical Christians and Baptists, like the other Churches in the Soviet Union, has been able in the last decade to make a number of foreign contacts. It is a member of the Prague Christian Peace Conference and of the World Council of Churches. The Senior Presbyter of Byelorussia, K. S. Veliseichik, was elected to the Central Council of the World Council of Churches in Uppsala in 1968. Nevertheless, resistance to ecumenical co-operation has not been overcome in all the congregations, and the World Council of Churches is attacked as the 'Whore of Babylon'. But the All-Union Council vigorously resists such tendencies to separatism, which in many congregations are connected with eschatological ideas of election.[135]

The Union has particularly close relations with international Baptist organisations. Representatives of the All-Union Council make regular trips abroad to the meetings of committees of the Baptist World Alliance and the European Baptist Federation. In 1966–8 M. Ya. Zhidkov, member of the Presidium, was the first Russian President of the European Baptist Federation. At its meeting in Vienna in August 1969, this European league of national Baptist Unions approved, with the votes of the Russian delegation, a declaration demanding for all men the right 'to confess their religion freely everywhere, without fear of discrimination or loss of social position and freedom'. The persecution of the free Baptists shows the relevance of these words in the Soviet Union today and it is a testimony to courage and independence that they were printed in the *Fraternal Herald*.[136]

The programme of visits and return visits of the All-Union Council in Moscow has been growing steadily in recent years and guests today come from many countries: from Switzerland, the U.S.A., Poland, West Germany and others. Contacts with the socialist countries are close, but closest of all are those with the Anglo–American countries where the Baptist faith is now centred.

REFERENCES

1. *FAZ*, 22 April, 1969.
2. A. E. Levitin-Krasnov in M. Bourdeaux, *Patriarch and Prophets*, p. 282.
3. *JMP*, 8/1969, p. 29.
4. Recent data on the Evangelical-Lutheran Church of Lithuania and the Methodist Church of Estonia in *RM*, II, October 1969, pp. 2–3.
5. *O-P*, XX, 1968, p. 149.
6. *Digest des Ostens*, 10/1068, pp. 6–8.
7. *StO*, 7/1969, p. 57. Cf. the letter of Levitin to Paul VI in the documentation section pp. 188 ff.
8. *Salzburger Nachrichten*, 29 April, 1970.
9. Levitin's letter to Pope Paul VI, documentation section pp. 188 ff.
10. *JMP*, 12/1968, pp. 35, 37–38; 5/1969, p. 29; 12/1969, pp. 23–24; *StO*, 1/1969, p. 17.
11. *VRSKhD*, 3/1969, pp. 107–11.
12. *JMP*, 12/1968, p. 19.
13. In mid-1972 the incumbency of dioceses was as follows: Alma-Ata and Kazakhstan, Metr. Iosif (Chernov); Arkhangelsk and Kholmogory, Bp. Nikon (Fomichev); Argentine and South America, Bp. Maxim (Krokha); Astrakhan and Yenotaevka, Bp. Mikhail (Mudyugin); Baden and Bavaria, Bp. Irinei (Susemihl); Berlin and Central Europe, Archbp. Leonti (Gudimov), Exarch of the Moscow Patriarchate; Brussels and Belgium, Archbp. Vasili (Krivoshein); Cheboksary and the Chuvash A.S.S.R. Archbp. Nikolai (Feodosev); Chernigov and Nezhin, Bp. Vladimir (Sabodan); Chernovtsy and Bukovina, Bp. Savva (Babinets); Düsseldorf, Archbp. Alexi (van der Mensbrugghe); Gorky and Arzamas, Archbp. Flavian (Dmitryuk); Irkutsk and Chita, Archbp. Veniamin (Novitsky); Ivano-Frankovsk and Kolomyya, Archbp. Iosif (Safrash); Ivanovo and Kineshma, Archbp. Feodosi (Pogorsky); Kaluga and Borovsk, Archbp. Donat (Shchegolev); Kazan and Mari A.S.S.R., Archbp. Mikhail (Voskresensky); Kharkov and Bogodukhov, Archbp. Nikodim (Rusnak); Kherson and Odessa, Metr. Sergi (Petrov); Kiev and Galicia, Metr. Filaret (Denisenko), Exarch of the Ukraine; Kirov and Slobodskoi, Archbp. Mstislav (Volonshevich); Kirovograd and Nikolaev, Bp. Bogolep (Anukh); Kishinev and Moldavia, Bp. Varfolomei (Gondarovsky); Korsun, Bp.

Pierre (L'Huillier); Kostroma and Galich, Archbp. Kassian (Yaroslavsky); Krasnodar and Kubanskaya, Archbp. Alexi (Konoplev); Krutitsy and Kolomna, Metr. Serafim (Nikitin), diocesan bishop of Moscow; Kuibyshev and Syzran, Bp. Ioann (Snychev); Kursk and Belgorod, Bp. Orest (Bychkovsky); Leningrad and Novgorod, Metr. Nikodim (Rotov); Lvov and Ternopol, Metr. Nikolai (Yurik); Minsk and Byelorussia, Archbp. Antoni (Melnikov); Mukachevo and Uzhgorod, Archbp. Grigori (Zakalyaka); Novosibirsk and Barnaul, Bp. Gedeon (Dokukin); Omsk and Tyumen, Archbp. Mefodi (Menzak); Orel and Bryansk, Metr. Palladi (Sherstvennikov); Orenburg and Buzuluk, Archbp. Leonti (Bondar); Penza and Saransk, Bp. Melkhisedek (Lebedev); Perm and Solikamsk, Bp. Ioasaf (Ovsyannikov); Poltava and Kremenchug, Bp. Feodosi (Dikun); Pskov and Porkhov, Archbp. Ioann (Razumov); Riga and Latvia, Archbp. Leonid (Polyakov); Ryazan and Kasimov, Bp. Boris (Skvortsov); Rostov and Novocherkassk, Archbp. Vladimir (Kotlarov); Saratov and Volgograd, Bp. Pimen (Khmelevskoi); Simferopol and the Crimea, Bp. Antoni (Vikarik); Smolensk and Vyazma, Bp. Feodosi (Prochyuk); Stavropol and Baku, Bp. Iona (Zyryanov); Surozh, Metr. Antoni (Bloom), Exarch of Western Europe (seat in London); Sverdlovsk and Kurgan, Bp. Kliment (Perestyuk); Tallinn and Estonia, Metr. Alexi (Ridiger), head of the patriarchal chancellery and president of the educational committee of the Holy Synod; Tashkent and Central Asia, Bp. Platon; Tula and Belev, Metr. Yuvenali (Poyarkov), head of the Foreign Department of the Moscow Patriarchate; Ufa and Sterlitamak, Archbp. Iov (Kresovich); Vienna and Austria, Bp. German (Timofeev); Vilnius and Lithuania, Bp. Germogen (Orekhov); Vinnitsa and Bratslav, Archbp. Alipi (Khotovitsky); Vladimir and Suzdal, Bp. Nikolai (Kutepov); Volhynia and Rovno, Archbp. Damian (Marchuk); Vologda and Veliki Ustyug, Archbp. Pavel (Golyshev); Voronezh and Lipetsk, Archbp. Mikhail (Chub); Yaroslavl and Rostov, Metr. Ioann (Vendland); Zhitomir and Ovruch, Archbp. Palladi (Kaminsky). The vicar-bishoprics were occupied as follows: Dmitrov (vicar-bishopric of Moscow), Archbp. Filaret (Vatskromeev), rector of the theological schools in Zagorsk; Rotterdam (vicar-bishopric of Brussels), Bp. Dionisi (Lukin); Tikhvin (vicar-bishopric of Leningrad), Bp. Meliton (Solovev), rector of the Leningrad theological schools; Volokolamsk (vicar-bishopric of Moscow), Archbp. Pitirim (Nechaev), head of the publishing department of the Patriarchate; Zaraisk (vicar-bishopric of Moscow), Bp. Khrisostom (Martishkin); Zürich (vicar-bishopric of the Western European exarchate), Bp. Serafim (Rodionov). *KIO*, XII, 1969, pp. 113–15 and current numbers of *JMP*.

14. *Die Russische Orthodoxe Kirche, Ihre Einrichtungen, Ihre Stellung, Ihre Tätigkeit*, Moscow 1958, pp. 41–2.
15. *StO*, 2/1969, pp. 18–21.
16. *JMP*, 12/1967, pp. 9–17.
17. *StO*, 7/1969, pp. 23–7.
18. *JMP*, 2/1968, pp. 5–12; 5/1969, pp. 12–18.
19. R. Stupperich (ed.), *Kirche und Staat in der Sowjetunion. Gesetze und*

Verordnungen. Ed. R. Witten 1962, pp. 35–7; R. Stupperich (ed.), *Die Russische Orthodoxe Kirche in Lehre und Leben*, p. 282.

20. The publications of the Patriatchate up to 1963 are listed in N. Struve, *Die Christen in der UdSSR*, Mainz 1965, pp. 499–500; *StO*, 5/1969, p. 24.
21. *Izv*, 23 April, 1970.
22. There is a detailed biography of Alexi in J. Chrysostomus, *Kirchengeschichte Russlands der neuesten Zeit*, Vol. III, pp. 79 ff.
23. G. Simon, 'Das russische Konzil wählte einen neuen Patriarchen', in *Herder-Korrespondenz*, XXV, 7, 1971, pp. 310–12.
24. *JMP*, 4/1969, pp. 33–4.
25. *BV*, 6/1968, p. 21; *StO*, 1/1969, p. 50.
26. *JMP*, 12/1967, p. 45.
27. *BV*, 6/1968, p. 21.
28. *JMP*, 8/1968, p. 14; *Eastern Churches Review*, I, 1966/7, p. 428.
29. *StO*, 2/1969, pp. 55–61 (the quotations pp. 58, 60, 61).
30. *StO*, 12/1969, p. 26.
31. *JMP*, 2/1968, pp. 21–4.
32. *StO*, 10/1969, pp. 23–7.
33. *JMP*, 11/1967, p. 43; *StO*, 11/1967, pp. 39–40.
34. *JMP*, 8/1968, p. 15; 9/1969, p. 18.
35. *JMP*, 11/1967, p. 12; 9/1968, p. 4; *Neues Forum*, 4–5/1967, p. 355; *StO*, 2/1969, pp. 18–21.
36. *Eastern Churches Review*, I, 1966, p. 60.
37. *StO*, 1/1968, pp. 52–4.
38. *JMP*, 10/1968, p. 18.
39. *Posev*, 4/1968, pp. 78–9.
40. *VRSKhD*, 3–4/1968, pp. 46–8.
41. *Posev*, 14 January, 1966, p. 4.
42. *JMP*, 7/1968, pp. 23–4.
43. *JMP*, 11/1968, inside back cover; 12/1969, pp. 22–3; *StO*, 12/1968, pp. 6–8.
44. *StO*, 4/1969, pp. 56–9.
45. *JMP*, 5/1968, p. 28.
46. *JMP*, 5/1968, p. 30; 8/1968, p. 43.
47. *Frankfurter Allgemeine Zeitung*, 7 September, 1968.
48. *öpd*, 29 August 1968, pp. 2–3.
49. *StO*, 10/1968, pp. 8–9; 1/1969, pp. 37–9 (quotation here from the declaration of 28 September 1968); *Osteuropa*, XIX, 1969, pp. 17–18.
50. *öpd*, 29 August 1968, pp. 2–3.
51. Ondra's and Hromadka's resignation letters in *RCDA*, IX, 1970, pp. 2–3.
52. *öpd*, April 1970, pp. 9–11.
53. *StO*, 8/1969, pp. 33–42 (the quotations pp. 33, 40).
54. *StO*, 8/1969, pp. 57–62 (the quotations pp. 57, 60, 61); 9/1969, pp. 45–62 (the quotations p. 51).
55. *JMP*, 10/1969, pp. 36–37.
56. *StO*, 6/1969, pp. 37–40.
57. *JMP*, 11/1967, pp. 66–71; cf. similar efforts of the Russian Orthodox Church in the Conference of European Churches, *JMP*, 2/1968, pp. 56–58.
58. *JMP*, 4/1968, pp. 31–35; *öpd*, 14 March, 1968, p. 3.

59. *JMP*, 9/1968, pp. 46–55 (the quotations pp. 54, 46, 53); extracts from the lecture in German in *Osteuropa*, XIX, 1969, pp. A 19–24.
60. *JMP*, 4/1968, p. 34.
61. *JMP*, 11/1967, p. 67.
62. *öpd*, 2 May, 1968, p. 3.
63. *JMP*, 12/1967, pp. 42–7; 4/1969, p. 4.
64. *JMP*, 2/1968, pp. 50–4; 5/1968, pp. 50–3; *StO*, 2/1969, p. 53.
65. *JMP*, 11/1969, pp. 47–57.
66. *JMP*, 3/1968, p. 5; 8/1968, pp. 7–14.
67. *NZZ*, 4 March, 1970; *FAZ*, 27 May, 1970.
68. *JMP*, 3/1968, pp. 1–2; 5/1968, pp. 5–6; 6/1969, pp. 4–11.
69. *FAZ*, 20 May, 1970.
70. *Mess*, 2–3/1968, pp. 74–84.
71. *JMP*, 11/1967, pp. 1–4.
72. *JMP*, 12/1967, pp. 36–8.
73. Schumann visited Zagorsk on 12 October, 1969, and Harmel on 25 July, 1969 (*StO*, 12/1969, pp. 6, 19).
74. Cf. pp. 84 ff.
75. *VRSKhD*, 3/1969, p. 22 (Letter of Father X to Father Sergi Zheludkov, undated).
76. Bourdeaux, *Patriarch and Prophets*, p. 282.
77. *Posev*, 11/1968, pp. 54–5.
78. *VRSKhD*, 4/1966, pp. 3–19; 1/1967, pp. 29–64; *Posev*, 11/1968, p. 53. The letter of November 1966 in partial English translation in Bourdeaux, *Patriarch and Prophets*, pp. 125–52.
79. *Posev*. 11/1968, pp. 53–60. Partial English translation in Bourdeaux, *Patriarch and Prophets*, pp. 332–9.
80. *VRSKhD*, 3–4/1968, pp. 68–76.
81. Bourdeaux, *Patriarch and Prophets*, pp. 331–2 (leter by Talantov, written after May 1967).
82. *Posev*, 9/1969, pp. 35–41.
83. *StO*, 4/1969, pp. 9–11.
84. *NZZ*, 31 October, 1969.
85. *Vedomosti Verkhovnogo Soveta RSFSR*, 1966, p. 819 of 16 September, 1966.
86. Bourdeaux, *Patriarch and Prophets*, pp. 284, 294.
87. *Posev*, 2/1970, pp. 38–9.
88. *VRSKhD*, 3/1969, pp. 101–6.
89. Ibid., p. 100.
90. *Problems of Communism*, 4/1968, pp. 60, 67, 69; *Posev*, 3rd special issue 1970, p. 43 (*Khronika tekushchikh sobytii* 5 [10]).
91. *Posev*, 10/1969, p. 7; 3rd special issue 1970, pp. 7–8.
92. *RCDA*, VIII, 1969, pp. 218–20.
93. *VRSKhD*, 3/1969, pp. 16–25 (Letter of Father X to Father Sergi Zheludkov, undated).
94. *Posev*, 12/1968, p. 57 (the first two quotations); *VRSKhD*, 4/1969, pp. 46–57 (quotation p. 57). The letter to Solzhenitsyn has not been previously published in the West.
95. *VRSKhD*, 4/1969, p. 55.

F

96. *VRSKhD*, 3/1969, p. 22; cf. Ch. I, pp. 20–1.
97. (A. E. Levitin-Krasnov), *Zashchita very v SSSR*, Paris 1966, pp. 100–1.
98. Literature on the Old Believers: P. Hauptmann, *Altrussischer Glaube*, Göttingen 1963, pp. 123–124; ibid., 'Das Moskauer Patriarchat und die anderen Kirchen und Religionsgemeinschaften innerhalb der Sowjetunion,' in R. Stupperich (ed.), *Die Russische Orthodoxe Kirche in Lehre und Leben*, Witten 1966, pp. 271–6; N. Struve, Christians in Contemporary Russia, pp. 219–25; W. Kolarz, op. cit., pp. 128–49; V. F. Milovidov, *Staroobryadchestvo v proshlom i nastoyashchem*, Moscow 1969.
99. *Posev*, 3/1969, p. 5.
100. Kolarz, op. cit., p. 97.
101. Hauptmann, *Das Moskauer Patriarchat und die anderen Kirchen und Religionsgemeinschaften innerhalb der Sowjetunion*, op. cit., pp. 260–1; *KIO*, V, 1962, p. 135; VII, 1964, p. 158; X, 1967, p. 136.
102. *Herder-Korrespondenz*, XXIV, 1970, p. 293.
103. *KIO*, X, 1967, p. 137.
104. *Kathpress*, 25 April, 1968.
105. Kolarz, op. cit., pp. 150–75.
106. *TASS* (Russ.), 23 September, 1968.
107. *JMP*, 12/1969, pp. 44–55; *RCDA*, VIII, 1969, p. 226.
108. *Herder-Korrespondenz*, XXIV, 1970, p. 293.
109. *Begegnung*, 10/1967, p. 14.
110. *Salzburger Nachrichten*, 20 February, 1970.
111. *RCDA*, IX, 1970, pp. 34–6.
111a. See Documents, pp. 236–7.
112. *JMP*, 7/1968, p. 57; *StO*, 2/1969, p. 48.
113. *RM*, II, May 1969, pp. 2–3; *Posev*, 2nd special issue 1969, p. 9 (*Khronika tekushchikh sobytii* 2[7]).
114. *KIO*, V, 1962, pp. 149–51; VIII, 1965, pp. 156–7; IX, 1966, p. 136.
115. *Digest des Ostens*, 5/1968, p. 82; 7/1968, p. 58.
116. *StO*, 5/1969, pp. 45–7; 11/1969, pp. 39–43.
117. *StO*, 3/1969, pp. 56–8; 8/1969, p. 42.
118. L. N. Mitrokhin, 'Chelovek v baptistskoi obshchine', in *Voprosy filosofii*, 8/1968, pp. 42–52.
119. *RM*, II, October 1969, p. 2; L. N. Mitrokhin, *Baptizm*, Moscow 1966, pp. 247–8, 252–3; cf. *Osteuropa*, XIX, 1969, pp. A 38 ff.
120. *KIO*, XII, 1969, p. 124.
121. Kolarz, op. cit., pp. 283, 303–12; *BV*, 5/1969, p. 79.
122. *BV*, 6/1968, pp. 22–3.
123. 'Statut des Bundes der Evangeliumschristen-Baptisten von 1966', in *Osteuropa*, XIX, 1969, pp. A 12–25.
124. *BV*, 1/1968, p. 67.
125. *BV*, 3/1969, p. 62.
126. *BV*, 3/1969, p. 69; 5/1969, pp. 77, 79; 6/1969, pp. 71, 74.
127. *FAZ*, 12 May, 1969.
128. *BV*, 1/1968, p. 65.
129. *BV*, 1/1968, p. 64; 4/1968, p. 77.
130. *BV*, 3/1969, p. 63.

131. *BV*, 6/1966, p. 17.
132. *BV*, 1/1968, p. 64; 3/1969, p. 63.
133. *BV*, 2/1969, pp. 75–9; 3/1969, pp. 76–7; 6/1969, p. 72.
134. *BV*, 2/1968, pp. 76–7; 3/1968, p. 79.
135. *BV*, 3/1969, pp. 67–8.
136. *BV*, 6/1969, p. 10.

V. State Pressure and Church Resistance

The Break-away Baptist Group, 'Initsiativniki'

'In our days Satan is dictating through the workers of the All-Union Council of Evangelical Christians and Baptists, and the Church accepts all their decisions which directly contradict the commands of God. . . . Because the leadership of the All-Union Council of Evangelical Christians and Baptists has submitted to human laws – has defiled itself with unworthy men – the Church has departed from the Lord's teaching, and this has caused the split in our congregations.'[1] With these words an 'Action Group [*Initsiativnaya Gruppa*] for the Calling of an All-Union Congress of Evangelical Christians and Baptists' in August 1961 addressed 'all registered and unregistered congregations'. This letter, signed by the leaders of the Action Group, A. F. Prokofiev and G. K. Kryuchkov, called in question the officially recognised leadership of the Union of Evangelical Christians and Baptists and marked the beginning of the biggest and most dangerous schismatic movement in any Soviet denomination since the Second World War. The *Initsiativniki* implied a challenge to the Union of Evangelical Christians and Baptists, who are probably the most lively religious denomination in the Soviet Union, just as much as to the state. What had happened?

In the years after 1958, when Khrushchev was at the height of his power, a renewed, comprehensive attack was levelled by state and Party against the denominations. Khrushchev's 'developed construction of Communism' was to be accompanied by a liquidation of the 'religious survivals'.[2] Repression, which occurred on a large scale, struck, among others, the Union of Evangelical Christians and Baptists, which after the Second World War had grown stronger and stronger to become an extremely lively joint evangelical movement. 'Thousands of workers filled with the Holy Spirit' were removed, in the Ukraine alone the authorities dissolved 'more than 800 congregations' and the obligation of registration for ministers was – as with other Church organisations – developed into an instrument for removing awkward presbyters and replacing them with those willing to co-operate. Thus not only did the authorities protect presbyters and Church councils with whom the congregations were dissatisfied, but the observation and infiltration of congregations by individuals acting as informants for Soviet officialdom took on proportions that had not been known in previous years.[3]

There were also, from the end of the 1950s, new regulations severely limiting the activity of the denominations, such as the prohibition on carrying out official Church acts outside the churches, linked with an obligation to report all such acts to the state bodies of control.

The new repressive regulations were established in an *ukaz* by the Presidium of the Supreme Soviet of the Russian Republic of 19 December, 1962, which really involved a thorough revision of the 1929 Law on religion; up to the present this *ukaz* has never been published. Excerpts from it became known accidentally through the indictment of the Baptists S. T. Golev, A. V. Bykov and others from Ryazan on 25 July, 1969, details of which reached the West. Particularly severe are those regulations of the *ukaz* which forbid ministers to look after any congregation outside the limits of their own locality, and which no longer allow any religious gathering or prayer meeting in a private home without special permission from the authorities. These and other limitations represent a severe tightening up of the 1929 Stalinist law.

Under these circumstances registration of new E.C.B. congregations, which had only taken place on any large scale in 1947-8, was as good as impossible. This led to a position where until 1960 probably only a third of the existing congregations were able to obtain their registration and thus their legitimisation. The leading organ of the Union, the All-Union Council of Evangelical Christians and Baptists (A.U.C.E.C.B.) in Moscow was also forbidden to take up any contact with the unregistered (and thus according to Soviet law non-existent) congregations, and to speak for them. These congregations were of course particularly exposed to state incursions and police measures.[4]

Thus the dissatisfaction in the congregations and the indignation of actively committed Christians against the Khrushchev repressions is only too understandable. In the Soviet Union today it is admitted, even on the atheist side, that 'rough treatment and administrative pressure' were also responsible for the formation of the schismatic movement among the Evangelical Christians and Baptists.[5]

But the wave of state persecution since the end of the 1950s had one further refinement. Not only were the congregations exposed to pressure from the relevant official departments (*ispolkomy*) and from officials of the Council for the Affairs of Religious Cults, but the central Church organisations, including the A.U.C.E.C.B., were themselves forced to dismiss over-active presbyters, dissolve congregations and restrict the scope of their own Church in every possible way. The All-Union Council had to do this in pursuance of the harsh religious laws of the 1920s, in particular the 'Law on Religious Associations' of 8 April, 1929; the spoken or unspoken concessions made to the denominations since the Second World War were now said to be illegal.

The most important proof of the submission of the All-Union Council to state demands is the Union statute, worked out and put into effect in 1960, and an Instruction to Senior Presbyters of the same year.[6] The excerpts from the Instruction that have been published so far leave very little doubt that they were dictated to the All-Union Council by the Council for the Affairs of Religious Cults, the supreme Soviet body of control. Here it is stated that congregations in the past had not heeded the Soviet laws on religion, and that Church activities that were expressly forbidden in the April 1929 Law were being carried on: '. . . There have been cases of young people under eighteen being baptised, material assistance has been given out of Church funds, Bible evenings and other special gatherings have been held, the reading of poetry has been permitted, excursions for young believers have taken place, funds for mutual assistance have been set up, there have been meetings for preachers and training of choir leaders. . . .' The Senior Presbyters are further exhorted in the Instruction to act against 'unhealthy missionary tendencies' as there must be an 'absolute end to the chase after new believers in our congregations'. The number of baptisms of persons aged between eighteen and thirty was to be reduced 'to the absolute minimum'. Children were no longer to be allowed to take part in the services.[7]

It is clear that the instructions of the All-Union Council were outspokenly self-destructive in character; hence the indignation in the congregations, which led to schism in many places, was at first directed chiefly against the All-Union Council and not against the Soviet state. The opposition accused its own Union leadership of bowing passively to all the demands of the Council for the Affairs of Religious Cults and of having led the Church into an 'adulterous alliance with the world, i.e. with atheism'.[8]

Thus the resistance within the Union of Evangelical Christians and Baptists against the policy of repression caught fire with the protest against these two documents approved by the All-Union Council. In May 1961 the opposition forces gathered around A. F. Prokofiev and G. K. Kryuchkov and demanded the convocation of a Congress of Evangelical Christians and Baptists to repeal the Statute and the Instruction.

To understand the resistance in many congregations to their own Union leadership, another factor has to be remembered. The Union, which was only formed in 1944 through the joining together of the Evangelical Christians and the Baptists, has always been threatened by separatist tendencies; these became more apparent the more the All-Union Council in Moscow tried – with the support of the authorities – to transform the Union into a centrally controlled Church organisation. The centrifugal forces did not come only from the individual groups of which the Union was formed (the Evangelical Christians and Baptists had been joined over the years by Pentecostals, Mennonites and the remains of the German Lutheran communities in Central Asia and Siberia); small splinter groups from the Union, rejecting the Soviet laws on religion either implicitly or openly, always existed. Among these relatively small groups were the 'Perfectionists', the 'Free Baptists' and the 'Pure Baptists' in the Ukraine.[9] A. F. Prokofiev, who led the Action Group until his imprisonment in 1962, had already been more or less outside the Union even in the 1950s. After he had spent the years 1941–51 in prison, he was sentenced again in 1954 for illegal missionary work, distributing home-made leaflets and letters, and giving religious instruction to children.[10]

A further reason why the resistance in the congregations to the Union leadership developed to the point of being a *raskol*, or schism, lies in the far-reaching independence of individual congregations *vis-à-vis* the Union, upon which the *Initsiativniki* logically lay particular stress. The Union always remained an organisation built up from the grass-roots, and the All-Union Council as well as the Senior Presbyters were much more dependent on the congregations than, for example, the Orthodox episcopate, so that an oppositional movement could form much more quickly, and escape the control of the Church leadership. Thus it is significant that the opposition which has also arisen since the beginning of the 1960s in the Russian Orthodox Church against the patriarchal leadership has not led to a Church schism.

The 'Action Group for the Calling of a Congress' developed therefore into an extremely radical movement, when it became evident that neither the Soviet authorities nor the All-Union Council of Evangelical Christians and Baptists was prepared to accede to the Group's demand for a congress: none of the thirty or so petitions which the *Initsiativniki* made to the central Soviet authorities between 1961 and 1966 received a written answer.

In February 1962 the Action Group met for a secret conference at which it transformed itself into an Organising Committee, headed by a five-man presidium, for the calling of an extraordinary congress of Evangelical Christians and Baptists. It was established that this congress was to warn the All-Union Council about its 'conscious departure from truth and the continuation of its constant anti-Church activity'. The Organising Committee went even further and threatened the All-Union Council with excommunication 'in accordance with the will of God'; it described its own task as the 'purification and restoration of the Church'.[11] Thus ten months after the foundation of the Action Group, the gap between it and the Union leadership was already almost unbridgeable. At a secret meeting in June 1962 the Organising Committee then excommunicated the three leading figures in the All-Union Council: the President Ya. I. Zhidkov, the General Secretary A. V. Karev and the Treasurer (later President) I. G. Ivanov; four other members of the All-Union Council, twenty senior presbyters and a number of presbyters were also excommunicated. At the same time the Organising Committee declared that it would 'take over the future leadership of the Church of Evangelical Christians and Baptists until the Congress';[12] it thus declared itself the only 'true' Church, and cast out the Moscow Union leadership and its structure as heretical. Only a small step was then needed to formalise what had already happened; in September 1965 the Organising Committee transformed itself into the 'Council of Churches of Evangelical Christians and Baptists', and the Church split became formally complete. By this time the Organising Committee had finally given up hope of permission being given to call a congress and of the All-Union Council capitulating and dissolving itself.

The formation of their own Church and their condemnation of the All-Union Council, which was tolerated and controlled by the Soviet government, is the understandable outcome of a deep concern for the survival of the Baptist congregations and above all of biblical mission in the Soviet Union; yet it was foolish to expect recognition and legitimisation from the Soviet authorities against whose repressions they were protesting.

Since 1962 a strong polemical battle has developed between the All-Union Council and the break-away group, which finds its chief expression in the constantly increasing illegal literature which is passed from hand to hand in the Soviet Union. The two *Initsiativniki* periodicals *Bratsky Listok* ('Fraternal Leaflet') and *Vestnik Spasenia* ('Herald of Salvation'), written by hand and then reproduced, appear fairly regularly. (Since the second half of 1971, *Bratsky Listok* has actually appeared in printed form.) The break-away 'Council of Churches' carries on the battle with the harshness, impatience and desperate martyr's courage of a group convinced that it alone has the gospel truth. The All-Union Council is described as a body which 'is not appointed by God or the Church, but carefully chosen and appointed by the Council for the Affairs of Religious Cults and other authorities working for the destruction of the Church'. The Union leadership, they say, had betrayed three basic principles of the Baptist faith: the independence of the congregations, the preaching of the gospel as the Church's main task and, most important, the separation of Church and state.[13]

In March 1965 the Organising Committee, as both previously and subsequently, refused discussions with the All-Union Council on reunification. They said that the All-Union Council had 'not only completely surrendered itself to the state authorities, but also exhorted the people of God to do the same'. By transgressing the basic principle of separation of Church and state, it had 'rejected obedience to Christ', and the members of the All-Union Council could 'never inherit the kingdom of God'. Even a conversation on reunification is described as 'irreconcilable with the holy scriptures and the will of God'.[14]

The break-away Council of Churches thus not only accused the All-Union Council of having submitted to state repressions, but in the sight of the *Initsiativniki* there was no longer any difference between the state authorities and the All-Union Council, which they saw as having become the destructive tool of militant atheism. The humiliating pressures to which the All-Union Council, like all Church bodies, had been exposed between 1958 and 1964 was simply ignored.

The Flexible Attitude of the All-Union Council

Although the Union of Evangelical Christians and Baptists sometimes reacted to the attacks of the *Initsiavniki* with sharp polemic, yet on

F*

the whole it responded to the schismatic threat with great flexibility. One important cause of this was certainly the realisation by the Union leadership of the danger of self-annihilation, and of its own guilt and shortcomings. For the All-Union Council must, of course, have been fully aware that its 1960 regulations had had catastrophic consequences for the congregations and that the reproaches of the *Initsiativniki* were fully justified, even though they should rightly have been directed against the Council for the Affairs of Religious Cults. Thus it could only be in the interests of the Union to comply with the justifiable demands of the *Initsiativniki* and to repeal as many as possible of the 1960 restrictions. That, however, would only be possible with the agreement of the Council for the Affairs of Religious Cults. And herein lay the second reason for the flexible attitude of the All-Union Council: the Soviet authorities were resolved to prevent a decay of the Union of Evangelical Christians and Baptists, which it controlled, and to obviate the formation of a numerically significant Baptist underground church. This confirmed a basic aim of Soviet religious policy over the last few decades, *viz.* the greatest possible unification and centralisation of Church organisations, if it does not appear opportune to destroy them. Soviet atheists explain this principle in this way: a schism may weaken the organisational strength of the Church but still lead to a revitalisation of religion, a growth in Church activity and a generally stronger interest in Church life; a Church schism therefore did not serve the interests of Soviet society.[15]

For these reasons the schismatic group was refused permission to call a congress and it remained limited to its secret meetings; on the other hand, for the first time since 1944, the legalised Union of Evangelical Christians and Baptists received permission to hold national congresses, which were primarily intended to help overcome the schism. In October 1963, 250 delegates met in Moscow, while at the October 1966 congress there were over 1,000 participants, including 711 delegates.[16] On neither occasion was the break-away group adequately represented; in any case many of its active members were then in prisons and camps.

The October 1963 congress not only repealed the 1960 Statute and Letter of Instructions to Senior Presbyters, but it also brought into effect a new Union statute which in almost all important points met the demands that had been made by the leaders of the Action Group, Prokofiev and Kryuchkov, in a 1961 draft statute.[17] This showed very clearly how the All-Union Council was yielding to pressure from below and entering into the 'new opportunities' offered by the revised state religious policy.[18]

Resulting from the demands of the *Initsiativniki* the 1963 Statute introduced a considerable democratisation of the Union. The All-Union Congress of congregational delegates was expressly recognised as the supreme organ of the Union; it was to meet at least every three years and elect the All-Union Council as the executive body. Alterations to the Statute (as Prokofiev and Kryuchkov had suggested) were now reserved for the Congress. While the 1960 version had allowed the All-Union Council to be in contact only with the registered congregations, this regulation was now dropped, as the *Initsiativniki* had demanded. Again following the suggestions of Prokofiev and Kryuchkov, the right of all Church members to preach, which had been severely limited in 1960, was re-established. Likewise the 1960 regulation that no services except funerals could be held in private homes was not included in the 1963 Statute; at the same time one may not conclude from this that Baptists today have the right to hold services in private apartments. The necessity to obtain permission for such meetings has been part of Soviet administrative law since the Khrushchev repressions.

In several points the 1963 Statute only met the *Initsiativniki* half way, but on these points the Statute which was accepted at the 1966 Congress and is valid today made some further partial concessions,[19] particularly regarding the appointment of the Senior Presbyters, who lead the congregations of certain areas as full-time ministers. Until 1963 they had simply been appointed and dismissed by the All-Union Council; the 1963 version called for the 'approval of the congregations in which they are members', but the new 1966 Statute established the election of Senior Presbyters by regional presbyters' conferences, according to the demand of the *Initsiativniki*. The 1966 Statute, in contrast to the others, also underlined the independence of the individual congregations and in this way too it seemed more acceptable to the break-away group.

But the Union of Evangelical Christians and Baptists not only tried through internal reforms to satisfy the opposition in the congregations; efforts were also made to persuade break-away groups to return to the Union. In a series of appeals and messages to all congregations the All-Union Council emphasised repeatedly that the doors stood wide open for all those who had left the Union. Within the Union no one need feel restricted in his faith (Phil. 3:15–16), for all believers were members of the body of Christ (1 Cor. 12:27).[20]

The October 1966 Congress also appointed a central commission on reunification, consisting of fifteen members, which was given the task of contacting the Council of Churches and of looking for those congregations all over the country where there had been schisms in order to encourage the break-aways to return to the Union. In 1967 and 1968 the members of the Commission visited more than 100 congregations, and many adherents of the Council of Churches rejoined the All-Union Council either individually or in groups; however, others rejected any contact or conversation.[21]

About 1,000 dissident Baptists are supposed to have returned to the Union congregations in 1967 and 1968, and the Senior Presbyter for the Ukraine, N. N. Melnikov, told the October 1966 Congress that in that year in the Ukraine alone 2,000 *Initsiativniki* had rejoined the Union. That the situation is still precarious is revealed by the stereotype assertion repeated by the late General Secretary Karev before the Plenum of the All-Union Council in March 1969: 'The move into the ranks of the dissidents has almost completely ceased.'[22]

The schism is still by no means overcome at the present time, and many congregations certainly vacillate between the All-Union Council and the Council of Churches. Even the 1966 Congress showed this; indeed, only two official observers from the Council of Churches were present, but a number of Church delegates sympathised with it. Other delegates expressly declared that they had previously belonged to the break-away group, but had now returned to the A.U.C.E.C.B. for the sake of unity. At the same time they criticised the All-Union Council and 'some presbyters' for their inadequate care of the congregations at the beginning of the 1960s; they also censured the Council of Churches for its pride and its flaunted 'sinlessness'.[23]

While the All-Union Council tries to win individual church members among the break-aways, efforts are also in progress to reintegrate the leaders of the *Initsiativniki* into the All-Union Council. In the spring of 1969, after some leaders of the free Baptists had been released after serving their terms of imprisonment in the camps, official conversations between the dissidents and the All-Union Council took place. The latter had renewed its offer of negotiation in a circular of March 1969 and expressed the opinion that there were 'no longer any reasons' for separation from the Union, especially since the Union had now printed Bibles and song-books, was holding theological courses and had achieved other concessions from the state.[24]

The conversations which took place at long intervals in 1969 on 19 April, 17 May and 6 December did not however bring any re-unification. Although there is no question of theological-dogmatic differences, it is impossible to see how there can be a merger between the Council of Churches and the All-Union Council as long as both sides continue to stand on the positions they have taken up to now. The All-Union Council openly confesses the mistakes it made at the beginning of the 1960s, but claims that these have been made good by the decisions of the 1963 and 1966 Congresses; it now expects the break-away Baptists to retract unjustified accusations, and to recognise unconditionally all existing Soviet laws on religion. The free Baptists, on the other hand, demand and practise an extended freedom of activity in the congregations and obviously still expect from the All-Union Council an admission of guilt and the abrogation of all state regulations. The reunification conversations are also made more difficult by the fact that the persecution of the dissident Baptists conti-nues with undiminished force.[25]

Before any closer examination is made of the controversy with the state and of the persecution, we must try to assess the numerical strength of the break-away group. Here, as in all questions affecting religion and Church in the Soviet Union, no reliable statistics are available. Although the stereotype assertion is always made that it is prohibited to make statistical surveys of believers in the Soviet Union, it is not fanciful to suggest that both state and Church bodies have access to quite precise data which may not, however, be published. The extent of the schism can only be assessed roughly.

Both Baptist sources and the Soviet press in recent years have repeatedly given the number of the *Initsiativniki* as about 5 per cent of the Evangelical Christians and Baptists i.e. 15,000 believers.[26] These figures thus assume that the Union of Evangelical Christians and Baptists has about 300,000 members. From other reliable data it is known that this can only mean the number of registered believers.[27] The total number of Church members having undergone believers' baptism in 1967–8 was at least 500,000.[28] It must be assumed that the dissidents found considerably more support in the unregistered than in the registered congregations, because relations with the All-Union Council were weaker there, and in 1960 the All-Union Council expressly had to forgo any contact with the unregistered congrega-tions. If one therefore presumes a Council of Churches membership

closer to forty or fifty thousand, this is supported by the fact that the
All-Union Council gave the number of believers in 1962 as 545,000
and in 1967 as 500,000.[29] However, the vigour of the reform Baptist
movement suggests that its membership could be much higher than
this.

Besides baptised believers, there are also in the Soviet Union a large
number of people who are close to the Baptists and take a greater or
lesser part in their church life; in 1954 the Union gave their number as
three million.[30] But it does not appear justified to count all these
people who are close to the Baptists among the *Initsiativniki*.[31]

The Persecution

It has been seen that the schism and the upheavals in the congregations
were caused by state repression against religious life, which the All-
Union Council was commissioned to carry out. The *Initsiativniki*
therefore turned with all their force first of all against the state-tolerated
and directed A.U.C.E.C.B. However, a collision with the state authorities and, as soon became evident, with the police and the law, could
not be long in coming, since the *Initsiativniki* disputed the state's right
to regulate religious life at will, down to the smallest details – a right
that the Soviet state had always taken for granted from the very beginning. The break-away Baptists have never questioned the Soviet
government and social system as such; on the contrary they always
emphasise their loyalty and have still not given up hope of legalisation.
Nevertheless, they were ready, potentially, to adopt an attitude of
opposition towards the Soviet state, because they did not recognise it
as the final power, authoritative in all spheres of life, and set higher
value on, for example, the command of the Gospel to evangelise than
on the Soviet prohibition of 'religious propaganda'.

The leaders of the Organising Committee, G. K. Kryuchkov and
A. A. Shalashov, formulated their demands to the state in a letter to
to Khrushchev of 13 August, 1963, saying that 'the Church must
remain free from interference by the world and secular powers in its
internal life.'[32] Under present conditions there is no prospect of the
state and Communist Party acceding to this demand.

The Organising Committee developed its ideas in detail in a letter
of 14 April, 1965, to L. I. Brezhnev, in his capacity as President of the
Constitutional Commission of the Supreme Soviet.[33] The letter, signed
by the President and Secretary of the Organising Committee, G. K.
Kryuchkov and G. P. Vins, shows a detailed knowledge of the evolu-

tion of Soviet religious legislation. Appealing to Lenin's decree on the separation of Church and state and the first constitution of the Russian Republic in 1918, the writers demanded the restoration of true freedom of conscience in the Soviet Union. They said that the 1929 Law on religious associations and the alteration of the Constitution in the same year, which removed the freedom of 'religious propaganda', had deprived citizens of the possibility of 'making use of the right of freedom of conscience'. The separation of Church and state had been violated in 1919 by the obligation to register congregations, by the fact that the authorities had to give their permission for general congregational meetings, were able to dismiss members of the Church executive bodies, and so on. Kryuchkov and Vins therefore demanded the repeal of the 1929 Law and an effective guarantee of freedom of belief; this was to be enshrined in a future Constitution in which 'freedom of religious propaganda' must again be established.

But the *Initsiativniki* did not wait for the new Soviet constitution, they immediately began to practise freedom of evangelisation inside and outside the existing Baptist congregations. Their preachers travelled around the country forming new congregations; religious instruction for children – forbidden in the Soviet Union – was organised; services and Bible studies were held in private homes or in the open air, and young people under eighteen were baptised, which was also forbidden. Handwritten spiritual literature also appeared in *samizdat* (privately printed sheets) in large quantities; a large part of this was devoted to the religious instruction of children and young people, and included a militant dialogue with atheism.[34]

The Soviet system reacted quickly and rigorously to this challenge of a fairly large group trying to escape its control. The first arrests of preachers and active workers among the *Initsiativniki* came in 1961. At first they were charged under the law of the Russian Republic of 4 May, 1961, protecting society against so-called parasites 'living on income not self-earned';[35] the Supreme Soviet of the Russian Republic on 25 July, 1962, then decided on an alteration of Article 227 of the Penal Code which was now adapted to meet the 'new exigencies'.[36] The other republics of the Union followed suit with similar alterations. While the article previously had only laid down penalties for the formation of religious groups harmful to health, it now also threatened the organisation or active participation in religious groups involving any encroachment upon 'personality or civil rights'. Group leaders who incited their members 'to avoid social activity or not to fulfil civil obligations' could also now be punished with five years' imprisonment; active participation and furtherance of such groups was published by three years' imprisonment.

It is obvious that these regulations allow for the widest interpretation. Every baptism, after all, is an encroachment upon personality; and if the Baptists encouraged their supporters not to join the social organisations and tried to keep their children away from the Young Pioneers and the Komsomol, they were thus demonstrating their rejection of social activity. The very fact that the *Initsiativniki* avoided noticing Party and atheist propaganda could be enough for the courts to apply Article 227. The readiness of the *Initsiativniki* to become martyrs was of course considered 'anti-social'.[37]

Trials have been held all over the Soviet Union against the dissident Baptists since 1962; information about them is received chiefly through their families, who at the beginning of 1964 formed a 'Council of Prisoners' Relatives' in order to gather and disseminate information and to fight corporately for the freedom of their relations.

In July 1964 the Council of Prisoners' Relatives issued its second list with the names of Baptists imprisoned at that time. The Council had collected information on 197 brethren; five of them had died from torture or through the inhuman conditions in the camps, while twenty-two had been released from investigation prisons or camps for various reasons. According to Baptist information Soviet courts up to the middle of 1964 had also taken twelve children in six families away from their parents, who were accused of having educated their children in a fanatical religious spirit.[38]

The fall of Khrushchev in October 1964 brought a *détente* in the whole religio-political front; while open criticism was made of Khrushchev's enforced ideological demands and his *administrirovanie* (arbitrary rule), there were scarcely any trials against those Baptists who, significantly, joined together in the autumn of 1965 in the 'Council of Churches of Evangelical Christians and Baptists'.[39] During this time a number of prisoners were actually released from the camps and rehabilitated.[40]

Between the autumn of 1965 and the spring of 1966, encouraged by the relative *détente* at home and strengthened in their self-awareness, the break-away Baptists came much more into the open than in previous years. They no longer held their services only in private homes and in remote parts of woods outside the towns, but gathered demonstratively in the main streets and squares. These meetings, usually with several hundred participants, took place in a number of cities, particularly on 7-8 November, 1965, and 1-2 May, 1966. There were mass youth baptisms in the presence of police who were unprepared for such demonstrations. Around this time, especially in the Ukraine, evangelistic groups of believers took to the buses and trams, where they sang Christian songs and engaged the other passengers in religious conversations. At the same time an intensive life developed in the congregations of the 'reform Baptists', or 'free Baptists' as they are sometimes called. Preachers and choirs made exchange visits, active Church workers met for small or large conferences and a 'congress of women believers' was held. Of course, all these meetings of active Church workers had to be underground events. In 1965-6 the top Party and state bodies were also flooded with a great quantity of letters, declarations and petitions. The reform Baptists again and again demanded freedom of evangelisation, the release of their fellowbelievers still in prison and permission to call a congress. They managed to have a delegation received by the Head of State, A. I. Mikoyan, in September 1965.[41]

The public appearances of the free Baptists reached their climax with a demonstration of about 500 delegates from more than 130 towns in front of the Central Committee building of the C.P.S.U. in Moscow on 16 and 17 May, 1966. The delegates asked to speak with the General Secretary of the Party, L. I. Brezhnev, to whom they wanted to hand a petition demanding an end to the repression and persecution. The Baptists asked for the release of their fellow-believers in prison and for the recognition by the Soviet authorities of the 'Council of Churches of Evangelical Christians and Baptists'. All citizens were to receive the right to give religious instruction and to take part in it; the 'interference of atheists in the affairs of the Church' was to cease.

Central Committee officials refused to receive the delegation which remained gathered outside the building throughout the day and the following night. On the next day, 17 May, at noon an official declared that ten Baptist leaders could be received on condition that the rest of the demonstrators dispersed. The leaders accepted but the crowd refused to disperse, whereupon the K.G.B. and police brought buses and transported the demonstrators away by force; as they got into the buses they were beaten by K.G.B. men, but still they sang in chorus.

Some of those arrested were released the next day, others were given ten to fifteen days in prison, and those who were considered organisers and leaders were held for judicial investigation. When the President and Secretary of the Council of Churches, G. K. Kryuchkov and G. P. Vins, and a preacher, M. I. Khorev, went to the Central Committee on 19 May to discover the fate of those arrested, they too were arrested. The result was a wave of trials against the independent Baptists throughout the Soviet Union.[42]

The attempts of the *Initsiativniki* since 1965 to evangelise publicly had already caused the Soviet authorities to prepare energetic counter-measures. On 18 March, 1966, the Presidium of the Supreme Soviet of the Russian Republic passed three edicts, prepared by the Council for the Affairs of Religious Cults, to give the courts and the local authorities a firmer basis in law for their action against the free Baptists.[43] Anyone organising and carrying out religious gatherings and ceremonies, or establishing special youth groups and work and literature circles could now be punished by the local authorities (*ispolkomy*) with a fine of up to 50 roubles. From March 1966 a second, complementary paragraph of Article 142 of the Penal Code of the Russian Republic threatened those who disobeyed the laws on the separation of Church and state more than once with imprisonment for up to three years, while those sentenced for the first time still had to reckon on one year in a labour camp. The third edict of the Supreme Soviet dealt with the interpretation of Article 142. Here the most important activities of the independent Baptists were specifically named as criteria for the application of this Article: the organisation of religious instruction for children, the carrying out of religious gatherings and ceremonies which 'disturbed public order', and the spreading of letters and documents 'which called on people not to fulfil the laws on religious cults'. A new Article 190/3 of the Penal Code of the Russian Republic, added in September 1966, once again made group activity which was connected with the disruption of 'public order' a punishable offence.[44]

The second wave of persecution against the *Initsiativniki*, which began in the spring of 1966, was accompanied by a violent press campaign. Personal attacks and slanders against individual believers in the local press often formed the prelude to intervention by the police and courts. Attempts by the independent Baptists to have their congregations registered and thus legalised were everywhere rejected by the authorities since the Baptists were not prepared to recognise in writing all the limitations on religious activity in the Soviet Union. Furthermore, measures were taken to restrict all organised activity of the *Initsiativniki*. Their prayer meetings in the open air or in private houses were dispersed by the police, often amid pogrom-like scenes. The preachers and flat-owners were imprisoned and subjected to interrogations not infrequently accompanied by torture. Believers lost their jobs and their children were discriminated against at school and removed from institutions of higher education. The courts often tried to make children denounce their parents; they were interrogated and made to sign protocols.

Those who took part in services of worship were given sentences of ten to fifteen days or heavy fines. The household effects of any one unable to pay a fine were confiscated. In Kiev alone from May 1966 to July 1967 ninety people were given fifteen-day sentences. The Council of Prisoners' Relatives gathered details of over 500 people who in the same period were fined a total of more than 30,000 roubles. But there were also cases of confiscation and destruction of houses where prayer meetings had taken place, and of believers being sent to psychiatric hospitals. Severe house searches and summonses by the authorities became a daily occurrence for the independent Baptists.[45]

In Moscow alone in the summer and winter of 1966 there were eighteen trials, directed mainly against the organisers and participants of the May Demonstration; the wave of trials covered the whole country. Three points were uppermost in the charges again and again: performance of and participation in illegal religious gatherings, which were usually presented as 'disturbances of public order', the production and distribution of religious literature, and finally the 'enticement' of minors into the faith.

The trials were usually conducted by the courts in a malicious and unfair way. Many defendants admitted that they did not consider all the regulations of Soviet laws on religion as just and therefore could not follow them; they appealed here not only to the Bible but also to Lenin's decree of 1918, the Soviet constitution and the U.N. Declaration on Human Rights, and they refused to plead guilty.

The readiness to suffer with which most defendants faced their sentence is incredible and almost alien to us: 'My spirit rejoices that God has found me worthy of such a high honour', said one woman, with amputated legs, in her final statement before the court that sentenced her to three years' imprisonment.[46] From information that has reached the West it is known that the Baptists are treated with especial cruelty in the camps if they confess their faith openly there too.[47]

Further arrests and trials are taking place all the time. However, it has proved impossible up till now to crush the movement. In Chelyabinsk, Oryol and Issyk in Alma-Ata Region, young people from a considerable area around met together in 1968 for illegal religious conferences, attended in each case by several hundreds of believers.[48]

In November 1969 the Council of Prisoners' Relatives, which constantly distributes documents about the persecution, held its first All-Union conference at a secret location. Its circular *To all Christian Churches, to all Christians of the World* stated that since 1961 more than 500 Baptists had been arrested and thrown into prison; in the autumn of 1969 alone the courts had again sentenced twenty-one people. The prisoners' relatives listed in their letter the names of the 174 Baptists at that time deprived of their freedom; more than 700 children were without their parents and wives without their husbands. Most of them, chiefly sentenced between 1967 and 1969, had been charged under Article 142/2 of the Penal Code of the Russian Republic, which was introduced in March 1966, to three years in labour camps; but the courts also handed out sentences of up to six years by applying other paragraphs.[49] According to the most recent prisoner lists to have reached the West, dated September 1971 and 1 January, 1972, 133 Baptists were in prison in the autumn of 1971; by the end of the year the number of those to have lost their freedom on religious grounds had again risen by twenty.

Among the prisoners, especially from Kirgizia and Kazakhstan, were a number of Germans; the prisoner list of November 1969 names twelve Germans among the seventeen imprisoned from Kazakhstan. However, the list is not complete and does not contain the names of the two young women, Ye. K. Chernetskaya and M. I. Braun, each of whom was sentenced on 11 March, 1966, by the District Court in Sokuluk, Kirgizia, to five years in a labour camp. These two had run an illegal Sunday school for children in Novo-Pavlovka village, to which mainly German parents sent their children; Maria Braun described herself before the court as a German.[50] She was released ahead of time, possibly before November 1969, after declaring that she had become an atheist.

A number of trials have attracted particular attention in the Soviet Union and abroad because of their harshness and ruthlessness. These include the case of Nadezhda Stepanovna Sloboda, who together with two relatives was sentenced on 12 December, 1968, by the Vitebsk

Regional Court to four years in a labour camp for organising an illegal
Baptist congregation since 1962. Mrs. Sloboda has five children;
already in February 1966 a court had deprived the parents of their
two eldest by taking them forcibly to a children's home because they
had been brought up by their mother in a religious and thus an anti-
social manner. The children ran away from the state home several
times and each time were forcibly taken back by the police, until the
mother was also locked away.[51] In February 1970 the three smaller
children were also taken from their home. More recently the two
eldest girls have been permitted to return.

Children are frequently those who suffer most in the persecutions.
In March 1969, 1,453 mothers complained in a letter to Brezhnev,
Podgorny and Kosygin about the severe discrimination to which
children of religious parents were exposed. They were mocked by
teachers and fellow-pupils, beaten and excluded from the community,
and often had no chance to go to institutions of higher education,
or were expelled from them. The new Family Law is also used against
religious parents; in Article 19 this provides for the removal of parental
rights if the parents 'exercise a harmful influence on the children by
immoral, anti-social behaviour'.[52]

The right of parents to religious instruction for their children,
which for a long time – officially at least – had remained uncontested,
has been specifically disputed in the trials of recent years. The indictment of the court in Sumgait, Azerbaidjan, against M. P. Kabanov,
N. T. Gurov and six other Baptists of 17 January, 1969, declared that
this parental right could not be recognised because the children would
be alienated from 'social life'. Children of Baptist parents, it said, did
not go to the cinema or the theatre, did not read any newspapers,
or join the Komsomol, and were generally removed from all the 'joys
of life'. The sentence of the court on 31 March, 1969, then established
in a typically discriminatory manner that Baptist children were
'usually recognisable by their appearance; the stamp of religiosity is
graven on their faces, and they are pale, sad, withdrawn and taciturn.'
The court stood by these generalised prejudices, which weighed
heavily against the defendants, although the school which Gurov's sons
attended expressly testified to their lively participation in social life.

The Baptists always plead not guilty before the court and they appeal
to the Soviet constitution and the freedom of religion established there.
The trials are thus held to extract proofs of guilt. The court at Sumgait
considered it as an important proof of guilt that Gurov 'himself

informed the court that he had read the Bible in believers' flats, where the sermons were accompanied with communal singing.' Communal reading of the Bible in other trials too is again and again taken as a confession of guilt. The Soviet courts can hardly show their true colours more plainly.[53]

A particularly harsh sentence was handed down by the court in Odessa on 27 August, 1969, when S. N. Misiruk was sentenced to four years in a labour camp followed by five years' exile and confiscation of property; his offence was inter-regional missionary work. In the trial of the most active workers of the free Baptist congregation, held in March 1969, in Odessa, the nine defendants received sentences of up to seven, nine and ten years. In this case, the conduct of the trial was particularly crude; it was held almost entirely *in camera*, and the police had the believers waiting outside the courtroom, being threatened by young *pogromshchiki*.[54]

The increasing brutality of the persecution by courts, police and administration in 1968 and 1969 led many independent Baptists to the conclusion that the Soviet state was aiming at their 'physical liquidation for believing in God'. But among the hard core of *Initsiativniki*, despair had the effect of strengthening their martyr's courage rather than making them ready to give up. Many of the more than sixty Baptists released from the camps in 1969 after serving their sentences immediately took up their illegal Church work again. However, the preacher M. I. Khorev, who had served a three-year sentence and meanwhile become almost blind, was arrested again on 18 December, 1969, a few months after his release. The Secretary of the Council of Churches, G. P. Vins, who was released from very severe prison conditions in 1969, was rearrested on 16 March, 1970.[55]

The future prospects for the break-away Baptist group appear gloomy. Although their unshakeable courage and readiness to sacrifice their lives for the faith is admirable, the independent Baptists are chasing an illusion if in the present harsher domestic political situation they expect the Soviet state to afford them free and uncontrolled scope for religious activity. This is all the more true since there is already an escape-valve in the A.U.C.E.C.B. which stops the pressure from hundreds of thousands, who want a religious life, from becoming too strong. By broadening the scope of the tolerated Union, it is hoped to squeeze the underground church of free Baptists into a small and insignificant group which can then be liquidated by police and administrative measures.

The All-Union Council has adapted itself to conditions in the Soviet Union and thus in recent years, without making any demands on principle, it has achieved much of what the free Baptists have struggled for in vain; for the Union congregations also carry on a thoroughly biblical mission to a modest extent and in private circles. M. Ya. Zhidkov, member of the All-Union Council, declared at the turn of 1967–8: 'We . . . consider it right to exploit the opportunities we have to the full and continually to press for the extension of these opportunities. They [the break-away Baptists] on the other hand reject all control and try to get immediate and complete independence. . . . We believe this is not the right way to remove the restrictions laid upon us.'[56]

Nevertheless, it is clear that the All-Union Council is largely indebted to the reckless courage of the free Baptists for the removal of restrictions. The *Initsiativniki* with their struggle for basic human rights have contributed greatly to critical awareness within Soviet society in recent years.

REFERENCES

1. *Nauka i religia*, 9/1966, p. 19; M. Bourdeaux – P. Reddaway, 'Church and State and Schism. Soviet Baptists Today' in *Survey*, 66, January 1968, p. 52.
2. Cf. Chapter III, pp. 69 ff.
3. *Posev*, 15 July, 1966, p. 3 (the quotations from the illegal organ of the 'Initsiativniki', *Bratsky Listok*, 2–3/1965); 25 November, 1966, p. 4; M. Bourdeaux, *Religious Ferment in Russia: Protestant Opposition to Soviet Religious Policy*, London 1968, pp. 26, 43.
4. *Posev*, 20 October, 1967, p. 6; Bourdeaux–Reddaway, p. 49.
5. L. N. Mitrokhin, *Baptizm*, Moscow 1966, pp. 88–9; 'Kto Takie "initsiativniki" u yevangelskikh khristian-baptistov?' in *Nauka i religia*, 7/1966, p. 24.
6. The 1960 Statute in Bourdeaux, pp. 190–209; extracts from the unpublished Instruction to Senior Presbyters: ibid., pp. 20–1; *Posev*, 15 July, 1966, p. 3, and A. I. Klibanov – L. N. Mitrokhin, 'Raskol v sovremennom baptizme', in *Voprosy nauchnogo ateizma*, III, 1967, p. 86.
7. The quotations from Klibanov-Mitrokhin, p. 86; cf. in particular Art. 17 of the Law on Religious Associations of 8 April, 1929 in *Kirche und Staat in der Sowjetunion: Gesetze und Verordnungen*, p. 16.
8. *Posev*, 15 July, 1966, p. 3.
9. Bourdeaux, pp. 9 ff.; F. Garkavenko, 'Baptizm: Vnutrennie techenia i borba', in *Nauka i religia*, 9/1966, pp. 23–4.
10. *RM*, November 1968, pp. 1–2; Bourdeaux, pp. 22–3, 50.
11. Documents pertaining to the conference of February 1962 in English in Bourdeaux, pp. 32–7.

12. Protocol of the secret conference of the Organising Committee, June 1962, in English in Bourdeaux, pp. 42–6.
13. Quotations from *Bratsky listok*, in *Posev*, 15 July, 1966, p. 3, and Bourdeaux, p. 76.
14. Quotations from a letter of the Organising Committee to the All-Union Council, March 1965, in Bourdeaux, pp. 100–2.
15. *Nauka i religia*, 3/1968, p. 37.
16. *BV*, 6/1966, p. 3.
17. The Statutes of 1960 and 1963 as well as Prokofiev and Kryuchkov's draft are printed in parallel form in: Bourdeaux, pp. 190–210.
18. Both were expressly admitted at the 1963 Congress, cf. Bourdeaux, p. 75.
19. The 1966 Statute in *Osteuropa*, XIX, 1969, pp. A 12–25.
20. *BV*, 5/1968, pp. 6–7.
21. Ibid., 5/1967, pp. 17–18; 1/1968, p. 68; 3/1969, p. 70.
22. *BV*, 5/1968, p. 76; 3/1969, p. 66.
23. *BV*, 6/1966, pp. 67 ff.
24. *BV*, 3/1969, pp. 71–2.
25. Ibid., 4/1969, pp. 69–72; *NZZ*, 14 June, 1970.
26. Bourdeaux, p. 142; J. Nordenhaug, 'A Visit with Russian Baptists', in *The Baptist World*, February 1967, p. 8; *öpd*, 25 January, 1968, p. 3.
27. F. Fedorenko, *Sekty. Ikh vera i dela*, Moscow 1965, p. 166, mentions 'more than 200,000' registered members. At the 1966 Congress, General Secretary Karev declared that at least 250,000 baptised believers belonged to the congregations: BV, 6/1966, p. 17. But comparisons with other figures make it more than likely that Karev only included registered members in this figure.
28. *StO*, 1/1968, p. 47.
29. Ibid.; P. Hauptmann, 'Das Moskauer Patriarchat und die anderen Kirchen und Religionsgemeinschaften innerhalb der Sowjetunion', in *Die Russische Orthodoxe Kirche in Lehre und Leben*, p. 268.
30. *BV*, 2–3/1954, p. 91.
31. As Bourdeaux attempts to do, pp. 3 and 141–2.
32. This letter in English in Bourdeaux, pp. 53–63, the quotation p. 59.
33. *Posev*, 5 August, 1966, pp. 4–5.
34. A discussion of the religious-educational literature of the *Initsiativniki*, from which he quotes at length, is made by Ye. Aleshko, 'Tletvornie zerna', in *Nauka i religia*, 3/1967, pp. 62–5.
35. *Vedomosti Verkhovnogo Soveta RSFSR*, 1961, pp. 286–7.
36. Ibid., 1962, p. 452.
37. Mitrokhin, *Baptizm*, pp. 86–7; *RM*, May 1968, p. 2; Bourdeaux, pp. 78, 170; *RA UdSSR*, June 1968, pp. 6–7.
38. Documents on the first two meetings of the Council of Prisoners' Relatives in February and July 1964 in English in: Bourdeaux, pp. 83–93.
39. *Posev*, 20 October, 1967, p. 6.
40. *RCDA*, VII, 1968, p. 39.
41. *Posev*, 25 November, 1966, pp. 3–4; Klibanov-Mitrokhin, p. 102; Garkavenko, p. 24; RM, May 1968, p. 2; *IZV*, 30 August 1966; Bourdeaux, pp. 114 ff.

42. *Posev*, 25 November, 1966, pp. 4–5.
43. *Vedomosti Verkhovnogo Soveta RSFSR*, 1966, pp. 219–20.
44. Ibid., p. 819.
45. The best information on the persecutions is given in the appeals of the Council of Prisoners' Relatives to the General Secretary of the UN, U Thant, 5 June and 15 August, 1967: *RCDA*, VII, 1968, pp. 23–40, and *Posev*, 20 and 27 October, 1967.
46. *RCDA*, VII, 1968, p. 27.
47. *Posev*, July 1968, pp. 5–6; *Problems of Communism*, XVII, 4/1968, pp. 96–7; *NZZ*, 5 December, 1968.
48. *Molodoi Kommunist*, 1/1969, p. 60.
49. *RCDA*, IX, 1970, pp. 14–17.
50. The sentence is published in English in R. Harris – X. Howard-Johnston (ed.), *Christian Appeals from Russia*, London 1969, pp. 59–62.
51. *Posev*, 11/1969, p. 12; 12/1969, pp. 58–9.
52. Ibid., 12/1969, pp. 57–63; cf. documentation section pp. 52 ff.
53. In recent years a number of protocol-type trial transcripts written by believers or trial documents have become known in the West. Materials pertaining to the following trials have appeared in the journal *Rossia i vselenskaya tserkov* (now *Logos*), 4–1/1968–69, pp. 26–84: trial of M. I. Khorev in Moscow 1966; trial of G. P. Vins and G. K. Kryuchkov in Moscow on 29–30 November 1966; trial of F. B. Makhovitsky in Leningrad on 25–28 November 1966; trial of N. P. Shevchenko, Ya. N. Krivoi, S. P. Solovyova *et al.* in Odessa on 2–7 February 1967; trial of T. K. Feidak and V. A. Vilchinsky in April 1968 in Brest. The Odessa trial has been published in English (extracts) in *Russian Christians on Trial*, E.C.M., London 1970.

Besides these some other trial documents have reached the West which have not yet been published. Quotation is made from these here and later in the text.
54. cf. German edition of this book, documentation section pp. 197 ff.
55. *NZZ*, 14 June, 1970.
56. *öpd*, 25 January, 1968, p. 3.

VI. The Underground Church

Richard Wurmbrand and his 'message'

The underground Church in Communist countries has always exercised a particular attraction and fascination for travel writers and for those anxious to help others, propagandists and those with Church interests. It has equally become a vehicle for a militant anti-Communism as well as for dilettante relief work. The less people know about it, the more speculation blossoms; emotion takes the place of critical examination.

It is claimed that the Orthodox underground Church alone in the Soviet Union has '45 million members', that there are 'tens of thousands' of Christians in prison there, and that the wife of the Soviet Prime Minister, Kosygin, is a secret convert – not to mention Khrushchev himself. On the other hand, many official Church bodies in the West are ill-informed about the situation in Eastern Europe and are ready to minimise and whitewash the persecution and discrimination against the Churches in Communist countries. Richard Wurmbrand, 'ambassador' of the underground Church in the U.S.A., uses this as a justification for making devastating criticisms of the Western Churches. At the same time he calls on persecuted Christians beyond the Elbe never to give in, and to resist the Communist state, the 'Beast of the Apocalypse', from underground. At the same time the defender of the underground Church utters a warning against the World Council of Churches, which is 'collaborating with the Communists'. Wurmbrand found this charge to be confirmed when, during the Plenary Meeting of the Council in 1968, he met 'bishops in a night club in Uppsala', where 'Russian wine was being drunk and obscene songs sung'.[1]

For several years now Wurmbrand has been travelling around in the West as a defender of the underground Church and calling for relief organisations to aid the Churches in Communist countries. He has been receiving mass support. In his last lecture tour of West Germany and Switzerland alone, in the spring of 1972, almost 150,000 DM. was collected.

In 1965, after a ransom payment, Wurmbrand was able to leave Rumania with his family, and since then has lived in the U.S.A. His activity has aroused considerable disquiet in Western Church circles. His books, pamphlets and relief work on behalf of the underground Church in Communist countries have largely met with mistrust and rejection from Church leaders in the West, while on the other hand his book *Tortured for Christ*, in which he describes his illegal missionary work in Rumania and the difficult years in Communist prisons, has sold more than a million copies throughout the world.

Thus Wurmbrand's uncompromising and often naïve attitude, which is determined by strong emotions, commands an audience. Nevertheless, he is subject to strong public attacks from both Church and political circles, and sees himself constantly required to prove the reality and truth of his own experiences. Through his extreme conclusions and the naïveté of his political and theological world view, he has partly forfeited credibility. But even if his religio-political judgments are much too narrow, there is still no ground for doubting the truth of his personal experiences.

Richard Wurmbrand was born in 1909 in Bucharest, the son of a Jewish dentist. He received a business training and in 1936 after a strong revivalist experience became converted to Protestantism. From 1939 to 1940 he was the secretary of the Anglican Christian Mission to the Jews (C.M.J.), and during the war he worked from 1941 to 1944 as preacher for the Swedish and later from 1945 to 1948 for the Norwegian Mission to the Jews. After the war Wurmbrand was active in the Rumanian representation of the World Council of Churches. However, he later cut himself off decisively from the W.C.C. when it took up contact with the officially tolerated Churches of the Communist countries. After the Red Army's occupation of Rumania, Wurmbrand, who knows Russian, conducted a revivalist Bible ministry among the Russian soldiers. This missionary work, taking no account of civil laws, or of social and intellectual differences, has since become the chief feature of his life. The mission to the Red Army, which Wurmbrand describes as having been extraordinarily successful, could only of course be carried on illegally. He became the leader of a Free Church group which distributed Bibles and religious literature in Russian barracks, addressed soldiers in the street, in shops and in trains, and drew them into religious conversations. Wurmbrand himself took a job for a while as a civil employee of the Red Army, in order to have constant contact with Russian soldiers. After the Communist take-over in Rumania in 1948, Wurmbrand was driven into illegality with his Protestant Free Church Rumanian congregation, because from the beginning he absolutely rejected the control and limitation of Church work by the new Communist authorities. He saw his call as underground missionary work, and in the following years he identified Christian witness more and more with martyrdom, and the Church organisations that accommodated themselves to the new conditions of life in a Communist country he regarded as guilty of treason.

Because of his illegal work in the Red Army and his contacts with Western 'imperialist' organisations, Wurmbrand was arrested openly in the street by the secret police in 1948. He then disappeared for years into police prisons, in which he even had to bear a false name because the authorities claimed first that he had escaped to the West and later that he had died. While ill with typhus after years of imprisonment he was sentenced at a secret trial to a twenty-year term. In his imprisonment Wurmbrand was tortured physically and mentally, and for a long time was close to death. He was bound, beaten, chased around in the cell like an animal, kept in isolation and subjected to brainwashing. Day after day he saw men suffering and dying. Wurmbrand was only able to survive illness and torture through his Christian zeal for conversions, which was sometimes almost compulsive but which brought many of his companions in suffering to the faith. At the same time this frequently aroused the indignation of his fellow-prisoners. Life in prison, isolated from the world, preaching among political and criminal prisoners, for which he continually received severe punishment, but which still remained his source of strength, have determined Wurmbrand's picture of Communism and of the Church in a Communist country. Since then he has been able to see the countries of Eastern Europe only as joyless and tormented prisons, where the Church, unless it is willing to become an accomplice to its own liquidation, can only work underground.

In 1956 Wurmbrand was released under amnesty after Stalin's death. After a short time as preacher to a small Lutheran congregation and after several controversial public appearances which brought down an official ban on his preaching, he retired completely into underground missionary work. He called for resistance to the 'band of robbers' – the Communist Party.[2] In January 1959 he was again arrested and this time sentenced to a term of twenty-five years. Once again he survived through conducting religious conversations with his fellow-sufferers and by his ardent missionary zeal. In July 1964 he was released after a total of fourteen years behind bars, but in spite of the thaw which was beginning in Rumania at that time, he continued to be in danger, since he was still, as ever, unprepared to adopt a loyal attitude to the socialist people's democracy. Therefore in 1965 the Norwegian Jewish Mission and the Jewish-Christian Alliance paid £2,500 in ransom money, and the Rumanian authorities thereupon allowed Wurmbrand and his family to emigrate to the West.[3]

Since then he has untiringly painted the horrors of his imprisonment, and held up the underground Church of Eastern Europe – suffering but 'happy' in its martyrdom – as a model for the lukewarm Churches of Western Europe and America.[4] In the process Wurmbrand's own experiences have imperceptibly become for him a myth, the yardsticks and perspectives of the underground Church phenomenon have contracted, and the political reality has become lost in clouds of homespun analogies and hopes.

For the uninitiated reader of Wurmbrand's books and listener to his lectures, the underground Church appears as a closed organisation, stretching across frontiers from the Elbe to the Yellow Sea, offering the only determined resistance to Communism, the 'most dangerous sin in the world'.[5] In reality the term 'underground Church' is a composite concept for the different religious groups in the Communist countries, belonging to various denominations and ecclesiastical traditions, which exist illegally but usually without any mutual connection or even sympathy. Wurmbrand himself provides proof of the lack of solidarity within the underground Church groups when he describes endless theological disputes in a prison cell for clergy of all confessions, in which there is hardly anything to be seen of the ecumenical spirit.[6] Wurmbrand himself brought a more ecumenical spirit into his contacts. Underground Church communities in Eastern Europe include the 'True Orthodox Christians' in the Soviet Union as well as the Jehovah's Witnesses and the Uniate Catholic Church of the Slavic Rite, which was officially and forcibly united with the Orthodox Church in 1946. In Czechoslovakia during the Prague Spring of 1968 the Uniate Church again received the chance to exist legally. Fellowship among underground Church groups is generally limited in its scope to the similarity of their political situation: either they have been completely outlawed and officially disbanded, or else they do not conform to the limitations of existing state laws and carry on illegal missionary work. In both cases they run into conflict – which, particularly in the first-mentioned case, is often bound up with a definite anti-Communist position – with the Party and the state. In all cases persecution has hit the underground communities hard and decimated them.

The hazy dividing lines between tolerated Church communities and underground circles also confirm that underground Church groups are not large bodies that have established themselves over a long period. Many congregations and committed Christians exist on the fringes of legality in their Church activity in the context of the recognised religious communities; this legality can at any time be limited by official repression. Statistics for Church groups outside the registered organisations in the countries of Eastern Europe are unobtainable. The largest group to exist independently of state control is now the reform Baptists, or *Initsiativniki*, in the Soviet Union. However, in Rumania there is at present no significant underground Church group, such as Wurmbrand frequently refers to. His personal circle of supporters and admirers in Bucharest can hardly claim to be an independent underground Church.

It is thus clear that the term 'underground Church' does not describe a clearly delimited phenomenon; it is used for heterogeneous groups, whose activities range from religious conversations with neighbours to the organisation of secret conspiratorial groups with plans for *coups d'état*. We should therefore use it with caution.

Wurmbrand, on the other hand, sees the persecuted Christian groups in Eastern Europe in the transfiguring light of early Christendom. For him the first three centuries of Christian history have returned; for the early Christian Church also 'worked secretly and illegally, and it triumphed'. These Christians had received no theological education and they had no Bibles, but 'God spoke to them'. In Eastern Europe 'the drama, bravery and martyrdom of the Early Church is happening all over again – now'.[7] Wurmbrand identifies the first Christian centuries with the history of suffering of the martyrs, among whose contemporary imitators he numbers himself. He sees Christ's followers, then as now, almost perfectly represented in the martyr figure. Only these for him are real Christians, for man only believes 'the things he is ready to die for'.[8] But as for the early Church the Constantinian era dawned, so Wurmbrand believes in the future of the underground Church. For it is 'the only force which can overthrow this awful tyranny [of Communism] by the power of the Gospel'. 'We *shall* win the Communists for Christ'; these, according to Wurmbrand's hopes, include not just any Communists, but Mao Tse-Tung, Brezhnev and Ceausescu.[9]

According to his opinion the underground Church, which he also occasionally compares with the *Völkermission* in the early Middle Ages or with the Reformation, has already won decisive successes. For Wurmbrand the fact that individual members of the secret police occasionally treat persecuted Christians with good will or privately confess their allegiance becomes the conviction that the police and indeed Communist governments have already been infiltrated by the underground Church.[10] As the *Völkermission* chased out the barbarian gods, so Wurmbrand hopes that the underground Church will break up atheistic Communism from within.

But as Wurmbrand loses his sense of proportion over the size and the opportunities of the Churches in Eastern Europe, he becomes ever less able to form a sober judgment of the present religious and political situation, with its background, in the Soviet Union, of five decades of Communist rule. His assertion that 'persecution in Communist countries has never been as bad as it is now' is not true of Eastern Europe. Neither is it true to speak of 'tens of thousands' of Christian prisoners.[11] Of the reform Baptists in the Soviet Union, at present the largest group to reject state control, a few hundred are in prison. We do not know how many Orthodox, Pentecostals, Roman Catholics and others are in prison, but it is certain that the number does not run into millions. The number of imprisoned Christians in other Eastern European countries is probably smaller. For China and Albania, where almost all public Church life is outlawed, an admittedly large, but unknown figure must be assumed.

We know that even today the forcible suppression of opposition and protest in the Soviet Union continues. In the autumn of 1969 two of the most prominent critics of the arbitrary incursions of state bodies into the internal life of the Russian Orthodox Church, A. E. Levitin-Krasnov from Moscow and B. V. Talantov from Kirov, were arrested. Levitin and Talantov have protested continually over the last few years in open letters, petitions and *samizdat* articles against the forcible closure of churches, discrimination against believers and terror against free opinion in the Soviet Union. Talantov died in a prison hospital in January 1971.[12]

In spite of these recent displays of force, which could mean death or other grim consequences for those concerned, we can still observe a certain hesitation on the part of the authorities and police in the persecution of opposition and protest. A universal and mindless attack is being avoided, because clearly a Stalinist wave of purges and arrests, which could easily be carried out technically, would have unpredictable consequences, especially among the intelligentsia. Only occasionally do the political police use the ultimate methods; but at the same time the deterrent effect of such measures has been nullified by the increasing solidarity among opposition circles, which have significantly grown in the last few years. It is characteristic of the present situation in the Soviet Union that for years Levitin, Talantov and others were able to spread petitions and articles; these admittedly did not on the whole question socialist conditions of state and society as such, but directed devastating criticism at institutions and the conduct of the authorities.

Other leaders of the opposition in the Orthodox Church, like the priests Eshliman and Yakunin or Sergi Zheludkov from Pskov, are still at liberty and have not disappeared into 'some prison or madhouse', as Wurmbrand thinks.[13] Elsewhere he makes the reader think that the 500 participants in a demonstration of the reform Baptists in front of the Central Committee building in May 1966 in Moscow were arrested and disappeared into prison.[14] In fact, however, most of the participants were released after interrogation, while several dozen leading Baptists were sentenced to between three and five years' imprisonment. Wurmbrand also must know that protesters in the Soviet Union are today no longer sentenced to 'twenty years'.[15] He seems, however, to make such exaggerations consciously in order to further his good cause, namely the mobilisation of public opinion in the West. But it is precisely his exaggerated formulations and subjective distortions that are provoking the mistrust of Western readers; and the 'unmasking' of Wurmbrand is made easy for Eastern propaganda.

A section of the illegal Christian groups in Eastern Europe are in conflict both with the state and the Party and with the officially tolerated Churches, from which they have frequently split off. Wurmbrand is one of those who not only reproach the tolerated Churches for their compromises with the authorities but are even convinced that the recognised Churches are instruments of the secret police for the destruction of the 'true Church'. The assertion that 'as a general rule, the leadership of the Churches is entirely controlled by the Communists'[16] is often repeated in the West, because it comes hard to accept the unconditioned political loyalty – particularly in foreign affairs –

of Eastern European Church leaders, although traditionally and until recently, Western European Churches have also been loyal to the state. The Churches in the Communist-controlled countries, however, were only able to maintain their legality by adapting to the new conditions of life. This is responsible for the loyalty towards the ruling regime, and for the necessity to give state authorities a controlling say in Church affairs. Only under these conditions could the Churches win a certain freedom of action, and they still remain a thorn in the flesh of the socialist countries. Legality, however, is an important condition for their activity, for this gives them a greater scope than the underground communities, for which they also remain the point of departure and a point to which to retreat. Thus we have no right to regard the Church leadership of Eastern Europe as a tool of the political police to undermine the congregations and deceive foreigners.

Wurmbrand is wrong in thinking that the large Baptist church in Moscow, which has room for about 2,000 and where 6,000–10,000 Muscovites assemble for worship every week, is only 'a church for duping',[17] even if a number of foreigners are thereby led to make the false assumption that there is unlimited religious freedom in the Soviet Union. It is also irresponsible to describe the leading personalities of the Russian Orthodox Church and of the Evangelical Christians and Baptists, Metropolitan Nikodim (Rotov) and the late General Secretary, Karev, as 'informers' or 'traitors'.[18] In his anti-Communist zeal, which blinds him to political realities, Wurmbrand even declares that the theological seminaries of the Orthodox Church in the U.S.S.R. were 'founded for atheists to prepare them for their atheist work as priests in the Church'.[19] Here, according to Wurmbrand, the devil has completed his work.

The self-styled 'messenger' of the underground Church, whom 'God has commissioned'[20] is also not afraid to cast unjustified suspicion on certain Church personalities. One of the leading men of the official Union of Evangelical Christians and Baptists, A. I. Mitskevich, is supposed to have said in Canada that every week in Moscow he had to report to a police officer on all that happened in the Church. Wurmbrand assumes that after these revelations Mitskevich must have decided 'not to return to Russia again'.[21] Nevertheless, it is a fact that Mitskevich not only returned, but since 1968 has been significantly involved in the establishment of regular theological education for new preachers through correspondence courses. Mitskevich has been appointed by the Union as director of these correspondence courses.[22]

G

Wurmbrand finds harsh words for the late president of the Prague Christian Peace Conference, Professor Josef Hromadka. He says he cannot accept that 'the Hromadkas are Christians', because they work together with the Communists.[23] But in the summer of 1968 it was Hromadka who showed courage and relative independence (although at a very late date) by protesting bitterly in letters against the invasion of Czechoslovakia by the Warsaw pact states. These manifestations have led to difficult controversies within the Christian Peace Conference and to massive political pressure from Moscow, as a result of which, on 14 November, 1968, Hromadka resigned as President of the C.P.C.[24]

The instances of such attacks by Wurmbrand could be multiplied. For him apparently every citizen in a Communist country who is not in prison is under suspicion. However these emotions, partly understandable on account of his personal experiences, are linked to an undifferentiating concept of Communism, which allows condemnation from a 'Christian' standpoint of everyone in Eastern Europe not actually suffering persecution. The most important trait of Communist ideology and political reality for Wurmbrand is its atheism. Communists 'are above all anti-religious'. 'Against it [atheistic Communism] we have to unite.'[25] Since however man – and above all 'the Russian' – is deeply religious, it follows that it 'is unnatural to be a Communist'.[26] Thus a view of Communism as satanic on the one hand is balanced on the other by the idea of its being made harmless. The latter view fosters the belief in an inner break-up of the regime through the underground Church.

With his rejection on principle of the socialist state and Soviet-style social order, Wurmbrand goes far beyond the position of the largest underground group, the reform Baptists. They reject state limitations and control of Church life, but are prepared to accept co-existence, and even try with all the means available to achieve legality in the U.S.S.R. Instead, Wurmbrand calls upon Christians in Eastern Europe to go underground. He should not, therefore, present his anti-Communism in the name of these reform Baptists or the opposition protesters in the Orthodox Church, yet he constantly does so.

In order to support the oppressed Church groups of Eastern Europe, a missionary society, 'Jesus to the Communist World' was founded – with Wurmbrand as a special attraction. In April 1969 it held its first international congress in London.

This missionary society seeks to bring material and moral aid to individual men and women who are in prison or in constant danger. Bibles and religious literature are to be flooded into the Communist-controlled lands. The mission also sponsors religious broadcasts which are beamed from the West into these countries. Material relief and the dissemination of religious literature would certainly deserve wide support if they were not inseparable from the organisation's urge to constant conflict. Wurmbrand's society not only fights against Communism in the 'red' countries but also sniffs out the Communist conspiracy in the Churches of Western Europe and America – which are pursuing a policy of 'complacency'[27] and among restless students and demonstrators. This hysteria goes even further, for Wurmbrand believes that the U.S.A. is directly threatened by Communism; both the Kennedy brothers and Martin Luther King are cited as victims of Communist conspirators: 'the Communists', he says, 'have already murdered many leading U.S.A. figures.'[28] Even if Wurmbrand reckons himself among the 'fools for Christ's sake',[29] it is difficult to see how, with such a narrowing of horizon, the 'sleeping West' is to be awakened and the Western Churches 'saved'.[30]

According to Wurmbrand, the decay and susceptibility of Western Protestantism is mainly due to modern theology with its dissection of the Bible, dogmas and Church history. So he calls on the Churches to 'give up the uninteresting subjects of the existence of God and Bible criticism' and instead to help the martyr Church. 'The professors who say God is dead are preparing the way for Communism.'[31] This anti-modernistic and anti-intellectual position is all of a piece with a two-dimensional world-view governed by black and white contrasts. For Wurmbrand's inflexibility, it remains quite inconceivable that various modes of behaviour should be possible at various levels. If on the same day that *Pravda* publishes a routine atheist article, Pope Paul VI also receives the Soviet head of state Podgorny, he sees this as a softening of the West and a victory for Communism.[32]

For such emotionally determined anti-Communism, the East–West confrontation imperceptibly becomes a moral world-drama in which a ceaseless struggle is waged between good and evil, light and darkness, for the final victory. This anti-Communism, which has put itself at the service of Christianity and the Church, argues along the same lines as Soviet propaganda and representative ideology, for which equally there is only a dualistic 'either/or' which, in the case of the Churches of Eastern Europe, means either opportunism or opposition. In this simple system of co-ordinates, the Church can only be either the

G *

'right hand of the Communists' or the 'true' underground Church. Such a world picture, with its own simple logic, can always ensure for Wurmbrand capacity audiences.

This world view does not at all correspond with reality, or with the problems faced by the Churches in the Communist-controlled countries. For them it is not a question of 'either/or', but of the necessity of living with the political and social reality around them. These Churches do not begin with the thought that Christianity is, *a priori*, bound up with a certain world order, but rather that at all times and in all political circumstances it has the task of reaching men.

One fixed point in the theoretical controversy and in the practical work of the Churches in Eastern Europe is the need to ensure that now and in the future, even in a society which has made atheism into its religion, there is still room for the Churches to exist. In this way the Churches stand opposed, on the one hand, to socialist ideology, and on the other, to an anti-Communism which claims that Christians living in a hostile society must inevitably react with hostility. The martyr stance can thus be transformed into the desire to co-operate in creative activity. Yet the Churches in Eastern Europe must always reckon with the possibility that one day, through circumstances and Christian responsibility, they may be forced to take an ultimate stand against their secular authorities.

REFERENCES

1. R. Wurmbrand, *Untergrundkirche und die hohen Herren*, leaflet circulated by the Hilfsaktion Märtyrerkirche (HMK); HMK, Rundbrief 2, March 1969; Rundbrief 3, May 1969; Rundbrief 26, June 1972. cf. Gerhard Möckel, 'Gefoltert für Christus? zur Aktivität Richard Wurmbrands', in *Evangelische Kommentare* 6/1970, pp. 354–8.
2. Wurmbrand, *Untergrundkirche*, op. cit.
3. R. Wurmbrand, *Tortured for Christ*, London, 1967, p. 48. The biographical details have been assembled from Wurmbrand's own information in his books. Meanwhile, the sharp polemic surrounding him has put in question many such details. It has been established among other things that before 1936 he was active as an atheist agitator and has never been ordained as a minister; also that he was unable to work in any of the small Protestant Churches in Rumania, and formed his own free church group. Even today he does not claim to belong to any denomination and considers himself as standing above them.

4. R. Wurmbrand, *Tortured for Christ*, London, 1967; The New Communist Propaganda Line on Religion (Hearing before the Committee on Un-American Activities, August 10, 1967), Washington, 1967; *in God's Underground*, London, 1968; *The Soviet Saints*, London, 1968; *Sermons in Solitary Confinement*, London, 1969; *If that were Christ, would you give Him your Blanket?* London, 1970.

5. Wurmbrand, *Tortured*, p. 72.

6. Wurmbrand, *In God's Underground*, pp. 218 ff.

7. Wurmbrand, *Tortured*, pp. 58, 82, 127.

8. Ibid., pp. 54, 59.

9. Ibid., pp. 70, 56 ff.

10. Ibid., p. 82; *Propaganda Line*, p. 535.

11. Wurmbrand, *Propaganda Line*, p. 550; *Tortured*, p. 126.

12. *International Herald Tribune*, 16 September, 1969; *öpd*, 30 October, 1969, p. 9; *NZZ*, 31 October, 1969. Cf. pp. 127–8.

13. *HMK*, Rundbrief 3, May 1969.

14. Wurmbrand, *Propaganda Line*, p. 542.

15. Ibid., p. 529.

16. Ibid., p. 535.

17. Ibid., p. 544.

18. Wurmbrand, *Tortured*, pp. 85, 103.

19. *HMK*, Rundbrief 4, July 1969, p. 6.

20. Wurmbrand, *Untergrundkirche*, op. cit.

21. Ibid.

22. *BV*, 4/1968, p. 77.

23. Wurmbrand, *Propaganda Line*, p. 549.

24. *öpd*, 20 November 1969, pp. 2–3.

25. Wurmbrand, *Tortured*, p. 80.

26. Ibid., p. 90.

27. Ibid., p. 66; HMK, Rundbrief 8, 2/1970, p. 14.

28. *HMK*, Rundbrief 4, July 1969, p. 6.

29. Ibid., p. 7.

30. Wurmbrand, *Tortured*, p. 77.

31. Wurmbrand, *Blut und Tränen*, Berghausen/Bd., 1969, p. 95; lecture in Nürnberg on 23 March 1969.

32. Wurmbrand, *Propaganda Line*, p. 528.

VII. Documents

For more than a decade now the 'silent' Church in the Soviet Union has been speaking more and more clearly; a stream of letters, petitions, protests, devotional articles and theological manuscripts has been reaching the West. Thus we know more about the internal life of the Churches in the Soviet Union today than at any time since the 1920s.

The documents and various material which are passed from hand to hand in Church circles in the Soviet Union represent a significant part of Soviet *samizdat* literature. They reveal a high degree of independence not only towards state and Party, but also towards their own hierarchy or Church leadership. In this way the Christian community is participating in the formation of a new self-awareness within Soviet society that resists arbitrary action by the authorities and limitations on personal freedom. The documents are revealing not only of the internal Church situation and the persecutions affecting, particularly, the reform Baptists, but also of the total personal commitment and inner strength of the believers. The documents which follow form a small selection of the material which has reached the West in recent years.

1. Letter of A. E. Levitin-Krasnov to Pope Paul VI: 'The Situation of the Russian Orthodox Church'

Levitin is one of the most important spokesmen of the independent critical movements within the Russian Orthodox Church. The letter to Pope Paul VI, which gives much information about the whole situation of the Church in the Soviet Union, was written in December 1967. (Russian text in *Religia i ateizm*, v S.S.S.R., March 1970, pp. 1–17.)

Not long ago we here in distant Moscow, on your 70th birthday, joined our prayers with the prayers of the Church for the health and welfare of Your Holiness. Already at that time I decided to write to Your Holiness and lay at the footstool of Your Apostolic Throne some of the thoughts of my greatest concern.

I of course know very well and understand the gulf which separates the Father of princes and kings from an ordinary person, a schoolteacher who, because of his religious convictions, is deprived of work in his profession. However, much is written in the West about our Church, and in this connection the writers analyse articles I have written dedicated to church subjects and published under the pseudonym 'Krasnov'. The fact that so much regarding the Russian Church has been published recently in the West by Catholic as well as non-Catholic authors, especially émigrés, witnesses not only to interest in our Church, for which we can only be thankful, but also to the fact that in the West they very poorly grasp the psychology of the modern Russian person and the position of the Russian Church. This is evident in the daily broadcasts of Vatican Radio in the Russian language. So let there be heard the voice of a person who never in his life has thought of anything but the welfare of the Church.

I have never had occasion to talk with a foreigner, but foreigners speak much about me. I cannot turn to any particular one of them, and do not even know how this could be done. Thinking about this, and praying, I decided to turn to the Great Foreigner, placed by God in so high a place that by comparison all earthly differences become insignificant.

Having been from early childhood a religious person, I already in my youth became acquainted with the works of the great Russian philosopher Vladimir Sergeyevich Solovyov, and from that time on the unity of churches has been the great dream of my heart. I did not follow Vladimir Solovyov in recognizing the dogma of papal infallibility, and remained a son of the Eastern Orthodox Church, to which I am eternally grateful for the great spiritual blessings which she has taught me. However, the dogma of papal infallibility is the only hindrance separating me from the Catholic Church, since I see nothing in other dogmas of the Catholic Church contradictory to Orthodoxy or hindering recognition of the Pope as the Supreme High Priest of the Universal Church. The Church has only one unseen Head – the Sweetest Jesus – but can have a visible High Priest symbolizing her unity, raised up above nations, free of all nationalistic and political passions.

It seems to me that the great mass of people in the Russian Orthodox Church hold these views. But of course what concerns me most is the fate of my country and of my own Russian Church. It is the aim of my life to serve the Church with my pen. Not to think about Her would for me be equivalent to not breathing. And so now I want to write about the Russian Church so that all corners of the earth may know her inner authentic life.

We believing Christians of the Russian land live under conditions vastly different from conditions in any other country. We live under a regime put together after the October Revolution which shook the whole world fifty years ago. In evaluating this regime one must first of all be objective and fair: one must not imagine the Soviet system as a paradise descended to earth, nor paint it only black. The Soviet system rests on sound foundations: the absence of private ownership of the means of production, and therefore the absence in the U.S.S.R. of rich persons – capitalists, bankers, merchants – briefly the absence of a bourgeoisie, is unquestionably a great historic achievement by the masses. Nor must one forget the great work carried through in the construction of industry, the liquidation of illiteracy (I myself in youth worked much at this) and the great contribution of the Russian people to all mankind in the victory gained over fascism.

At the same time the Soviet system gave birth to Stalinist tyranny, to the Yezhov and Beria secret police, which were the worst crimes against mankind. And the Stalinist terror has left its traces: for thirty years there developed a generation of bureaucrats accustomed to uncontrolled power and a generation of people used to subordination, frightened and timid. But now a new generation is arising, which did not know Stalin. The most interesting thing in Russia now is the youth. Youth strives for culture and knowledge, and intensely seeks the meaning of life. Splendid, good-hearted, inspired with good-will – this is Russian youth. Help them O Lord!

What does Russian youth want? One can answer in two words: socialist democracy. Socialist democracy in our country is not simply a slogan, it is the only possible reality of the next century. Our people do not want capitalism. They are so unaccustomed to it that school teachers have to spend much time just to explain to senior pupils what is a capitalist and who is a landlord and how one differs from the other. One who sides with capitalism in the U.S.S.R. is considered as much an anachronism as a royalist in France, a supporter of the restoration of the colonial system in India, or the return of North America to the British Empire. At the same time the Russian people, and especially Russian youth, hate Stalinism and Maoism in all their aspects and variants. They want complete freedom of opinion, free scientific research, freedom of philosophical and religious convictions. An economy without private ownership and complete freedom of opinion – this is socialist democracy.

In pre-revolutionary times democratic literature liked to quote Chernyshevsky, who held that history is not the Nevsky Prospect (the main street of St. Petersburg), neither is it traced in free, broad, even lines. History moves with crest and trough, and the Lord gives nothing without a price, whether to persons or to nations. God does not need either people or nations who are sluggards. I consider the parable of the talents to be at the very base of Christian sociology. The Russian person was never a lazy slave, hiding his talent in a napkin and burying it in the ground. And now, in the person of youth, the Russian people audaciously undertakes socialist democracy. The movement for socialist democracy, for its complete achievement, becomes each year more powerful, broader, better organized and more deeply respected. In 1956, when

I came from seven years' imprisonment and returned to the same school in which I had taught before my arrest, I literally did not recognise the youth there, because after the death of Stalin and the XX Party congress they had become so mature, understanding life, freedom-loving and audacious. And this process has continued and deepened with each succeeding year. The process of inner renewal of the Russian people goes on with seven-leagued boots, and the time is near when Russia will become 'the world's brightest democracy', as was prophesied by Gorky.

Religion plays a very special role in this process. During the years since the October revolution traditional religiosity in large measure disappeared in the U.S.S.R. The third generation is already here. The generation of grandfathers, those who lived in the epoch of revolution and who made the revolution, were not passive in their attitude toward religion. Its leading and most energetic representatives passionately hated the Orthodox Church, seeing in her the chief support of the Tsar's regime. This impassioned hatred of the Church soon moved on to uncontrolled anti-religious fanaticism. One of the worst recollections of my childhood is that of the chapel on Krestovsky Island in Petrograd (now Kirov Island), with ikons thrown about on the floor and even the eyes poked out of their faces. A priest during these years literally did not dare show himself on the street, he would be met with hooting and insults.

During the Patriotic War my cousin George Romanov died at the front, near Smolensk, and I pray for him daily. Our relationship had been poisoned from early childhood because of his passionate hatred of religion; he grew up to sing the horrible anti-religious songs, which I cannot even now remember without shuddering. He was not an exception but typical of youth of that day – this Russian boy with a shining face, ash-blond hair, irrepressible gaiety and friendliness.

The second generation – of 'fathers', to which I belong, had and has a different attitude toward religion; we were brought up and lived in the era when religion was driven deeply underground, the great majority of churches closed, clergy imprisoned, and the struggle against religion conducted by purely administrative methods; it was not permitted to talk openly about religion, but with quiet steps it passed out of life. Fyodor Dostoyevsky brought into the Russian language a new verb, 'stushevatsya', which, he said, means to go out, to leave not noisily but quietly, unobtrusively, to change yourself into nothing. Religion in the pre-war years 'went out' of the minds of the vast majority of Russian people, especially of the Soviet intelligentsia, and only the Patriotic War called forth a powerful wave of religious feeling in the popular masses, showing that the dissappearance of religion had only been imagined, that religion continued to live underneath the surface. However, the complete absence of religious up-bringing and religious teaching had done its work. The second post-revolutionary generation was the most estranged generation of any ever inhabiting the earth; it did not hate, it simply was ignorant of religion.

Modern youth holds a quite exceptional place in the matter of religion – the third post-revolutionary generation. As a rule these are persons who have no conception of religion, having received a clearly expressed anti-religious upbringing. Although it may appear strange, this has not only a negative but also a positive side for the promotion of religion. The positive is this, that modern youth simply does not know the negative aspects of pre-revolutionary Orthodoxy, which led to so much hatred and bitterness on the part of the people. They do not remember the times when religion was obligatory, when the Church was an official institution, a support for Tsarism. They do not remember the pre-revolutionary clergy, an inherited caste, in which as a consequence there were many persons ordained to church service without any inner calling, by inertia, and looking upon their responsibilities with purely professional unconcern. Our youth is often without religion, frequently infected with anti-religious prejudices, as a result of which they look upon religion as the root of darkness and ignorance. Among them, however, one does not find the anti-religious fanaticism and animosity of their grandfathers, and all the efforts of professional anti-religious propagandists in Khrushchev's time to spread anti-religious fanaticism ended in complete failure. But among them there is no deep unwillingness to know or to become aware of religion, none of the cold, suspicious unconcern which characterised their fathers. The average representative of the younger generation approaches religion with mixed feelings of incredulity and interest. We spoke just now about the average representative of the younger generation, but the method of averages, according to economists, is faulty even when applied to the material level of life, and still more so when applied to complex psychological situations.

Modern youth in Russia is a disturbed youth, it seethes and passionately seeks for something. A religious reaction is characteristic of quite a large number of these boys and girls. It would be no exaggeration to say that in these young people the religious reaction, in intensity and strength, is no less than the feeling of fiery enthusiasm among the earliest Christians. More and more frequently there are cases in Moscow where the sons of communists and even of old chekists (security police) are baptised. Quite often there are baptisms of persons of Jewish nationality. Looking at these people who have come to the Church from outside, who a few years ago had not the slightest comprehension of religion, looking at these boys and girls whose coming to religion usually provokes sharp family collisions, leading to loud quarrels and even to complete alienation from their parents – one involuntarily thinks of the words of the Gospel: 'The wind bloweth where it listeth, and thou hearest the sound thereof, but canst not tell whence it cometh and whither it goeth; so is every one that is born of the Spirit' (John 3 :8).

The official Church here, as is well known, does not engage in missionary work; the higher clergy warns priests against it, and if individual priests nevertheless lead persons to the faith, this is at their own risk, without any support from the bishop.

In most cases the process of conversion to Christ takes place instinctively, and a special role in it belongs to the laity. The apostolate of the laity, of which so much was said at the last Vatican Council, and on which so much is now written in the West, has been an actuality here with us in Russia for some years. In the great majority of cases of conversion, the role of the priest is only to conduct the sacrament of baptism, whereas conversion itself and catechetisation, i.e., preparation for baptism, is often done apart from the clergy.

Young people newly coming to the Church are usually filled with the desire to proselytise, and they in turn lead other boys and girls, their companions and friends, to God. There are frequent cases where a young person who has come to the faith converts to Christ his future spouse, and so a Christian family is formed, consisting of two young people who only a short time before were unbelievers. Not wanting to be wordy, I would like to give a few examples of such conversions.

A few years ago a simple old woman was approached by her neighbour, a young engineer, who had just completed the Institute, had married and become a father. 'I know that you are a believer,' he said. 'Can't you tell me about God? The thing is this, as a graduate in physics I am not satisfied with the philosophy of dialectical materialism, and I should like to know the point of view of believing persons.' 'But I am not able to do this,' said the woman. 'Tell me what you can.' After this the conversation went on and the woman led the neighbour to an acquaintance, a religious person better informed on theology, when the conversation took on a more systematic and serious character. After two months the engineer said to his wife, 'You know, after long meditation I have decided to be baptised.' The reply of his wife was, 'But I was baptized a week ago, and our child too.'

A young man, K., an 18-year old member of Komsomol, son of a security police officer, at about this time chanced to enter the Cathedral in Moscow. Here he saw a great number of pilgrims approaching the relics of Saint Alexi the Protector of Moscow. Out of curiosity he also went forward. At the tomb there stood the old Archimandrite Zosima, a great ascetic monk, now dead. He looked penetratingly at the young man and asked, 'You are not baptised?' 'I am not baptised.' 'Then go to P. to priest X. He will baptise you.' The young man went to this suburban church, soon was baptised and became a warm witness to the Christian faith. It is true that after a while he cooled off; in conversation he told me incidentally that he does not consider his leaving the faith to be a permanent step. But this is the only case of apostasy that I know of.

At about this time a Tartar, A., was baptised under the influence of a conversation with a believing woman tailor. A. soon thereafter married a Russian

G**

woman, whom he led to the faith, and now for several years this couple has led a strictly Christian mode of life, taking Holy Communion monthly, attending church, and paying very great attention to religious matters.

A young man, Ye., son of a factory director, whose father and grandfather were communists, a few years ago, at the age of 16, came to the faith. This gave rise to conflict with his parents, resulting in the young man's leaving home. Soon however he returned, his relationship with his father became normal, although both sides retained their respective convictions. Last year he married, his wife being baptized a month before the wedding.

A companion of this young man, a worker in physics, a Jew L., a searching, eager youth, for several years wandered about searching for a world-view, was attracted to Freud, then studied Nietzsche and then turned to Berdyaev. Berdyaev turned out to be a splendid missionary. L. went on from him to the Gospels. Now at this time the young Christian has been leading a strictly religious mode of life. Three months ago he married a young woman, daughter of fanatical atheists, who had been baptized two years earlier, to the horror of her parents.

A few years ago a copy of the Gospels came into the hands of student A. But he did not read them, and quite forgot about it. A month or so later, being in low spirits, he opened the Gospels and was astonished. He read without stopping, but did not accept them at once; some parts he liked, but parts he did not agree with. Faith came unexpectedly, when he read about the raising up of Lazarus. This portion, which is the stumbling block for many, became for him the source of faith. 'I suddenly understood how it really was, and I believed,' said the student, now a physician. He has become a deeply believing person, and so has his wife, daughter of unbelieving parents. She had been led to the faith at Troitse-Sergieva Lavra (Zagorsk).

We have spoken above about Nikolai Berdyaev, who was the missionary for the young Jew. In another case the missionary turned out to be Fyodor Dostoyevsky. The artist B. under the influence of *The Brothers Karamazov* became interested in monasticism, began going to Zagorsk, and was baptised. Now he is a leading Christian and expresses religious ideas in his artistic creations.

A year and a half ago a certain Yevgeni K. was baptised, who has now become well known because of a political trial that took place from August 30 to November 1. This young man in childhood showed great interest in social problems. At the same time he enjoyed literature and himself wrote rather good poems and stories. When I gave him a Testament, I was shocked by his reaction. Regarding the Sermon on the Mount he said, 'this is a splendidly written pronouncement; it has a publicity agents' approach, all the slogans are properly pointed up.' (This was about the beatitudes.) After that I did not talk with him any more about religion, feeling it was useless. But unexpectedly he himself raised with me the question of religion. At a difficult time in his life he said to me, 'I tried to pray. It worked. Made me feel better.' Then several months passed. These were hard months for Yevgeni; he was suffering official persecution and they even sent him to an insane asylum for observation (incidentally he was analysed as completely normal). Coming out he said, 'I prayed all the time. I should like to be baptised as soon as possible.' Today he is a believing Christian, he did not deny his faith either in the K.G.B. prison or at the trial.

Along with these young people I want to speak about more mature ones who have come to the Church out of unbelieving circles in recent decades. Their path to Christ led through Stalinist prison camps; in the midst of despair and sorrow, they gained the great treasure of faith. I can speak here of my friend Vadim Mikhailovich Shavrov, who has told the story of his conversion in his well-known autobiography, 'Early Thoughts and Recollections'.

As I look upon these people, I can clearly see the contour of the future Church and future Russia. We have said that in the midst of the people there is an apostolate of the laity. One could speak of the living incarnation in Russian life of yet another aspect which in the West is the subject of theoretical discussions. I speak of the ecumenical problem. I can remember clearly when the Orthodox Church was much disturbed over the relative freedom acquired by sectarians after the revolution. The sects made great progress in the 1920s, and the vast majority of those converted to the sects were deserters from Orthodoxy. Propaganda against Orthodoxy was the basis for Baptist activity, of Evangelical Christians, Adventists, Dukhobors and others. Orthodox propaganda, fed at that time by the traditions of official missionaries of the Pobedonostsev school, responded to the sects with bitterness and anger, almost hatred. It would have seemed that there was no force that could modify this mutual antagonism. What then happened? For several decades Orthodox Christians and sectarians suffered together in Beria camps, slept side by side in prison bunks, gulped the same prison soup out of the same rusty bowls. So now the Church and the sects practically do not compete with each other. We have given above some examples of conversion to Christianity through the Orthodox Church. The Baptists can be proud of even more conversions; however their conversions come from unbelieving youth. The Baptist Church as compared with the Orthodox is more easily understood by the less educated, and thus a strange selectivity takes place: people less mature in spiritual life, of more rationalistic minds, go to the Baptists, whereas people capable of deep mystical experience go to Orthodoxy.

One can see a new spirit in relationships between Orthodoxy and the sects; the old mistrust and bitterness is entirely gone, there is rather mutual respect and sympathy. Common problems facing both the Church and the sects favour still closer relationships. (Of course all this does not apply to the fanatical sects, with which Orthodox can have nothing in common, and whose spread in the U.S.S.R. can be explained by the decrease in religious education and the absence of Orthodox churches in some places). Thus in Russia there is an authentic ecumenism, in living religious practice, and this ecumenism takes place without conferences, official speeches or great banquets, as in the case of Amsterdam ecumenism, but perhaps just because of this it is authentic ecumenism. There is also great warmth in relationships between Orthodox and Old Believers.

The unjust, forcible reunion of the Uniates which took place in the early post-war years shattered the relationship between Orthodoxy and Catholicism, but only for a short time. At present interest in the Catholic Church is to be noted among Orthodox youth, who are particularly attracted by the world-wide spread of the Catholic Church. The blessed personality of Pope John XXIII has great respect among believers in Russia. The reforms of the Vatican Council are studied with great attentiveness. And all of this does not in the least weaken loyalty to our national Church, which in a true sense is our Mother, because from Her we have received our spiritual life, both we and our ancestors and all our Russian land.

Your Holiness, Blessed and Great Father!

If only I could find words to tell you of all we have lived through, of our joys and our sorrows! Of our sufferings and our hopes! Of our love and of our anger! But I feel my inability to express these basic feelings. I can therefore only release my tears silently bowing before your Holy throne, and continue my simple story of the Russian Church.

One of the most pressing problems for our Church is the question of her inner renewal. This term calls up very bad associations for us. At one time we spoke of Church renewal as the modernistic trend which in the 1920s broke off into its own formation. I joined this movement, became a deacon of an Archbishop of the Living Church and very close to him. Now, as a result of living experience, I clearly see the errors of that movement. The unprincipled cringing before state authority, which some of the bishops served shamelessly, the breaking of canons which were intended to preserve the moral purity of the clergy, the violent forcing of reforms contrary to the will of the people – such were the sins of the Renewal movement. However, all of these sins cannot weaken the merit of the idea of renewal in itself, the transfiguration of the Church.

The renewal of the Church must express itself first of all in the enlivening of preaching. Church oratory is quite a special area and for us in Russia it has its own long history. The 1920s were years of the highest development of preaching. I had the pleasure of listening to the sermons of such great church orators as Alexander Vvedensky, Antonin Granovsky, Alexander Boyarsky, and therefore I know how enormous can be the influence of preaching on the hearts of the people. I know this, but my young friends do not. Preaching was silenced during the 1930s and has not been revived. In Moscow at present there are only a few priests who preach systematically, all the rest are silent or read their sermons from slips of paper, careless and cold sermons, more likely to cool off than to stir up their listeners. The task of restoring church preaching is a difficult problem. The difficulty lies not only in external hindrances, which can be overcome, but in the lack of living experience; the tradition lapsed and must be restored. Nevertheless, looking at our talented, eager, and above all warmly enthusiastic church youth there cannot be the shadow of doubt that it is capable of solving this problem.

A second important question before the Church is the rebirth of patristic theology and religious philosophy. In one of my articles some ten years ago I referred to the dangerous position of Russian theology in view of the absence of serious theological work at the Academies. Speaking of theological academies, I must say that the situation has not improved; instruction as before is done from text-books seventy years old, and master's dissertations are of a very low level. These weaknesses are partly compensated for by theological works written outside academic walls, which are widely distributed in typewritten copies. Here must be mentioned first of all the work of the late Archbishop Luke (Professor V. F. Voino-Yasenetsky), 'Spirit, Soul and Body'. This great bishop, who was also a remarkable surgeon, can be considered the foundation stone of typewritten apologetical literature which has penetrated into the most distant corners of our unbounded land. Other works to be mentioned would be those of A. Lamishnin, Fioletov and Belov, written on a relatively high level, and using the latest facts of scientific knowledge, the very lively and clearly expressed works of Father A. Men, dealing with the history of religion, the interesting articles of Priest S. Zheludkov, and the anonymous work, 'Did Christ Ever Live?' All of these works in only small measure serve to fill the great gap in our theology. We shall hope that soon there will appear new works and new names and that the winds of lively thought will penetrate into our Academies.

The third current task is that of liturgical reform. We have spoken above about the new Christians in the Church, persons who have come from entirely different milieux. They absorb the Gospels with a full heart, but there are some specific aspects about their acceptance; they completely lack the childhood memories which are woven into our reception of church life; they do not understand the Church-Slavonic language at all. Church rituals lack meaning, and many church customs which have been deeply rooted throughout the centuries and are natural for us appear to them strange or ridiculous.

All of this leads up to the fact that religious youth attends church very little; they receive the sacraments and form little groups around certain priests and religious teachers. They turn to the works of N. Berdyaev and S. N. Bulgakov, they read typewritten articles, but to church they go very little and even unwillingly. Still more alien does the Church seem to young unbelievers who begin to be interested in religion. Frequently worship strikes them as cold and turns them away. All of this makes liturgical reform absolutely necessary; the question is how to carry it through.

First of all one must say that any obligatory liturgical reform, the enforced embracing of new customs, is entirely unacceptable, and could only arouse deep dissatisfaction among the faithful. Our Church had, in this connection, the tragic experience of the reforms of Patriarch Nikon, which led to schism. Here we may take account of the experience of the Catholic Church and the decisions of the last Vatican Council. Liturgical reform must be introduced not by breaking down tradition but by the gradual introduction of new customs allowing them to exist side by side with the old. Thus, together with the liturgy in Church-Slavonic there could be liturgy in the Russian language. Along with traditional liturgy (largely beyond the royal doors of the iconastasis) there could be the liturgy of Bishop Antonin, a combination drawn from ancient liturgies, Syrian, Coptic, etc., celebrated with the royal doors open, etc. All of these novelties of course must be sanctioned by highest Church authority and practised only with the sanction of the diocesan bishop.

Now we address ourselves to the most important subject for the Russian Church – the episcopacy. If permitted to use a political term in the spiritual world, one could say that the Church is at present living through a 'crisis of authority'. As is well known, the 'crisis of Church authority' is to be noted in the loss of authority by the bishops and even by the Holy Patriarch among believing Christians; it found its expression in a series of documents which had very wide circulation. We speak of the petition presented by two Moscow priests, Fathers Nikolai Eshliman and Gleb Yakunin, also the petition of twelve believers in the city of Kirov, with B. P. Talantov as leader, also the letters of Archpriest Vsevolod Shpiller, and finally the articles of the writer of these lines.

In the West these documents generally aroused favourable reaction. However, there were also critical voices. It fell to me to bear many of these charges, for the reason that my articles were noted for their sharp tone. Thus I received an article by Abbot Dumont, in which while recognising the correctness of the facts which I presented, he criticises me for using such sharp words in addressing the bishops. The émigré bishops belonging to the Patriarchate, Metropolitan Anthony Bloom and Archbishop Vasili Krivoshein, use the columns of foreign papers for similar charges. What can one say about this?

Only that all these worthy persons are completely ignorant of Russian conditions. Here in Russia we never had the modus of parliamentary debate. Our discussions were always heated and sharp. This is to be explained not by any sort of crude habits (the Russian person in spite of his external crudity is very mild and not ill-willed), but by love for truth and by being passionately caught up in ideas. The Russian person, using the words of Dostoevsky, 'does not eat an idea, the idea eats him up', and consequently the parliamentary structure of speeches, easy flowing formulations, purposely minimising and politely emphasising – are alien to him. As a matter of fact, taking typical Russian persons, could one imagine Patriarch Nikon, on the one side, and his adversary, Protopop Avvakum, on the other, fencing with brilliant phrases, exchanging bows and compliments? Could one imagine Dostoevsky or Leo Tolstoy pronouncing parliamentary speeches, referring to their opponents as 'most esteemed gentlemen', etc.? It is true that this parliamentary manner was adopted at the beginning of the XX century by the Europeanised Russian intelligentsia, who sent their representatives to the Tauride Palace. Bishops Anthony and Vasili come out of these circles of the intelligentsia. Yet perhaps they will remember how little the Russian people cared for the fine manners of their fathers.

I learned how to polemicise from the great Russian writers V. G. Belinsky, A. I. Herzen, C. E. Saltykov-Shchedrin, F. M. Dostoyevsky, and they, in spite of the variety of their world-views, were alike in lacking a parliamentary manner. And this manner of expressing harsh truth to the great ones of this world, without modification or equivocation, so characteristic of Russian people, seems to me to accord with the Gospels, for even our Divine Saviour spoke exactly in this tone to the scribes, the pharisees and the merchants in the temple. Even Saint Nicholas, the most revered saint of the Russian people, polemicised with the heretics in a far from parliamentary manner; the sweetening of address was in general not characteristic of the Church Fathers, who had rather a stern masculine style. But this does not mean that we do not love our Patriarch and the other hierarchs of our Church.

I assert that I love His Holiness Patriarch Alexei, whom I have known for forty years, far more than he is loved by the climbers who, in order not to disturb him, deceive him and urge him on to actions which compromise him in the eyes of the faithful. I have no personal dislike of any of the hierarchs, even of Metropolitan Nikodim, whose capacities I greatly value, and it is not my fault if many of them provide occasion for very sharp criticism. Let them stop giving such occasions, and we shall stop criticising them.

As regards showing esteem, politeness, adhering to external forms, they are good only when sincere. Easy flowing formulations are not suited to the followers of Him who said, 'let your words be yea, yea, nay, nay; for whatsoever is more than these cometh of evil' (Mat. 5:37). Thus we say 'yea, yea' when we see how bishops, such as the late Pope John XXIII fulfilled his archi-episcopal duties and in everything followed the example of our Beloved Teacher and Lord Jesus Christ; and we say 'nay, nay' when they do not do their duty and depart from the path of Christ.

Here I do not go into the quarrel which recently arose in the Russian Church, because its essentials are well known and the positions set forth in the articles of the above mentioned clergy and laity cannot leave any doubt for anyone.

Your Holiness, Mighty Teacher and Father!

I began this letter by saying that already in my youth I dreamed of the union of the Orthodox and Catholic Churches. Later, in prison camps, where I spent most of the time in prayer, I constantly prayed to the Lord for the Catholic Church, her leading pastors and for you personally, whom I have known from the press to be the leader of the foreign policy of the Vatican and later Archbishop of Milan. Even now I daily remember you in my prayers. Although my many sins before the Lord make my prayers feeble and weak, yet my prayers come from a sincere heart. Once F. M. Dostoyevsky wrote that the Russian person is 'all-person'. And actually nationalistic antagonism, chauvinism, is not characteristic of the Russian people. And this inspires hope for the union of the two great Churches of Christ.

Church circles listened with tenderness and joy to communications telling of your contacts with the Holy Ecumenical Patriarch Athenagoras. All of us here welcome the efforts for peace made by His Beatitude Pope John XXIII and by Your Beatitude. The majority of Orthodox cannot accept the dogma of papal infallibility in the sense in which it is professed now in the Catholic Church. Yet they can accept other doctrinal decisions of the Catholic Church, although not as dogma but as theologoumena, not obligatory but permissible for each local (independent) Church. And, finally, the concept of a single High Priest of the Universal Church is close and understandable for many Orthodox. This was recognised by the late Patriarch Sergi, who was one of the most profound theologians, in one of his articles written two years before his death.

All of us are grateful to Catholic public opinion for the attention and interest it has shown in our national Russian Church. And I am thankful to the foreign public for its attention to my works. This is quite natural and understandable, as every writer wants to be read and known. However, I must say with regret that the Western public has a mistaken conception of me. In the West they generally publish my articles written with reference to the petition of the two Moscow priests against the Moscow Patriarchate. The question naturally arises as to the reason for this choice. There, in the West, they have my three-volume work, 'History of the Renewal Movement,' written jointly with V. M. Shavrov (I know from the London radio that they have it), and my memoirs entitled, 'The Fall of the Renewal Movement', which includes unique material on the recent history of the Russian Church; also my modest apologetical works, which are interesting at least because they are eagerly read here by young people. Perhaps the publishers are motivated by political demagogy. If so, it is really too bad.

To be sure, politics is an inseparable element of life, but, in the first place, religion cannot be equated with politics, and then, in politics in particular one must above all be objective and fair.

Your Holiness!

I turn to you as one coming from the Russian land. I am a hot-blooded person, not used to compromise, one who has lived a very difficult and hard life, one who at times fell into error but who always above all loved truth. To reveal the truth, to tell the West about the life of our Church, that is what I have tried to do in this letter.

I beg for your Holy Prayers and Apostolic Benediction!

[Signed:] ANATOLI LEVITIN-KRASNOV

3rd Novokuzminskaya Ul. 23
Moscow Zh-377

2–3. Alexander Solzhenitsyn's letter to the Patriarch and Zheludkov's reply

During Lent in 1972, Alexander Solzhenitsyn appealed to the new Patriarch, Pimen, in a remarkable and moving letter. As the best-known spokesman in both East and West of the non-conforming intelligentsia, and their undisputed moral leader, Solzhenitsyn has for the first time in this letter publicly declared himself a believing member of the Russian Orthodox Church. At the same time he aligned himself wholly with the critics of the Church leadership, although at no time did he dispute the latter's canonical position. The idea of a schism is clearly alien to Solzhenitsyn, as it is to most of the opposition thinkers within the Church. Solzhenitsyn sees the main task of Church and Christendom as the moral renewal of society. Only if the spirit of sacrifice and self-denial occupies the highest place in the scale of values does the future seem to him worth living for. Solzhenitsyn's letter proves once again the close links between the opposition literary intelligentsia and the independent forces within the Russian Church which, through Solzhenitsyn's voice, have undoubtedly gained in strength.

However, the reply by the well-known Father Sergi Zheludkov from Pskov reveals the one-sidedness of Solzhenitsyn's viewpoint. Zheludkov, who in his theological writings has moved a long way from academic Orthodox theology, defends the position of the Church leadership with regard to the Soviet state because he sees no alternative way of preserving the Church's legal existence. This is a vividly clear instance of the probably insoluble dilemma between compromise and resistance. Often the dividing line between the two can only be determined by a personal decision in which both sacrifice and reason must find their place. (Solzhenitsyn's letter in Russian in *Posev*, 5/1972, pp. 8–9.)

To Pimen, Patriarch of All Russia: a Lenten Letter

Most Holy Father

The subject of this letter weighs down like a gravestone upon our heads and crushes the breasts of those Russian people in whom the Orthodox faith has still not been quite extinguished. Yet another little stone has been added by your pastoral letter on Christmas night. Now, further silence becomes impossible.

What brought pain to my heart was the passage where you spoke at last of the children – it was perhaps the first time in half a century that a person of such eminence had spoken in such a manner, saying that parents should inculcate in their children, along with a love for their native land, a love for the Church (and presumably for the faith itself?) and that they should reinforce this love by their own good example.

I heard this – and there rose up before me my own early childhood and the many church services I attended then and the very first impression which they made on me, singular in freshness and purity, which no personal suffering and no intellectual theories were able later to erase.

But what are you saying? Why do you address this honest appeal only to Russian émigrés? Why do you appeal only for *those* children to be brought up in the Christian faith? Why is it only the distant flock which you warn to be 'discerning of slander and falsehood' and to gird itself with righteousness and truth? What about *us* – are we to be discerning? What about *our* children – should we inspire in them a love of the Church or not? Yes, Christ's commandment was to go and seek the hundredth sheep which had strayed, but that was when the ninety and nine were safely in the fold. But when the ninety and nine are not in the fold should not our first concern be for them?

Why, when I come to church to have my son baptised, should I have to produce my identity card? Under what canonical obligations does the Moscow Patriarchate need to register those who are baptised?

One is only the more amazed at the strength of spirit of the parents and at the undefined spiritual opposition handed down through long centuries with which they go through this registration, though it leaves them open to denunciation.

And afterwards they suffer persecution at their place of work and are held up to public ridicule by ignoramuses. But that is where their will to resist comes to an end; the sacramental life of children within the Church usually ends with baptism and the succeeding ways of bringing them up in the faith are totally barred to them, as is access to participation in church services. They are sometimes barred from receiving communion and even from simply attending services.

We are robbing our children when we deprive them of something which they can never experience again – the pure angelic perception of worship which as adults they can never recapture nor even realise what they have missed. The right to continue the faith of their fathers is annulled, as is the right of parents to bring up their children in their own outlook on life – while you, hierarchs of the Church, have accommodated yourselves to this, even abetting it and finding in it a true sign of *freedom of religion.*

In a state of affairs, that is, where we have to hand over our defenceless children, not into neutral hands, but into the domain of atheist propaganda of the most primitive and dishonest kind.

In a situation in which our young people who have been snatched away from the Christian faith – lest they should be infected by it! – are left for their moral upbringing only the abyss between the propagandist's notebook and the criminal code.

Half a century of the past has already been lost, and I am not talking about trying to save the present. But how are we to save the *future of* our country? – the future which will be made up of the children of today?

In the final analysis the fate of our country, in the true and profound sense, depends on whether the idea of the *rightness of force* becomes finally embedded in the national consciousness, or whether it will be purged of obscurantism and will shine forth once again with the *force of righteousness.*

Shall we succeed in reviving in ouselves at least some elements of the Christian faith, or are we going to lose the very last of them and abandon ourselves to considerations of self-preservation and personal gain?

A study of Russian history over the last few centuries convinces one that it would have followed an incomparably more humane and harmonious course if the Church had not renounced its independence and the people had listened to its voice, in the same way as in Poland, for example.

Alas, for us it has long since been a different story. We have lost the radiant ethical atmosphere of Christianity in which for a millennium our morals were grounded; we have forfeited our way of life, our outlook on the world, our folklore, even the very name by which the Russian peasant was known. We are losing the last features and marks of a Christian people – can this really not be the *principal* concern of the Russian Patriarch?

The Russian Church expresses its concern about any evil in distant Asia or Africa, while it never has anything at all to say about things which are wrong here at home.

Why are the pastoral letters which are handed down to us by the supreme Church authorities so traditionally submissive? Why are all ecclesiastical documents so complacent, as though they were being published among the most Christian of peoples?

As we turn from one complacent letter to another we can but ask whether, one unpropitious year, the need to write them at all will disappear: there will be nobody to address them to, no flock will remain, apart from the people on the Patriarch's own staff.

Seven years have now passed since two very honest priests, Yakunin and Eshliman, confirmed by their own sacrificial example that the pure flame of the Christian faith had not been snuffed out in our land. They wrote their well-known letter to your predecessor, setting out for him with a wealth of detailed proof that voluntary internal enslavement, even self-destruction, to which the Russian Church had been reduced.

They asked that anything that was untrue in their letter should be pointed out to them. But every word of theirs was the *truth*, and none of the Church leaders took it upon himself to refute them.

And what answer did they receive? It was the simplest and harshest – for telling the truth they were punished by being barred from celebrating at the altar. To this very day you have not redressed this. Moreover, that terrible letter from the 12 citizens of Vyatka remained similarly unanswered while its authors were crushed.

As of today the one fearless archbishop, Yermogen of Kaluga, is still exiled in his monastery-prison because he would not allow his churches to be closed or his icons and books to be burned in a belated burst of rage by that atheism which succeeded in destroying so much in other dioceses before 1964.

Seven years have passed since all this was proclaimed from the rooftops – but what has changed? For every church in regular use there are 20 which have been demolished or are ruined beyond repair and a further 20 standing desolate and profaned. Is there a sight more heartrending than these skeletons now taken over by the birds or the store-keepers?

How many towns and villages are there in the country which do not have a church at all within a hundred or even two hundred kilometres? The northern regions of our country, the age-old repository of the Russian spirit and possibly where the future of Russia most truly lies, is now completely without churches.

The activists, people who make financial sacrifices and others who leave money to the Church find that their every effort to *restore* even the smallest church is blocked by the biased legislation on the so-called *separation* of Church and state. We do not dare even to raise the question of the ringing of church bells – yet why has Russia been deprived of its ancient adornment, its finest voice? But churches apart, the Gospel is nowhere to be obtained in our country, so that copies of it have to be brought to us from abroad, as our missionaries once took them to Siberia.

Seven years have passed, and is there anything at all which the Church has defended? The whole administration of the Church is still conducted secretly by the *council for religious affairs*, including the appointment of pastors and bishops (even those who commit outrages, so as to make it easier to ridicule and destroy the Church).

The Church is ruled dictatorially by atheists – a sight never before seen in two millennia! The whole of the Church's property and the use of Church funds – the mites contributed by pious fingers – is under their control. Five million roubles at a time are donated to outside funds with grandiloquent gestures, while beggars are thrown off the church porch on their necks and there is nothing with which to repair a leaking roof in a poor parish.

Priests have no rights in their own parishes; only the act of worship is still entrusted to them for the time being, so long as they do not go outside the church for it, and they have to ask permission of the town council if they want to visit a sick person or enter the churchyard.

By what reasoning is it possible to convince oneself that the planned *destruction* of the spirit and body of the Church under the guidance of atheists is the best way of *preserving* it? Preserving it *for whom*? Certainly not for Christ? Preserving it *by what means*? *By falsehood*? But after the falsehood by whose hands are the holy mysteries to be celebrated?

Most Holy Father. Do not ignore altogether my unworthy cry. Perhaps such a cry will not reach your ears every seven years. Do not let it be supposed, do not make people think, that for the bishops of the Russian Church earthly power is more important than heavenly power or that their temporal responsibilities are more awesome to them than their responsibility before God.

Let us not deceive ourselves before men – and even less in prayer – that external chains have power over our souls. Things were no easier at the birth of the Christian faith; nevertheless it held out and prospered. And it showed us the way: *sacrifice*. Though deprived of all material strength, it is always victorious in *sacrifice*.

Within our own living memory many of our priests and fellow-believers have accepted such a martyrdom, worthy of the early Christians. But in those days they were thrown to the *lions*, whereas today you can lose only your material well-being.

In these days, as you go down on your knees before the Cross brought out into the middle of the church, ask the Lord what other purpose but sacrifice can there be in your service to your people, who have almost lost their Christian countenance and even the spirit of the faith?

ALEXANDER SOLZHENITSYN

Lent,
Week of the Adoration
of the Cross, 1972

LETTER OF FR. SERGI ZHELUDKOV TO A. SOLZHENITSYN

Christ is Risen!

Dear Alexander Isaevich,

I have the honour of greeting you on the Bright Festival of the Hope of all mankind. 'O Easter! our salvation from grief.' May I also congratulate you on receiving the literature prize. Thanks be to God, Who has brought you to this day through all the trials of your unusual life. May you have many more blessed years.

This Easter message must also serve as an answer to your 'Lenten letter to the All-Russian Patriarch'. With my deep personal respect for you, I am all the more at liberty to express to you my concern over this document which may evoke the most unexpected interpretations, even for the author. I must say that in this case your moral sensitivity has to some degree deceived you. You have made a written accusation that has been publicised throughout the world, against a man who, as everyone knows, has no possible chance of replying to you. In this respect you have repeated the moral mistake of the two well-known priests whom you mention. And you also repeated their chief mistake – you did not tell the whole truth, you gave half-truths.

The *full truth* is that the legal Church organisation cannot be an *island of freedom* in our strictly unified society, directed from a single Centre. There may be various opinions as to the historical significance of such a strictly unified and controlled social system. The most extreme judgment is that in our country literature and art are perishing, economics and science are lagging behind, morality is decaying, the people are becoming dull and stupid. . . . This extreme judgment presupposes that the destiny of Russia lies in sacrifice. At the price of its own culture our nation saved Europe from the Tatars and saved the whole world from fascism; today it is undergoing a grandiose experiment, on view to the whole world, that is not leading anywhere. This is the opinion of some. Others, on the other hand, cherish bright hopes. . . . My opinion here is of no value and it is not asked for. But one thing I must state with great conviction. There exists this strictly centralised system, and within it, surprisingly, is preserved an alien body – the Russian Orthodox Church. It exists in very strictly determined conditions. We are *not permitted* to work at the religious education of children, or of adults, just as we are not permitted to do many other things necessary for the existence of real church life. *We are permitted only one thing* – to conduct divine worship in our churches, whereby it is supposed that this is something from the past preserved only for a disappearing generation.

What can we do in such a situation? Should we say: all or nothing? Should we try to go underground, which in the present system is unthinkable? Or should we try somehow to accept the system and for the present make use of those opportunities that are permitted? The Russian hierarchy took the latter decision.

Hence today all the evil about which you very rightly wrote, as well as all the evil you did not mention. But there was no other choice. You make appeal to the Catholics in Poland; all honour and glory to them, but they have a quite, quite different history. You justly write about the abuses that have not existed during two thousand years of Christian history. But never, never before have our completely unique conditions of human existence been known.

This is the whole truth. The late Patriarch Alexi, unable to answer the accusations of the two priests in words, answered in deeds – he forbade them to serve as priests and thereby he involuntarily confirmed the relative truth of their argument. It is good that it happened that way, and it was precisely in the courage of the two priests that the moral beauty of their action lay, which cannot at all be said, forgive me, of your amazingly pretentious document. Our present Patriarch Pimen also has no opportunity of answering you in word. By what deed do you suppose he could answer you? Only by giving up his position. But there is no one better to take his place. And anyway one man cannot change anything. So everything would stay the same. One of the consequences of your accusatory letter will be a still greater discrediting of the Church hierarchy in the eyes of those who do not understand the whole truth. Do not misunderstand me – I am not telling you to be silent; but if you do write, do not choose someone who cannot answer you and tell the whole truth. At the time when you were being heaped with slander, Alexander Isaevich, we were all grieved for you. But now you are offending the defenceless Patriarch and us – not with slander, but with talented half-truths, which to many may seem more dangerous than lies.

There must be no unwillingness for sacrifice and martyrdom in the Church of Christ. We have enough willing martyrs, both inside and outside the Church (the distinction is rather conditional), and I am sorry that you did not even mention the names of the churchmen Boris Talantov, who died in prison, and Anatoli Levitin, now suffering in prison. I would say that our duty today is to give due appreciation to their deeds, and ourselves each one to work as best we can in the opportunities open to us. In particular, there is now a problem of the Christian education of children in the scattered families of the emergent Christian intelligentsia. In general, we must make a healthy acknowledgment of reality: the Russian Church hierarchy in its present composition and in our present system cannot in any significant way affect the system. It is easy and safe, Alexander Isaevich, to accuse the bishops, but in fact the work of the Lord today is hard. The destiny of the Russian Church is inseparably linked to the fate of the people. If 'there is a future', then there will also inevitably be a renaissance of Russian Cnristianity.

Christ is Risen!

Sincerely,

God's unworthy servant in the priesthood,

[SERGI ZHELUDKOV]

Easter 1972

4. Letter of the 1,453 mothers

In the persecutions of the reform Baptists, it is above all the families and children who have to suffer. In a letter signed by 1,453 mothers the Baptists protested against discrimination exercised towards their children and particularly against the placing of some by force in state children's homes. (Russian in *Posev*, 12/1969, pp. 57–63.)

To the General Secretary of the Central Committee of the Communist Party of the Soviet Union, L. I. Brezhnev.

(the letter is directed to twenty-five other named Soviet officials, organisations and journals)

To the Council of Evangelical Christian and Baptist Churches. To the Council of Relatives of E.C.B. prisoners, sentenced for the Word of God in the U.S.S.R. from Evangelical Christian and Baptist mothers living in the U.S.S.R.

'*Let all the earth fear the Lord: let all the inhabitants of the world stand in awe of Him*' (Ps. 33:8).

'*And, behold, I come quickly; and my reward is with me, to give every man according as his work shall be*' (Rev. 22:12).

DECLARATION

We Christian mothers living in the U.S.S.R. are compelled to appeal to you, the authorities, regarding the following.

We believe profoundly in God, the Creator of the universe. We are deeply convinced of His infinite love to man, to whom He has given a way of access to Himself by sending to earth His Only-begotten Son Jesus Christ, who, by His sufferings, death on the cross and resurrection, has redeemed the whole world from sin. We pray for all people that God might send them spiritual insight and repentance, that He might forgive them their sins and not allow their immortal souls to perish. Among these we also pray for you.

As law-abiding citizens of our country, we live and work in peace and quiet, not doing anyone any harm. Most of us have several children. 'All human beings are born free and equal in dignity and rights,' says the first article of the Universal Declaration of Human Rights, which you accepted.*

This applies both to you and to us. You too, like us, were nursed by your mothers. How much love there was in those cradle-songs they sang to you, as they held you in their arms! They too wished you happiness, as we wish our children. It was they, our parents, who made the laws which still remain the basic laws of our country. Those laws are as follows:

1. Constitution of the U.S.S.R., Art. 124. 'In the interests of guaranteeing freedom of conscience for all citizens, the church in the U.S.S.R. is separated from the state and the school from the church. Freedom to hold religious services and freedom of anti-religious propaganda is recognised for all citizens.'

Art. 126 grants children the right to participate in youth organisations, circles, etc.

2. The Decree of the Council of People's Commissars of 23 January 1918, Point 9: 'The school is separated from the church. The teaching of religious doctrine in all state and social as well as private institutions of learning, where subjects of general instruction are taught, is forbidden. Citizens may teach and be taught religion privately.'

Point 3. 'Every citizen may profess any religion or none. Any deprivation of rights in connection with the profession of any faith or none is countermanded.'

[The authors then quote Articles 2, 5, 12, 18 and 19 of the Universal Declaration of Human Rights].

We cite an extract from the Convention on the Struggle against Discrimination in the Field of Education, Art. 5, Para. b: 'Parents, or where appropriate legal guardians, should have the opportunity, first, within limits determined by the legislature of each state, of freely sending their children not to state but to other institutes of learning which measure up to the minimum demands laid down or affirmed by competent educational organs, and, secondly, to guarantee their religious and moral education according to their own convictions; no individual and no group of people as a whole should be forced to have religious education that is incompatible with their convictions.'

This was ratified for the U.S.S.R. by the Supreme Soviet on 2 July, 1962.

You are well aware that in the country which you govern there live hundreds of thousands of believing citizens. However, as atheists yourselves, you have permitted fanatically-minded atheists harshly to oppress believers. After the death of V. I. Lenin you permitted the passing of the decree 'On Religious Cults' of 8 April 1929, in which believers are forbidden to profess their faith. In the March decree of 1966 this regulation is upheld and applied to Art. 142 of the Penal Code of the R.S.F.S.R. and to corresponding articles of other Union republics, with a prohibition on prayer meetings, children's and women's

* In fact the Soviet Union, with five other countries, abstained from voting on this resolution (Translator's note).

meetings; it is forbidden to help one another in trouble, etc. Recently this decree has acquired an unusual violence, aiming at physically annihilating believers. The whole press, the cinema, schools, lecture organisations, television, etc., are filled with lying propaganda against believers. Lacking patience to wait for a change in the spiritual formation of believers, you have given unlimited power to atheists to destroy religion by persecutions, beatings, arrests and death of believers. You did this through the organs of the K.G.B., the procurators' offices and the police.

We bore those insults patiently, drawing strength and comfort from our meek Teacher and Saviour Jesus Christ. Thousands of letters of believers from every part of our huge country were sent to you with the request to regulate relations with believers. We expected, according to common sense, that measures would be taken by you to end the cruel persecution of believers.

And indeed measures were taken. Now persecutions burst upon believers with renewed force. Impossible fines, beatings, dismissals from work, from institutes of learning, confiscation of flats, arrests of fathers, husbands and (which seems incredible) of mothers – such has been the answer to all our complaints to you up to this day.

Last year (1968) which was named international human rights year, 64 Evangelical Christians and Baptists were arrested and sentenced, and about two hundred children were again deprived. Right up to the present day they are still tearing from our midst the fathers of our children and even children themselves who have scarcely begun life. You are throwing their pure hearts, unstained by vice, into the company of criminals, among people who are morally quite depraved; for several years on end they are witnesses of such corruption as you would never permit your own children to see. The deep wounds of the soul which they receive there in the camps will never be effaced. Their tears have been collected by God and will lie on your conscience as a millstone of ineradicable guilt.

But the object of this declaration to you is not to recount our personal sufferings as mothers. Oh, if only these persecutions affected us alone! But our children are persecuted along with us.

Today we direct your attention to the sufferings of our children whom you are tormenting, presenting this to society under the guise of 'saving them from the destructive and harmful influence of Christian upbringing'. They are witnesses of searches. It is they who even as children have come to know the horror of their fathers and mothers being arrested. Many of them have experienced the terror of interrogations at procurators' offices and at the K.G.B., so that at the sight of a policeman they break out in a cold sweat. Many of them have been given the permanent nickname 'obscurantist' among their unbelieving schoolfriends.

After a whole series of experiences, we have come to the conclusion that by their activities atheists are not re-educating but facilitating the physical annihilation of our children. Is this really their aim? If we could cite here all the concrete facts, we would write a whole volume. We cite only a few instances which are sufficiently graphic and convincing.

The children of Nadezhda and Ivan Sloboda were taken away – and what sort of education did they receive? These children were stolen from their parents.*

On the question of the seizure of these children you gave two replies: first to Mrs. Vezikova (the children's aunt), that they had been seized because of their religious upbringing, according to Art. 447, Para. 6 of 16 March, 1966, and you justified the act. The second time you replied more diplomatically to the above cited complaint of the parents that it was for 'their incorrect upbringing and development', but you again upheld the seizure (see reply of Vice-President Procurator General of the U.S.S.R. of 31 April, 1968, to No. 8/546/1966).

Twice the children ran away from the children's home to their own house, grieving and pining for their parents' love. Twice a rough hand, wielding sword and authority, tore them away again from their parents' home.

To our great horror on 11 December, 1968, their mother, Nadezhda Stepanovna Sloboda, born in 1930, was sentenced to four years' imprisonment by the decree of March 1966, according to Art. 142 of the Penal Code of the R.S.F.S.R. and part two of the corresponding article of the Belorussian S.S.R., based on the law 'On Religious Cults' of 8 April, 1929, for witnessing to Christ. She still had three small children at home. When a representative of authority arrested her and took her along the street, the children ran after her crying 'Mummy! Mummy!' (the youngest child is three years old).

The eldest children wrote a letter from the children's home to the government about their sufferings and asked for permission to spend at least their winter holidays at home. Probably consent was given as a joke, for when they arrived home, the sun of their mother's love and tenderness no longer warmed their childish hearts, their mother's loving hand no longer touched their heads: their mother was already in prison. Oh, the horror of violence! Whose heart does not shudder to see and hear this? Did not yours? For this is happening here with us, in our time, under your rule of the country.

In Leningrad the E.C.B. believer Yevgenia Alexeyevna Azarova, living at 67 Stachek Passage, Block 5, Flat 560, is suffering persecution accompanied by threats that her children will be taken away. Azarova's husband, a young man in his prime, died in 1965 in an industrial accident. She was left with five little ones.

They are threatening to take away the children of the believer V. F. Bytina

---

* The full text of the letter of Nadezhda and Ivan Sloboda to Mr. Kosygin is given at this point. It is omitted here, as it was known previously and has been published in *Christian Appeals from Russia*, ed. Rosemary Harris and Xenia Howard-Johnston, Hodder and Stoughton, London, 1969, pp. 87–9.

who lives in Bryansk Region, Bryansk District, Netinka Industrial Settlement, 13 Lugovaya Street. She has been given a week to think it over.

In Kiev they have threatened to take away the children of the believers S. I. and T. S. Zadorozhny, who have seven small children. Their father was thrown on the rails under a tram by volunteer police at the instigation of the militant atheist Kovalev, who is locally well known, and it was only by the grace of God that he is still alive. Now, by the efforts of the same Kovalev, they are threatening to take away his children. Can they be all right, if the parents have already been asked to come to the Executive Committee with all their children? The oldest girl is twelve.

The Beating of Children at the Instigation of School Teachers

In previous letters to you we have written a great deal about beatings of our children in the schools, about their being frightened, about their shock during searches, etc. One little girl of four immediately runs under the table every time the doorbell of the flat rings. She was at home during two searches and was a witness of believers being rounded up by the police. Poor child, no one could allay her fear that a merciless hand would drag her out even from under the table, as happened with children in Tashkent, when they were pulled out from under the beds.

You were sent a complaint of 11 December, 1968, from the E.C.B. believer Nina Rudich of 109, Shevchenko Street, Bobrovitsa, Chernigov District, Chernigov Region. We cite it in full.

To the President of the Council of Ministers of the U.S.S.R., Mr. Kosygin

To the President of the Presidium of the Supreme Soviet of the U.S.S.R., Mr. Podgorny

To the General Secretary of the Central Committee of the C.P.S.U., Mr. Brezhnev

from Nina Mefodievna Rudich, E.C.B. believer of Bobrovitsa, Chernigov Region, Chernigov District

DECLARATION – COMPLAINT

I, a believing mother anxious about the future of my sons, appeal to you who have the power to halt the arbitrary action and lawlessness to which my sons are subject in the Bobrovitsa village school.

All mankind, led by our country, watches over the happiness of children in the whole world. I am shocked to the bottom of my heart and I cannot understand why in our country, a free country, the children of believers are suffering – and not only that: there are even attempts on their lives.

Like me, my sons Vasya and Volodya in their short lifetime have suffered a great shock with the death of their father, my husband. He was disabled during service in the ranks of the Soviet army and he fell ill during military service. On 15 April, 1963, I attended his funeral.

Children who in early years have suffered such a hard emotional blow, such a loss as a loving father, now also have to undergo hard experiences and suffer for their belief in God, even to receive psychological shocks.

From the beginning of this school year, the teacher, Miss M. I. Cherednichenko, forced my youngest son Volodya to wear a star. To achieve this she stood him in the corner, or beside his desk in the classroom, first periodically, then every day, and said: 'You'll stand there till you wear the star.'

The pupils, encouraged by the teacher's example, started to stand him in the corner before lessons began as well. The teacher gave him the nickname 'Little Jesus' (and lowered his behaviour mark by four), which made the pupils hostile towards my son. Rejecting the path of reasonable explanation, she deliberately whipped up the whole class, until three of his classmates, V. Menshun, A. Ovodov and V. Shestun, did something terrible. On 19 November, 1968, on the way home from school, these children threw my son Volodya on to the roadway under a moving tractor. It was only thanks to the quick reaction of the driver, who braked sharply, that he was not killed.

But they did not stop at that. They dragged him to the gutter, and threw him down in the mud and went on hitting him about the head with their fists and kicking him in the stomach, shouting, 'You're disgracing our class because you don't wear a star!'

Now he is unable to go to school, but the doctors pay no attention at all, attempting to present his illness from another angle, making out that he must have tests in a psychiatric hospital. Yet he obviously has a 'general trauma of the organism'; and in order to remove responsibility from the teacher, they diagnose it as a general type of cold: 'catarrh of the upper respiratory channels', although his throat is perfectly all right and he has no cough. In fact, I told the doctor myself at the very start that it was from a beating. Are our doctors really so incompetent that they cannot distinguish between an illness from a cold and from a beating?

All this was done to cover up for the teacher, who incited the pupils who committed this terrible act.

We do not demand that the guilty ones be punished, but we appeal to you as people who have the power to stop this arbitrary action and lawlessness towards my sons, so that it should not happen again. Even if he gets better, we have no guarantee that a similar thing will not be repeated. Therefore we ask you to give the order to stop this arbitrary action and lawlessness towards my sons, so that there should be no disgrace to our country where freedom, brotherhood and equality are proclaimed but not put into practice. I am waiting for the realisation of these beautiful expressions in deed and you have the obligation to do so, if you want to put this freedom, equality and brotherhood into effect.

Respectfully yours,

N. RUDICH

This is 'ideological education' in the struggle against religion.

In the village of Strasheny, Kalaretsky District, Moldavian S.S.R. on 6 October, 1968, believers were assaulted by a group of Komsomol members and volunteer police as they were getting on to a train to return from a service. We cite an extract from the believers' letter: 'During the beating-up there were shouts of "Hit them, chaps!" As a result, many believers have injuries. Thus Andrei Stepanovich Nikt, of Strasheny, has a swollen right eye and a bruised face as a result of blows. I. F. Severin received several blows about the head, and his wife, who is pregnant, was seized by the throat and nearly throttled. Girls were shamelessly seized and thrown down in any manner. Children were screaming in fright. When they were beating up her father, a twelve-year-old girl, Praskovia Buyuk, lost consciousness from fright and blows; in the train she fell into a fever and we do not know how it will end. An elderly man, D. A. Trifan, who took part in the Second World War, was beaten up and fell on the roadway from a blow and lost consciousness. The assault continued in the train. All this happened at the instigation of the secretary of the party organisation, I. D. Pelitu, the president of the village Soviet, I. K. Rotar; the president of the comrades' court, Anatoli Muntyan; the surgeon's assistant, Vitali Muntyan; the headmaster of the school, M. A. Buza, and of other administrative workers who were present at the assault.'

You have already received the letter about this from the believers who suffered.

There are some cases of assault on children resulting in such severe concussion of the brain that there is little hope of their recovery. For example, Nadya Bulchuk from Lutsk has been unfit for work for three years now and cannot study because of the foul act done to her by a member of the Komsomol who beat her up for her belief in God.

The boy Vladimir Shtundyuk, a pupil of School No. 15 in Lutsk, was beaten up and has a broken collar bone.

In Gorky the child of the believer Serafima Yudintseva, whose father is languishing in prison for his faith in God, is subject to constant beatings in school.

The same things are happening with almost all believers' children in every town and village of our country. We are unable to include every case in this declaration.

Interrogation of Children of Believing Parents by the Authorities

In Brest on 24 October, 1967, they interrogated Tamara Ferenets, born in 1953, a pupil of the eighth form in School No. 15. This was carried out by the investigator A. I. Ogarkov, in the presence of the head of the school, F. M. Potash. The investigator carried on the interrogation for three and a half hours. He shouted at her and demanded testimonies against believers. The girl got neuralgia from fright.

On 26 September, 1967, Irina Sych, born in 1953, of 6/1, First Kievsky Lane, was taken away with her father at 7 a.m. to the police-station and then to the procurator's office, where she was interrogated for an hour and a half. The girl was ill and not going to school; Ogarkov was the interrogator.

On 20 September, 1967, Lidia Korol, pupil of School No. 14, born in 1955, was interrogated in school during lessons for two hours. Anatoli Skovorodko, born in 1950, was kept without food at an interrogation from 7 a.m. to 7 p.m. in 1967.

In Brest, besides all this, they have also conducted interrogations of nine or more other children. The same questions were put to everyone: 'Who is the presbyter? Who preaches? Where do you meet to pray? Do you read the Bible? Do you pray at home? Who teaches singing, playing, etc?'

In Voznesensk, Nikolaevskaya Region, interrogations of children took place in July and August 1960. They chased the children through the streets by car, which aroused the indignation of those around. Similarly the children of Vera P. Kvashenko, a girl of twelve and a boy of seven, were interrogated from the morning until 5 p.m. without food and as a joke were forced to kneel down and pray. They threatened to take the children away from their father and to arrest him, although he was not a member of the E.C.B. church.

Valentina N. Boiko, born in 1931, in the ninth month of pregnancy with her seventh child, was frequently summoned with all her children to interrogations accompanied by shouts and threats. On 16 July, 1968, they took two of her small children to the police-station for interrogation. On the next day they came to the house and searched for the other children in the attics, in the garden and all over the village. The investigation was carried out by Ipatiev of Nikolaev and another man who concealed his name.

In Shakhty, Rostov Region, Leonid Oleinik, a pupil of the fourth form at Intermediate School No. 1, was summoned to the investigator of the procurator's office, Skakun, where he was subjected to an interrogation about believers. Skakun with his assistants even dared show the boy photographs of a man with a severed hand, a gouged-out eye, a disfigured face, and declared: 'That's what we do with people like you who don't give information.' The frightened boy was compelled to sign a protocol written by Skakun.

In Barnaul after their father's arrest, the children Dimitri V. and Antonia M. Minyakov were taken for interrogation while ill with high temperatures, after which the children fell seriously ill.

There were similar interrogations of children in Zhitomir, Tashkent, Rostov, Kiev, Oryol, Chelyabinsk and in other towns and villages of the Soviet Union.

Expulsion from Schools and Colleges for Faith in God
This phenomenon has been legalised by you, since you have not reinstated a single person upon the complaints of these expelled. This has become common

in all institutes of intermediate and higher education. After preliminary conversation with the believing children, they are told to renounce their faith or
be thrown out, they are given a mark of two for social sciences and the pupils
are expelled. Your replies to complaints confirm the expulsions.

In this way A. P. Alexeyev and G. G. Kuznetsov from Kiev were expelled,
also Yevdokia Volostnova and her brother Pavel. Veniamin M. Karatayev was
converted by his mother's grave, on the day of the funeral, after which he was
dismissed from the fifth year of a Moscow institute as a believer in God. Ya.
Klopot-Makarchuk was expelled from the fourth year of a medical institute
for her convictions: there have been many others.

*   *   *

At present the situation of believing children and parents has become
very serious. You have published a law 'On Family and Marriage', of which
Article 19 is on 'Loss of parental rights'. It states: 'Both parents or either one
of them can be deprived of parental rights if it is established that they are
deviating from the fulfilment of their obligations in the upbringing of their
children, or are misusing their parental rights, treating the children cruelly,
exerting a harmful influence on them by immoral, anti-social behaviour, or
alternatively if the parents are chronic alcoholics or drug-addicts.' This is
being used as a basis for depriving us of parental rights. Attempts at this have
already been made in the case of the family of A. T. Kozorezeva and her eight
young children, whose father is languishing in prison for his faith in God.
From threats and attempts you have proceeded to actions.

On 14 March at Nikopol there opens the trial on loss of parental rights for
Pyotr M. and Maria G. Zhurba, of 29 Altaiskaya Street, for bringing up their
children as Christians. They are Lyuda (14) and Olya (13). Art. 19 of the law
'On Marriage and the Family' will be applied. We cite the full text of the
Investigation Report by the procurator of Nikopol, Kovgan.

The Procuracy of the U.S.S.R.

The Procurator's Office of	To the People's Court, Nikopol
the Nikopol District	From the Procurator of Nikopol District
Dnepropetrovsk Region	
11 February, 1969	'On the loss of parental rights for
No. N-10,	P. M. ZHURBA and M. G. ZHURBA'
Nikopol	29 Altaiskaya Street

INVESTIGATION REPORT
(according to Art. 118 of the Civil Code of the Ukrainian S.S.R.)

On the basis of materials from the Commission on Minors, on the question
of the loss of parental rights for P. M. and M. G. Zhurba, it has been established
that their children Lyudmila (born in 1955) and Olga (born in 1957) are under

the influence of believing parents; from early childhood they have been subject to a religious influence, which does not correspond to the aims of state education; they regularly attend meetings of a religious sect and take part in its ritual.

The Commission on Minors with justification raises the question of loss of parental rights for P. M. and M. G. Zhurba.

On the basis of the above and according to article 161 of the Legal Code on Marriage, the Family and Guardianship, and Art. 19 of the Laws on Marriage and the Family. . . .

I request

1. That the case be accepted for trial and the question of the loss of parental rights for Pyotr M. and Maria G. Zhurba be considered.
2. That the defendants P. M. and M. G. Zhurba of Nikopol, 29 Altaiskaya Street, be called to the trial, as well as a representative from the Commission on Minors as a witness.
3. That I be informed of the date of the hearing.

Appendix: 20 pages.

The Procurator of Nikopol District
Junior Legal Adviser,
KOVGAN

We are not ignorant of the directives to school heads to take note of all children of believing parents and to give information about them to central organisations.

Thus on 24 December, 1968, in School No. 41, Barnaul, Seryozha and Sasha Zhirnokleyev, pupils of the fifth and seventh forms, were requested to fill in the following atheistic questionnaire:

1. Name, age.
2. What do you understand by the word atheism?
3. Do you believe in God?
4. Were you baptised or not?
5. Are there believers in your family?
6. What festivals are observed in your family?
7. What is your attitude to religion?
8. What omens do you believe in?
9. What would you say if you met a believer?

Similar questionnaires are being used in many places in the Soviet Union.

All this gives us cause to suspect the existence of new large-scale and mass measures to separate our children from us as mothers, to make them captive from their youth, to deprive them of a mother's tenderness, to harm their souls with sufferings that are indescribable in human language, to kill them physically, to make a mockery of them (as of the Sloboda children), to create tragedy for their childish souls.

No, you cannot kill the word 'Mummy' in a child's soul and you cannot take away their grief with any atheistic children's rattles! Who can measure even a tiny part of the despair of a child's heart when it is torn away from its mother? It is terrible to think that this is happening in our time and not in those described by Beecher-Stowe in her book, *Uncle Tom's Cabin*, where the child Harry is sold. And all this is happening while on the international scene you 'defend' children suffering from racial discrimination!

We can boldly say that our children are well brought up and disciplined, they are not tainted by vices and among tens of thousands of juvenile delinquents you will not find our children.

On the basis of the law 'On Marriage and the Family', Art. 19, we are faced with the fact of our children being taken away, and of going to prison ourselves because of their religious upbringing. It is terrible! Terrible! The world has never known anything like it! These methods have been borrowed from the ancient Egyptian Pharaoh who was a child murderer, from Herod, from Nero, notorious in every century for their blood-thirstiness. And this in face of the Declaration of Human Rights, which you signed.

Your aim of depriving children of religious upbringing is quite clear to us, not because you are concerned about the souls of our children, but in order to halt the growth of the Church. But Christ said: 'I will build my Church and the gates of hell shall not prevail against it.'

We as mothers, because of our unlimited love for our children, cannot give in to you over the ruin of our children. We cannot and will not be silent any longer. These are our children, we gave them birth, we will defend them with all our strength and we have the right to do so. Not one right-thinking person can deny this right of a mother. Even animals protect their young at the cost of their lives.

We are guaranteed the right to love, protect, bring up and defend our children by every law: by international laws, by the laws of the country in which we live, by the law of the human conscience, by the law of common sense and by the law of our Creator and Saviour!

We invite you to repent of the fact that for decades you have been tormenting our children and as a consequence of this to cease from the violence.

1. Cease the interrogation of minors.

2. Create normal conditions in schools, stop assault and slander.

3. Grant the opportunity to our children to study in institutions of intermediate and higher education, or else publish a law making known the prohibition on the instruction of children of believers for religious reasons.

4. Give a clear public interpretation of Art. 19 of the law 'On the Family and Marriage', stating that this article does not apply to believers and preventing local authorities from interpreting it otherwise and applying it to them.

5. Categorically prohibit them from threatening us with the removal of our children and from actually removing them.

6. Immediately return to parents these children who have been taken away.

7. Free Nadezhda S. Sloboda from prison and return her daughters Galya and Shura to her.

Attend to this letter, or these actions of yours will not remain unpunished by the Lord who will exact a penalty for every child's tear. Cease breaking international and common human laws, as well as your own.

We shall pray about this and we are fully determined to act, pressing to us the trembling hearts of our defenceless children; if necessary we will die for them.

March 1969   Appended is a list of signatures of E.C.B. Christian mothers numbers 1 to 1,453

* An answer may be sent to these addresses:

1. Shakhty, Rostov Region, 26 Stepanova Street, T.F. Popova.
2. Kiev, Ukrainian SSR, 7/1 Brestlitovskoye Chaussee, Flat 54, N. Cherepok.
3. Nikopol, Dnepropetrovsk Region, 29 Altaiskaya Street, M.G. Zhurba.
4. Barnaul-17, 77 Polyusny Passage, Anna Gibert.
5. Leningrad, 67 Stachek Passage, Block 5, Flat 560, Ye.A. Azarova.

5. *Fraternal Leaflet* Nos. 7–8/1971

Fraternal Leaflet is one of the periodic publications of the reform Baptists; this is the first issue to be circulated among believers in printed form. The network of secret printing presses which the Baptists have built up since the end of the 1960s is an entirely unique phenomenon within the whole sphere of Soviet *samizdat*. Together, the printing presses appear to form the publishing agency *The Christian*. Neither the literary intelligentsia nor the dissidents among the various non-Russian peoples of the Soviet Union have so far been able to circulate their materials in printed form.

The jubilee issue of *Fraternal Leaflet* gives us an impression of the spirit of the whole reform movement among the Baptists. On the one hand there is the joy and thankfulness for the fruitful work of preaching the Gospel and the readiness to sacrifice everything for this; on the other hand the harsh and uncompromising accusations are repeated here against the officially tolerated All-Union Council, whose workers are described as traitors and apostates. The struggle within the Baptist Church of the Soviet Union has its tragic side, but this is no new phenomenon in the history of Christendom. Young, vital revivalist move-

H

ments within the Churches have always tended to set themselves up as perfect and to claim a monopoly of the truth.

'Stand firm in one spirit, with one mind striving side by side for the faith of the Gospel' (Phil. 1:27)

FRATERNAL LEAFLET

7–8. 1971   published since 1965

Council of Churches of Evangelical Christians and Baptists

JUBILEE MESSAGE
To All Evangelical Christians and Baptists

> *'Who is there like You, Lord. . . . You lead this people by Your mercy, this people whom you have delivered; You guide them by Your strength into the dwelling place of Your holiness.'* Exodus 15:11, 13.

Peace to you and joy, beloved brothers and sisters in the Lord!

The Council of Churches wholeheartedly greets and congratulates all of you on the tenth anniversary of the spiritual awakening of our brotherhood!

Ten years is a short instant in the life of the Church of Christ, but it has been a blessed instant. It has been great neither in time nor in our efforts, but great in the acts of God, in the revelation of his grace and power, great in the closeness of the Lord to His people.

Having been under way for ten years, we testify with solemn reverence: all that has been and is noteworthy and radiant in the service of our brotherhood, everything down to the last iota, is the working of our all-merciful Lord and Saviour Jesus Christ. Without Him all our actions would have been unfruitful and our whole life a cold night without a glimmer of hope. We, simple and uneducated, powerless and stumbling along, have tried in everything to humble ourselves to the Lord when He called us to this journey. We have walked this thorny path subject to railing, ridicule, blows and threats, supporting one another. Our severe path has passed through iron bars and barbed wire. But we went on and kept up the struggle. We walked onward only because God was with us.

Out of love for God and neighbours we went arousing and witnessing to small and great, exposing and admonishing, as He commanded (Eph. 5:11).

Our clothing did not grow old and our shoes did not wear out – He gave us what we needed. Our bread did not run out, for he who gathered much did not keep the excess, but distributed to those who had none – as Christ taught. And when there began to be a general scarcity, He Himself came and asked, 'Children, do you have any bread?' And we shared Christ's bread, and thousands were filled.

When we were in special danger, we remembered that he who touches us touches the apple of His eye. Sorrow wrung our hearts when we lost friends and heroes. But we knew that by their death they glorified God and moved His work forward. And he comforted us.

From experience we became convinced of the unlimited love of Christ. He is for us all in all. In Him we live, move and have our being. And we have nothing to glory in except the name of the Lord. Our merit before the Lord is just like that of a beggar before one who out of his mercy took off his rags, gave him a royal adoption and led him into the palace of his glory. Therefore we tell Him from our heart: 'Everything is from You! Yours, Lord, are the blessings, Yours is the bread, Yours is goodness, Yours are strength and wisdom, Yours is eternity. And we will be happy if You accept our praise and remain with us in the future, according to Your promise. We have tried to sanctify Your name, and You have sent us all we need for life and well-being and have delivered us from the evil one. So accept our hosanna, hear our halleluia O Most High, for Yours is the kingdom and the power and the glory for ever, Amen.'

In these days of Jubilee we direct our grateful gaze towards the past, remembering what dark days for the brotherhood God transformed into bright days of awakening and joy.

The year was 1961. . . . The brotherhood was subjected to heavy trials. Freedom of religion was brutally suppressed. The activities of unregistered congregations was totally forbidden. Across the whole country there were mass arrests, and confiscation of houses used by believers for meetings. Even the registered congregations were closed by the hundred. During the first half of 1961, 300 such congregations were closed. The A.U.C.E.C.B. (All-Union Council of Evangelical Christians and Baptists) reckoned that at this rate of padlocking, all congregations would be closed in 2½ to 3 years.

But it was not this which threatened our brotherhood. Persecution is nothing strange for the Church of Christ. She has the Almighty Defender, Who possesses all power in heaven and on earth.

The frightening thing was that during the persecutions, when the Church was especially in need of universal, persistent prayer for God to send down strength and defence, the brotherhood was under the leadership of people whose apostate actions insulted the greatness of God and turned away His face. The godless world, which constantly interfered in the affairs of the Church, spent a long time carefully forming this leadership out of people who had betrayed the Lord and His teaching. Therefore in the years of testing there resulted not only no call to prayer, but there was even revealed an open betrayal and co-operation with the persecutors. From without the world advanced against us. From within – Church leaders who had apostatised from

God. The atheists hung their padlocks on the doors of the prayer-houses, and the apostates, sending out secret instructions, 'hung padlocks' on the lips of the preachers and worshippers.

God has written on the holy pages eternal words about how the Church and its servants should behave in conditions of persecution.

In the first century, enemies of the truth advanced from all sides on the Church of Christ. There arose Herod and Pilate, the heathens and the people of Israel. Spiritual and political authorities, both those who knew God and those who denied Him, showed a striking unity in the struggle with the Church.

How did the Apostles and the Church receive this blow?

The 4th chapter of the book of the Acts of the Apostles testifies that they took four most important steps along the path of commitment to the Lord, and He granted them blessings and victory.

1. There was a holy disobedience: in reply to the threats and the ban on evangelising, the Apostles declared: *'We cannot but speak that which we have seen and heard'* (v. 20).

2. They told everything to the Church: *'Having been released, they came to their own people and repeated what they had been told'* (v. 23).

3. They prayed earnestly: '. . . *they raised their voices with one accord to God.* . . .' (v. 24).

4. They acted: '. . . *they were all filled with the Holy Spirit and spoke the word of God with boldness'* (v. 31).

Alas, the unfaithful sevrants of our brotherhood took these four steps in the reverse direction.

In questions of worship they obeyed men rather than God, they hid from the Church the intentions of outsiders to bring down the brotherhood, for they themselves were implementing their plans; they did not issue a call to prayer for the sending down of power for faithful worship of the Lord during persecutions; they limited the preaching of salvation and acted not for the upbuilding, but for the destruction of the work of God.

This was a time of troubles. . . . Sorrow seized the hearts of all the Lord's children. The opponents of the truth had a foretaste of victory. They judged the Church by its apostate servants. But the apostates are not the Church. Thanks be to God, there has not been nor will there be a day when the Lord does not have His dedicated slaves. They were there then, and they acted at that dreadful hour. Elders who had grown grey in the struggle and young people full of strength, in spite of all anti-evangelical bans, independently carried on the service as much as they were able. 'Philips' went on the road. Moved with boldness for God, youth came together for combined fellowship. Prayers and fastings were conducted.

But this was by no means being done everywhere, and the Church was in need of general prayer and united action.

And then in the spring of 1961, when the darkness seemed particularly impenetrable, the leaders of the unregistered Church in Uzlovaya (Tula Region) were the first to place before a members' meeting the question of the necessity of forming an Action Group with the participation of leaders of registered congregations also, for the calling of all believers to prayer and combined action in the matter of defending the truth and calling for an All-Union Congress of Evangelical Christians and Baptists. The whole meeting unanimously commissioned the brethren with this task, prayed fervently and with benediction, and thanked God.

On 13 August, 1961, the Action Group visited the A.U.C.E.C.B. and delivered a letter to that effect. Within ten days the first message of the Action Group had been sent out to all congregations. All the people of God then raised their voice to God, and the Lord sent His answer.

It is impossible even to describe what blessings and transformations the Lord sent to the whole brotherhood in the past ten years. His works are too eloquent for words.

Congregations which had earlier been disbanded now renewed services.

The illegal, anti-evangelical limitations and bans introduced by workers of the A.U.C.E.C.B. were revoked.

The Spirit of the Most High inspired the hearts of His children with great power and a spirit of sacrifice. They brought to the altar of the living Church not only the fruits of their service and labour, but also their life, blood and tears. . . . And we praise God for this sacrifice.

It is impossible to recall without thankfulness how the brotherhood offered for the families of those suffering for the name of the Lord about 2 and a half million roubles (over £1 million) over this period.

Is it possible not to be delighted with the work of the publishing agency *The Christian*, which gave the brotherhood over 40,000 copies of the New Testament, hymn-books and other religious literature . . . ?

The good heralds *Fraternal Leaflet* and *Herald of Salvation* came to our congregations and into our homes for joy and encouragement.

In spite of difficulties and sorrow over separation, even the relatives of prisoners accomplished their work.

Our poets sang of Christ and His Church. It was not the heathen muse which brought them inspiration, but the One Who is fairer than the sons of men. Their verses, in accord with the awakening, called to faithfulness, holiness and unity:

> The hearts of the young, today may they be
> Beating as one on the breast of Christ,
> And tomorrow perhaps one of them may be raised
> To the tree of the cross by a crowd filled with rage.

These lines were written by brother N. P. Khrapov, who spent 26 years in fetters, and a considerable number of those years due to these lines, but the poem 'Greeting to you, radiant people of Christ' has become now the believers' favourite hymn.

And is it possible to be silent about notable cases of personal sacrifice? In the beginning of the movement, one couple gave up three gold coins, carefully preserved for many long years. A sister from an A.U.C.E.C.B. congregation turned over a thousand roubles of her personal savings for the needs of the publishing work. And recently a brother, also from an A.U.C.E.C.B. congregation, also gave more than a thousand roubles, although he himself does not have an abundance. All of them had prayed that the Lord would show them where there was a need and He showed them.

Is not the hand of our Heavenly Father in all these matters? Are not these His bounties?

But we have one more aspect of God's blessings – blessings in His refusals! In them there appeared the wisdom of His guidance.

Here are a few of them:

To begin with, the Action Group had no intention whatever of calling a congress under its leadership. Its goal was to sound the alarm. The leaders of the Action Group reckoned that they would be imprisoned less than a month after issuing their first declaration. 'Then let us go to prison,' they declared, 'but the brotherhood will be awakened, and the A.U.C.E.C.B. with general support and prayers will be able to call a congress. The Church will throw off the yoke of human regulations, the ignominious harness will be broken, and the brotherhood will be united.'

But all of the following years of enmity showed how hopelessly they had become hardened in their apostasy, and such a congress would have led to more difficult consequences, By cancelling the documents the bitter fruits would have been pulled off, but the tree was firmly rooted and would have continued to bear them. Now we can say with certainty that if the A.U.C.E.C.B. had agreed to that congress ten years ago, this movement would have died, having hardly been born, and we would never have had what we now have. But they did not agree to such a congress, and God turned this refusal to the good of His work.

In 1966 we asked to have 10,000 Bibles, 5,000 hymn-books and other spiritual literature printed at a state-owned printing establishment, but this was not granted us, and as a result our brotherhood has its own publishing agency.

The Council of Churches was unable to act otherwise than according to the laws and showing respect for the authorities, and as it never received a reply to its legitimate petitions, it had the right to act independently.

Thus by their silent refusals the Lord set us on the path of ever greater independence, sending us incomparably more than anything we could ask or think (Eph. 3:20).

So let us praise the Lord in our meetings that He heard all our sighs and prayers. May praise resound to Him for all the bounties and refusals, for joys and sufferings, for material and spiritual gifts, for gold and for the widow's mite. But most of all let us praise Him for the sacrifice of His precious blood by which He paid the debt of the whole world.

Being saved by Him, we shall also continue to carry the light of His teaching, to attain unity, holiness and virtue.

Our path may be hard and thorny, but in the face of all sufferings we abound in joy, for we are saved, and before us goes the One Who has already walked this path and knows the place of the promised haven. Hold fast, Church of Christ! *'Your God has destined you for strength'* (Ps. 68:28). Go then, Golgotha-Christians, after your Teacher, there awaits you eternal joy and rule with Christ.

'Let us rejoice and be glad and offer Him praise . . . ' (Rev. 19:7).

6. Open Letter of the reform Baptist congregation at Uzlovaya, Tula Region

In August 1971 the Uzlovaya congregation appealed to the United Nations Organisation as well as to the Soviet government in protest against the police search for G. K. Kryuchkov, President of the Council of Churches, who is clearly under a new arrest warrant. Kryuchkov is one of those Baptist leaders who were released in 1969 after serving their term of imprisonment. But even after the bitter experience of a labour camp they were still not prepared to give in and to rejoin the official All-Union Council of Evangelical Christians and Baptists. After unsuccessful talks on reunification in 1969, which were expressly encouraged by the Soviet authorities, a sharp new wave of persecutions overwhelmed the reform Baptists. Kryuchkov has been able to avoid this so far only by going underground.

To the General Secretary of the United Nations Organisation, U Thant.

Copies to the General Secretary of the C.C. of the C.P.S.U., comrade L. I. Brezhnev; the President of the Council of Ministers of the U.S.S.R., comrade A. N. Kosygin; the President of the Presidium of the Supreme Council of the U.S.S.R., comrade Podgorny; The Council of Relatives of E.C.B. Prisoners.

From the church at Uzlovaya, Tula Region, U.S.S.R.

Open Letter

> '*For Thy sake we are being killed all
> the day long; we are regarded as sheep
> to be slaughtered.*' (Rom. 8:36)

Dear U Thant!

You know that because of the illegal interference by the state into the spiritual life of the Church, with the aim of liquidating and destroying it, it is now ten years since there arose in our country a movement within the Church for the separation of Church and state, for the purification and sanctification of its members.

This movement is led by the Council of Churches, elected by Evangelical Christian and Baptist (E.C.B.) believers from the whole country, the President of which is the former pastor of our local church, Gennadi Konstantinovich Kryuchkov.

At the commission of the believers he has been a servant of the Church for ten years now, and for all these ten years he has been persecuted because of this by the authorities.

Now a nationwide search for him has been declared, as if he were a common criminal.

But all our Church has known brother Kryuchkov from his youth and their impression of him is completely positive. He is a straightforward, modest, honest person, the father of nine children, and God has blessed him as a servant of the Church.

Since 1951, when he became a member of the Church, he has taken a most active part in its life and work, enjoying the love and respect of all the believers.

At his factory they considered him to be the best worker.

At the time when Kryuchkov served as a pastor, the life of the Church in our country was becoming daily more impossible because of illegal interference by atheists. The authorities forbade us to meet, broke up prayer meetings and beat up believers.

The apostate leadership of our Church, the All-Union Council, was acting iu concert with the atheists and still is today.

In August 1961, at a members' meeting of our congregation, Kryuchkov put forward a plan of action for the revival of the Church in our country, which the Lord had revealed to him. We approved these plans with complete unanimity and we entrusted him with the leadership of an Action Group for the calling of an All-Union congress of E.C.B. believers to resolve internal Church problems.

We had not made a mistake, for the Lord worked through him! The best testimony to this fact is the thousands of reawakened believers in our country.

But as soon as brother Kryuchkov was elected by us for nationwide work, persecution was immediately unleashed against him. He was unable to live at home with his family, because K.G.B. collaborators kept a constant surveillance on his house.

Then on 30 May, 1966, Kryuchkov and almost all the members of the Council of Churches were arrested and imprisoned for three years.

In the camp he was subjected to mockery, blackmail and provocation. K.G.B. officials offered him freedom and an absolutely secure life if he would agree to collaborate with them, but Kryuchkov refused; then they told him he would never get out.

Criminal proceedings were opened against him for which they sought false witnesses among the prisoners, promising them release in exchange.

Thus one prisoner, trying to curry favour, gave Kryuchkov a New Testament in which had been placed a diagram of the administrative chain for an atomic reactor, which was supposed to be a state secret. After that a careful search was made to recover this diagram, but Kryuchkov had already found and destroyed it.

Notwithstanding this, a new, false case was concocted and again he faced trial. As a sign of protest, for 17 days before the expiry of his term of imprisonment, Kryuchkov refused food. He would have died there in the prison, if his wife and other believers had not found out about this and sent telegrams to the Government demanding his release. After such publicity the case was dropped and he was set free.

Because of these illegal actions, we know his innocence for a certain fact. We further know that he is being persecuted as a true servant of the Church.

After returning from imprisonment, Gennadi Kryuchkov had several conversations with the authorities concerning the normalisation of relations between Church and state. As a result of this the Council of Churches, for the first time in all its years of petitioning, received official permission for an All-Union conference of pastors of the E.C.B. Church. At this conference the members of the Council of Churches were re-elected and Kryuchkov remained President.

Together with all E.C.B. Churches in the whole country, the Council of Churches appealed to the Government with a request for recognition, for the right to carry on unhindered the spiritual work which had been entrusted to it by the Churches, and for permission to use as a permanent office the room provided by brother N. I. Vladykin in his own house. His address is Tula, ul. Krasnodontsev 14.

As a reaction to this the authorities again began to persecute and repress the Council of Churches and its supporters. Once again it became impossible for brother Kryuchkov to live at home with his family.

Brother Vladykin's home was confiscated and a sewing workshop installed there, while he himself was thrown into prison. But thanks to this brother's fortitude (in prison he refused food and water for 21 days) he was released,

H*

but to this day his house has not been returned to him. At present he is wandering around with his family, without any permanent home.

Thus once again we saw and understood that our atheist authorities still had no intention of normalising relations with the Church and would shun no methods in order to destroy its leaders.

The liberty and possibly the life of Kryuchkov is in serious danger. In these circumstances it would not be surprising if he should share the sad fate of Martin Luther King.

Yet the authorities come to Kryuchkov's house and assure his family: 'In the presence of the children we declare that he can return home, we won't touch him.' They say the same to several believers.

But the facts speak differently: at the military registration office Kryuchkov's wife was informed that a criminal case was in preparation against him and that he was being sought. Several searches have been carried out at his home. From all parts of the country one hears that a nationwide search for him has been declared and photographs of him have been circulated.

On 13 August, the day of the ten-year jubilee of our internal Church movement, our evening service was suddenly visited by a police officer along with the secretary of the local executive committee and other individuals.

There is a photograph of Kryuchkov in Sosnogorsk (Komi Autonomous Republic) on the wall under the general heading 'Wanted by the Police', where photographs of criminals and recidivists are displayed alongside his. The caption under his photograph reads:

Gennadi Konstantinovich Kryuchkov, born in Volgograd, previous sentence. Wanted by the Criminal Investigation Department of the Ministry of Internal Affairs of Tula Regional Executive Committee for leading illegal groups of evangelical-baptist believers, and for spreading literature of a slanderous character.

(We have sent copies of the photographs to U Thant).

The chief of police in Tula told Kryuchkov's wife that if they found him and he tried to escape, he would be shot. There can be no doubt that they could easily provoke such an escape attempt. These words by the chief of police are not meaningless, since such actions by the authorities are not new to us.

N. Khmara was tortured to death in prison as a young man. I. A. Afonin, a member of the Action Group and father of nine children, died in prison at the age of 45 in July 1971; P. F. Zakharov, after insults and torture in prison, died at the age of 49; the old man, A. F. Iskovskikh, who had spent the greater part of his life in prison as a Christian, has also died behind bars.

S. T. Golev, a member of the Council of Churches, elderly and ill, has spent about 20 years in bonds; at present he is virtually condemned to death in prison for his nationwide work for the Council of Churches.

Lidia Mikhailovna Vins, ill and advanced in years, President of the Council of Baptist Prisoners' Relatives, is languishing in bonds for writing petitions about the 200 persecuted for their faith in this country.

Brother N. P. Khrapov has spent 26 years of his Christian life in prison.

The list of those persecuted for their faith, whose only guilt lies in the fact that in questions of faith they obey only God and not atheists, could be prolonged indefinitely.

We appeal to you, U Thant, because we do not want at some time to have to add to this tragic list the names of the remaining members of the Council of Churches also. We have already several times appealed to you in letters with similar requests and for some reason have never received an answer. None of you has ever had an official meeting with the Council of Churches. We want to know how you and the world public stand with regard to those who are persecuted for Christ.

Reviewing the facts about the inhuman attitude to us as Christians, we do not despair and we do not consider our situation hopeless. Suffering for Christ and the Church is a common and usual thing, for Christ Himself said: 'They persecuted Me and they will persecute you.'

But we speak about this because all those who live on this earth, and especially those in authority, bear responsiblity before God and men for their attitude towards illegalities committed before their eyes.

We pray to God that He might give you wisdom to use every opportunity so that this illegality might be stopped.

Yours sincerely,
THE MEMBERS OF THE UZLOVAYA E.C.B. CHURCH

22 August, 1971
Please address reply to:
Tulskaya oblast,
g. Uzlovaya, pos. Lyubovka,
ul. Bratyev Lapshinykh 5,
K. F. Yakimenkova.
(Signed on behalf of Uzlovaya church by 70 people.)

7–8. The Unrest in the Catholic Church of Lithuania

Since 1969 the Catholic Church of Lithuania, with a membership of about two million people, has become a new centre of internal Church unrest, and of remarkable activity. Hundreds of priests and thousands of lay men and women are protesting together about the restrictions on Church life, about the imprisonment and fining of priests and the prohibition of **any** form of religious instruction, even a short preparation of children for their first communion.

Protests at the discrimination against the Catholic Church in Lithuania have in only a few years taken on massive proportions. Nowhere until now have so many people signed petitions for religious freedom as has happened in that country. A special feature of the protest movement is the close interweaving of nationalist and religious elements. The demand for freedom for the Catholic Church is linked in the mind of every Lithuanian with the memory of the annexation of the country by the Soviet Union in 1940, the deportation of tens of thousands of Lithuanians and the suppression of all nationalist manifestations. The Lithuanian Catholic Church is a symbol of national unity and national self-awareness in face of the Russian and Orthodox environment.

Lithuania today is one of the most serious trouble-spots in the Soviet Union. In May 1972 there were demonstrations and riots in Kaunas, the second largest city in the country, with thousands of young people demanding 'Freedom for Lithuania!' in the streets. The police had to be reinforced by troops in order to restore order. The Church did not side with these violent manifestations; nevertheless, it has had an important role in the formation of an independent self-awareness in Lithuania. The next two documents appeared in English in *East–West Digest*, 3/1970, pp. 77–81; 11/1972, pp. 425–7).

To the Chairman of the U.S.S.R. Council of Ministers

Copies to the Chairman of the Lithuanian S.S.R. Council of Ministers; Catholic Church leaders in Lithuania

Declaration by the Priests of the Catholic Church in Lithuania

In his article 'To the Country Poor', Lenin, generalising the tasks of the Social Democratic Party, wrote: 'Social democrats demand that every person must have full liberty to freely profess any religion' (*Writings*, vol. 6, Vilnius, 1961, p. 364).

By criticising the Tsarist government and the means it used against those who had different beliefs, Lenin wrote: 'Every person must have full freedom not only to profess any religion he wants, but also to publicise and change his faith . . . this is a matter of conscience and let no one dare to interfere in these matters' (*Writing of Lenin*, vol. 6, Moscow, 1946).

The Constitution of the U.S.S.R. guarantees to its citizens freedom to practise any religion. The laws of the Soviet Union will defend the rights of the faithful to practice their religious rites. Article 143 of the Penal Law speaks about the penalties, if anyone interferes in the exercise of these rights. But in reality it is not so. The laws which protect the rights of the faithful are broken without any consideration. The Catholic Church in Lithuania is condemned to die. The facts declare this. If in 1940 there were four seminaries for priests in Lithuania and about 1,500 priests, then after 1944 there was only one seminary left, in Kaunas. About 400 seminarians used to flock to it from all the dioceses. In 1946, in the very midst of the school year, only 150 seminarians were permitted to stay. During the last few years, in all the five courses in the seminary, the limit is 30 seminarians. If a seminarian leaves or becomes ill, no one is allowed to take his place. About 30 priests die in Lithuania every year, but only 5–6 are ordained. This year (1969) only three new priests were ordained. Already, at this time, many priests have to serve in two parishes. There is a good number of parishes where the pastor is 70 years old. Even invalids have to serve as pastors, for instance, in Turmantai.

Young people who want to enter the seminary meet many more difficulties than those who intend to go to other schools of higher education. The candidates are not chosen by the representatives of the Church, but by the officials of the government. This is not normal. What would we say if candidates for music would be selected by veterinarians or other specialists?

In January 1969, the priests of the diocese of Vilkaviskis addressed themselves to the Chairman of the U.S.S.R. Council of Ministers concerning this abnormal situation in the interdiocesan seminary in Kaunas. During the month of February of the same year they contacted the still active bishops and administrators of the dioceses about this same matter. Because of these moves, two priests, the Rev. S. Tamkevičius and the Rev. J. Zdebskis, lost their work certificates. They had to seek other work, they cannot perform their priestly duties.

In 1940, there were twelve bishops in Lithuania, today there are only two left: Bishop Matulaitis-Labukas, born in 1894, and Bishop L. Pletkus, born in 1895. Two still effective and able bishops: J. Steponavičius (for nine years) and V. Sladkevičius (more than ten years) have been deported to far away parishes [house arrest, trans.], although according to Articles 62–69 of the Penal Code deportation is foreseen only for five years and that for grave offences. What have our shepherds done, without any court action or proven guilt, to be punished for an indeterminate time?

From time immemorial Vilnius is the centre of religious life, but today this city is not allowed to have its bishop, even though other smaller religious communities, for instance, the Orthodox, have their bishop, and others some equivalent religious leader.

According to the Church Canon Law, the capitular vicars are only temporary administrators who are chosen when a bishop dies or leaves the office. The archdiocese of Vilnius and the diocese of Panevezys now have been administered by capitular vicars for 9 years, and that of Kaisiadoriai for 23 years.

It is not always, even for those who have official authorisation, that the bishops and administrators are permitted to visit the parishes and confer the Sacrament of Confirmation according to the canons of the Church. In the dioceses of Panevezys this sacrament has been conferred only once since 1961. In other dioceses it is permitted to be conferred only in the centres, for instance, in Vilnius, Kaunas, but very rarely in the regional cities. Those who want to receive the Sacrament of Confirmation have to travel from distant places, endure all the hardships with their small children. Thus great pressures and difficulties are created.

The pastoral work of the priests is being hindered in a number of ways: one is not allowed to help the neighbouring parishes in religious services nor to invite the necessary number of priests on special occasions of devotion. The faithful who want to confess have to wait for a long time; suffer inconvenience and lose much of their precious time. On special days of devotion in some churches about 1,000 people come for confession. Even if only three minutes were given to each penitent, one priest would have to hear confessions for 50 hours, and this is impossible.

Specialists in all fields come together for conferences to perfect themselves and learn from the experiences of others. The Church Canon Law also require that the priests should make a three day retreat at least every three years. Such retreats at this time are forbidden not only at the diocesan centres, but also in the deaneries: even priests of one deanery are not permitted to get together.

Official representatives of the government (delegate of the government for religious affairs, leaders of the regions and districts) give various directives to the priests, by word of mouth only. It sometimes happens that these orders contradict one another. For instance, a representative of the executive committee's chairman of the Varena region forbade the pastor of Valkininkai to accompany the burial procession to the cemetery, while an agent for religious affairs instructed that the priest can go to the cemetery, but he cannot accompany the procession from the home to the church. On 15 April, 1969, an agent for religious affairs in Svencioneliai, in the presence of government officials and the members of the church committee, told the pastor that when there is a priest in the procession of the deceased no hymns are allowed, but this can be done without the priests. If a person is buried with religious rites, an orchestra is not permitted; collective farms and organisations cannot help materially.

Catholics in Lithuania cannot avail themselves of the freedom of the press for their religious needs. They cannot make use of the radio and television, of cinemas, schools, lectures. We do not possess even the most elementary religious textbook, prayerbook or other religious writings. During the Russian occupation not even one catechism was printed. Only in 1955 and 1958 a Catholic prayerbook was printed and in 1968 a liturgical prayerbook. But both of the editions had a very limited number of copies so that only a few families could acquire them. Besides, the liturgical prayerbook was supposed to include a short explanation of the truths of the faith, but the delegate for religious affairs would not allow this to be printed. The priests and the churches received only one copy of the Roman Catholic Ritual and documents of Vatican II were available only for the priests, one copy each. The faithful did not even have a chance to see these books.

Although the Constitution of the U.S.S.R. guarantees freedom of conscience, and parents do want and request that their children be educated in a religious spirit, nevertheless priests and catechists are forbidden to prepare children for their First Communion. The delegate for religious affairs allows the children to be examined only singly. Those who do not follow this unwritten law are severely punished. For instance, the government officials have fined the Rev. J. Fabijanskas for catechisation; the Rev. M. Gylys and the Rev. J. Zdebskis were sent to a forced labour camp. In Anyksciai, Miss O. Paskeviciute prepared children for their first confession. For this she was deported to a forced labour camp, where there followed her overexhaustion, sickness and death. Parents themselves have the right to prepare their children, but they have no means: they are not prepared for this job, have no time or religious books. In like manner, during Tsarist times, workers and serfs could not make use of the right to give their children higher education.

Children who frequent the church experience much abuse. They are made fun of, wall bulletins write about them. In schools, children are constantly taught that religious parents are backward, have no knowledge and can give them no directives. Thus the authority of the parents is destroyed. When children cease to respect their parents, it is difficult to control them both in the school and outside its walls. Besides, religiously-minded children are not allowed to take an active part in the liturgy, sing in the choir, participate in processions, serve Mass. Thus the rights of the faithful children and parents are severely violated. They are harshly discriminated against, coerced and forced to compromise others. For instance, on 26 December, 1967, the secondary school headmaster Baranauskas and other teachers in Svencioneliai kept the II-VI class students for two and a half hours until they forced them to write letters against the local pastor Rev. Laurinavičius. For one of those youngsters, J. Gaila, an ambulance had to be called because of threats. Second class student K. Jermalis was sick with fright for a couple of months. The pastor, who allowed the children to serve Mass and participate in a procession, was removed from Svencioneliai. The offended parents of those children appealed to Moscow. How much time was lost, expense incurred, health impaired? Just recently the Rev. A. Deltuva was fined 50 roubles because he allowed the children to serve Mass.

According to the law, the convictions of one who believes and one who does not should equally be respected, but practice is different. In many hospitals, for instance, in Vilnius, Utena, Pasvalys, Anyksciai, even when sick people ask to receive the sacraments, their request is refused. In 1965 a driver, K. Semenas, and Miss B. Sudeikyte married in the Church. By this act they lost their previous grant of a piece of land where they were going to build a house. Notwithstanding the fact that all the material was bought for the construction, they were told: 'Let the priest give you land.'

In Pasvalys, Anyksciai and other places, taxicabs cannot even bring the witnesses of the marrying couple to the church. There is much suffering for the intellectuals who secretly baptise their children, marry or attend Mass in the church. These facts are brought up at their work, and they are often reprimanded or even lose their jobs. For instance, in 1965 Miss P. Cicenaite, a school teacher in Daugeliskis, was dismissed from her work by the school director because she would not forsake the Church. When the school officials told her to leave, she, wishing to have her book 'clean', wrote a request to be released from work. Often the faithful are dismissed from work or are punished because of their convictions, this fact though is concealed by some other motive.

In 1956 the Pension Act by-passed the servants of the Church. Organists and sacristans can only dream about pensions. For instance, Mr. P. Pagalskas joined a collective farm when the Soviets came to Lithuania. Like all other citizens, he delivered his horse and farming tools to the authorities. He worked in the office of a collective farm as an accountant, and on Sundays used to play the organ in the church. When he had the misfortune to get sick and became an invalid and could not work in the office, he night-watched the animals on a collective farm. When he reached old age (b. in 1889), he applied to the Social Welfare Office of the Ignalina Region. An answer came back from this office that organists do not receive any pension.

Many of the churches are not allowed to ring bells, use loudspeakers or any other technical aids. Materials are not allotted for the upkeep of the churches. The cities are growing, but since 1945 only two churches have been built in Lithuania (one of which, in Klaipeda, has been turned into a music hall), many older churches are serving as storage places, museums and so forth.

These and many other painful facts which which we have mentioned here show that the priests and the faithful are discriminated against and they cannot fully use those rights which the U.S.S.R. Constitution guarantees them.

Consequently, we have dared to address ourselves to you, Mr. Chairman of the U.S.S.R. Ministers, hoping that you will correct this unnatural situation of the Catholic Church in the Lithuanian S.S.R. and see to it that we, the Lithuanian priests and faithful, like all other citizens, will be able to exercise the rights as they are foreseen in the Constitution.

Signed by the Priests from the archdiocese of Vilnius

August 1969   [40 signatures]

To the Secretary-General of the Communist Party of the Soviet Union, Moscow Kremlin.

Memorandum of the Roman Catholics of Lithuania

After the Second World War nations have risen from the ruins and desire a permanent peace. A genuine peace is grounded on justice and respect for human rights. We, Catholics of Lithuania, painfully deplore the violations of the believers' freedom of conscience and the persecution of the Church that persist in our nation to this very day.

It is now more than ten years that Bishops J. Steponavičius and V. Sladkevičius have been subjected to the hardships of exile, without a proper court verdict and without a set term, although they have not committed any crimes.

In November of this year two priests, J. Zdebskis and P. Bubnys, were sentenced to one year in prison for having instructed youngsters in the foundations of Catholic faith, at the request of their parents in fulfilment of their own priestly duties. These priests helped the youngsters to prepare themselves for the First Communion not in school but in the church and used no compulsion – only those who wanted to received the instruction.

Meanwhile, the believing children of believing parents are compelled to study atheism in schools. They are even forced to speak, write and act against their consciences, yet those who coerce them are neither reprimanded nor tried.

The priests are no longer capable of providing proper service to us, believers, because they are too few. There are many cases where one priest serves two and sometimes even three parishes. Even aged and invalid priests are compelled to work. This is so because the seminary of priests is administered not so much by the bishop as by a state representative. The state authorities have limited the enrolment in the Seminary to a mere ten theological students a year.

The appointment of priests to specific parishes is also directed by a state official.

Although the penal code of the Lithuanian S.S.R. provides for punishment of those who persecute believers, in practice such penalties are never enforced. In 1970 the Board of Education of Vilkaviskis dismissed the teacher, Mrs. O. Briliene, from her job because she is a believer. Meanwhile, the authorities in Vilkaviskis refuse to employ her even as a street-sweeper. Nobody punishes such officials, although because of their arbitrariness the members of the intelligentsia are afraid to practise their faith publicly.

State authorities do not allow the believers to restore churches that have burned down, as for example, in Sangruda, Batakiai, Gaure. It is only with the greatest difficulty that permission is given to furnish a little chapel in a residential building, but one is never allowed to transfer it to a churchyard.

We could point out many more cases of discrimination which have embittered our lives and have sown disillusionment with the Soviet Constitution and laws. We therefore ask the Soviet Government to grant us the freedom of conscience, which has been guaranteed by the Constitution of the U.S.S.R. but which has not as yet been put into practice. What we want is not pretty words in the press and on the radio but serious governmental efforts that would help us, Catholics, to feel we have equal rights, as citizens of the Soviet Union.

December 1971

ADDITION TO THE MEMORANDUM

Seventeen thousand fifty four signatures are enclosed with the memorandum. It must be noted that the memorandum was signed by only an insignificant portion of religious believers in Lithuania, since the organs of the militia and the K.G.B. have used all kinds of means to interrupt the collection of signatures. Several persons active in the collection of signatures were arrested in Kapsukas, Sakiai, Islauzas, Kapciamiestis.

If the state organs will continue giving the same kind of treatment to the complaints of the believers, we will feel compelled to turn to international institutions: to the Pope of Rome, the Head of our Church, or to the United Nations Organisation, an authoritative institution that protects human rights.

In addition, we would like to inform you that this memorandum is the result of a national calamity: social ills, such as juvenile delinquency, alcoholism and suicides, have increased tenfold during the period of Soviet power in Lithuania. Divorces and destruction of unborn babies have also reached a dangerous level. The further we move away from the Christian past, the more the terrible consequences of compulsory atheistic education come to light, the wider the spread of the inhuman way of life, deprived of God and of religion.

We are addressing ourselves to you as the highest authority of the Party with a request for the most serious and responsible consideration of the facts presented by us and for the adoption of an appropriate decision.

REPRESENTATIVES OF LITHUANIAN CATHOLICS

January 1972

To: Mr. Kurt Waldheim,
Secretary-General of the United Nations

Appeal of the Lithuanian Catholics

Taking into consideration that Lithuania is not represented in the United Nations Organisation, we, Catholics of Lithuania, must address ourselves to you, Mr. Secretary-General, through appropriate channels.

Our appeal was caused by the fact that religious believers in our republic cannot enjoy the rights set out in Article 18 of the Universal Declaration of Human Rights. On these grounds our clergy, groups of believers and individual Catholics have repeatedly addressed themselves to the highest state organs of the Soviet Union, demanding that the violations of the rights of the believers be stopped. Several petitions of believers were transmitted to the Soviet government, including: a statement of the Catholics of Prienai, signed by 2,000 persons, sent in September of 1971; a statement of the believers of the Parish of Santaika, region of Alytus, bearing 1,190 signatures, sent in October of 1971; a statement of 1,344 parishioners of the Parish of Girkalnis, region of Raseiniai, sent in December of 1971. All these statements were transmitted to various of the highest offices of the U.S.S.R., but not a single one of them has sent an official reply, although state agencies are under an obligation to respond to citizens' statements within a month. The unofficial reply (to those statements) manifested itself by increased repression towards the believers.

The Catholics of all Lithuania, in addressing a memorandum to the Secretary-General of the Communist Party of the Soviet Union, Mr. Brezhnev, were determined to remind the Soviet leadership of their lack of human rights, but the organs of the Soviet militia and K.G.B. have suppressed the mass collection of signatures by means of threats, arrests and iron handcuffs.

Such action by the authorities has prompted the conviction that the present memorandum, signed by 17,000 believers, will not attain its aim if it is sent by the same means as previous collective declarations. Therefore we, Catholics of Lithuania, are addressing ourselves to you, Honorable Secretary-General, and are asking that you relay the said memorandum, signatures included, to the Secretary-General of the Communist Party, Mr. Brezhnev.

Respectfully yours,

REPRESENTATIVES OF LITHUANIA'S CATHOLICS

February 1972

9. The Voice of the Old Believers

The situation of the smaller denominations is not greatly different from that of the Russian Orthodox Church or the Baptists. They are exposed to the same repression, and since the end of the 1960s they have also produced critical, independent voices protesting against the interference of state authorities in internal Church affairs, against infiltration and deception by officialdom. The personal accusations levelled in the following document cannot in the nature of things be checked. Up to now it is the only document of oppositional direction to have become known in the West from Old Believer circles. (Russian in *Posev*, 3/1969, p. 5.)

Report on the persecution of Old Believers, Ancient Orthodox Christians in the U.S.S.R. and of priests who are members of the 'Moscow and All-Russian Archiepiscopacy' (January 1969).

The 'Moscow and All-Russian Archiepiscopacy of Old Believers' in the U.S.S.R. serves the spiritual needs of millions of Old-Orthodox Christians and has more than a hundred of its own parishes. The Archiepiscopacy is headed by Archbishop Yosif, who is advanced in years and seriously ill in bed. There are four* other bishops, of whom one has been prevented by the Soviet authorities from celebrating the office in public – he has been barred from the notorious so-called registration, introduced by the authorities to enable open interference in the internal affairs of the Church and the imposition of pressure on priests and believers. There are also more than 100 priests.

Besides this, the Soviet authorities are corrupting the Old Believer Christian Church from within by means of infiltrating their agents among its pastors and using cunning methods to recruit traitors among the unstable section of priests and Christians. These are provocations, threats and so on. Thus for example, the secret organisation of the authorities, the K.G.B., has penetrated into the very heart of the Archiepiscopate at Moscow, Zh-52, Rogozhsky Posyolok, d. 29, and placed its own important agent, Protodeacon Georgi Alexandrovich Ustinov, there as secretary. They try to deprive believers of their pastors, whom they illegally bar from their rights to celebrate the office; they summon them to interrogations without any reason, they look for excuses to close churches and to take away registration, and so on. The aim is to prevent the priest from serving God, without worrying about the means used. Priests are watched, both in their churches and where they live. The clergy and believers live in constant fear of slanderers informing on them, and they are constantly being threatened by someone or other, in order to force them to stop celebrating the office.

Ustinov, that Judas, is especially dangerous for Old Believer faithful and clergy. He has the position of secretary to the whole Archiepiscopate, which is very convenient for keeping his eyes on them, since all incoming and out-going correspondence passes through his hands; correspondence with the parishes, priests and believers, declarations, complaints of believers about persecution by local Soviet authorities, and so on, as well as the answers of the Archbishop and his officials – all this immediately becomes known to the K.G.B. Recently some 'Nekrasovtsy' Old Believers (who were formerly led in Turkey by the Cossack Nekrasov) returned from Turkey to the U.S.S.R. A good young Old Believer priest was appointed for those who had returned, but immediately after this he suddenly and mysteriously died. People think

---

* Earlier the number was given as three bishops since the bishop dismissed by the Soviet authorities was mistakenly considered as no longer of episcopal status. According to Church canons he is notwithstanding still a bishop.

that this priest refused the suggestion of the Soviet authorities through the K.G.B. to collaborate and play Judas to these Christians; therefore the authorities hastened to remove him, so that there would be no time for him to reveal the secret, vile machinations of the Soviet authorities against Christ's Church. The believers see no other reason for the death of this good young priest.

The discrimination against believers and priests is demonstrated by the following facts alone: a higher flat rent is demanded from Old Believer priests in comparison with the price paid for living space by other Soviet citizens, and other taxes are also imposed. For example, if a priest receives (say) 400 roubles, then 180 roubles are demanded from him in tax (i.e. 45%). Believing students are excluded from Soviet higher educational establishments. This happened to the honours student Yevgeni Bobkov who was expelled from Moscow State University. The Soviet papers also propagate slander against believers, giving the signal for religious persecution of Christians, as, for example, in the newspaper *Moskovsky Komsomolets* of 11 April and 13 October, 1959, and other subsequent issues. Believers are given no chance to defend themselves against the slander, despite the beautiful articles in the Constitution: you will not find a single article by a believer in the Soviet press in his own defence; they will not even print his reply. This one fact shows that in the U.S.S.R. those in authority are guilty of arbitrary action.

The Soviet authorities also hinder Old Believers in the repairing of their churches, even in Moscow: they demand the payment of 'baksheesh' to the extent of 70 per cent of the cost of the church repairs and render no work or assistance in exchange for this money. Therefore the churches often look shabby from the outside. The authorities allow Old Believers to publish only 4,000 church calendars, and even then the Soviet printers hold up the work and do not publish them until a good part of the current year is gone.

But regardless of all the shameful methods of persecution of Old Believers they know the cunning and hatred of the devil towards Christians and wage a steadfast spiritual struggle with the powers of darkness and demand from the Soviet authorities the opening of new churches and parishes for thousands upon thousands of believers. Recent examples have occurred in the following towns: Alma-Ata, Barnaul, Vitebsk, Dzhambul, Leningrad, Frunze, Beltsy (Moldavian S.S.R.), Semyonov (Gorky Region), Melenki (Vladimir Region), and in other districts.

The Soviet authorities do not reply to the legal letters and demands of their own citizens, since they know that the number of believers is increasing and Communist propaganda is bankrupt. They remain cynically silent, violating the elementary principles of relations between their own institutions and the Church in correspondence with its communities.

Besides this, the very fact of opening Christian churches will be a witness to the collapse of the Communist ideology. Therefore they conceal the legal requests of believers, knowing that they are doing something underhand.

Chronological Table

1905–7	First Russian Revolution.
1917	October Revolution.
August 1917 to September 1918	Local Council of the Russian Orthodox Church.
23 January 1918	Decree on Separation of Church and State.
1917–25	Patriarch Tikhon.
1922–7	Climax of the Church Schism though the 'living Church'.
1923–7	Recognition of the Soviet State by the Russian Orthodox Church and other denominations.
1917–28	Relative freedom for the non-Orthodox denominations in the Soviet Union.
8 April 1929	Law on Religious Associations.
1934–8	Climax of Stalin's terror; far-reaching destruction of Church institutions.
8 September 1943	Election of Metropolitan Sergi as Patriarch (died 15 May, 1944).
27 October 1944	Uniting of Evangelical Christians and Baptists.
31 January to 2 February 1945	Local Council of the Russian Orthodox Church.
1943–9	Time of Church reconstruction.
1945–70	Patriarch Alexi.
1958	Beginning of the Prague Christian Peace movement.
1959–64	Church persecution under Khrushchev.
18 July 1961	Synod of Bishops of the Russian Orthodox Church.
1961	Beginning of the *Initsiativniki* split from the All-Union Council of Evangelical Christians and Baptists.

1961–2	The Russian Orthodox Church, the Georgian Orthodox Church, the Armenian-Gregorian Church, the Evangelical-Lutheran Churches of Latvia and Estonia and the Evangelical Christians and Baptists join the World Council of Churches.
November 1965	Protest letters by Frs. Eshliman and Yakunin. Formation of opposition elements within the Russian Orthodox Church.
1–4 July 1969	Zagorsk Conference of all Religions in the U.S.S.R.
1963, 1966, 1969	All-Union Congresses of the All-Union Council of Evangelical Christians and Baptists in Moscow.
30 May–2 June 1971	Local Council of the Russian Orthodox Church in Zagorsk. Election of Pimen (Izvekov) as Patriarch.

Select Bibliography

Books

Bourdeaux, M., *Religious Ferment in Russia. Protestant Opposition to Soviet Religious Policy*, London 1968.

——, *Patriarch and Prophets. Persecution of the Russian Orthodox Church Today*, London 1969.

Chertikhin, V. Ye., *Ideologia Sovremennogo Pravoslavia* (The Ideology of Contemporary Orthodoxy), Moscow 1965.

Chrysostomus, J., *Kirchengeschichte Russlands der neuesten Zeit*, 3 vols., Munich–Salzburg 1965–8.

——, *Kleine Kirchengeschichte Russlands nach 1917*, Freiburg 1968.

Codevilla, G., *Stato e Chiesa nell'Unione Sovietica*, Milan 1972.

Curtiss, J. S., *The Russian Church and the Soviet State, 1918–1950*, Boston 1953.

Feron, B. *Gott in Sowjetrussland, eine Bestandsaufnahme*, Essen 1963.

Fletcher W. C., *Nikolai: Portrait of a Dilemma*, New York 1967.

——, *The Russian Orthodox Church Underground, 1917–1970*, London–New York–Toronto 1971.

—— and Strover, A. I. (ed.), *Religion and the Search for New Ideals in the U.S.S.R.*, New York 1967.

Galter, A., *The Red Book of the Persecuted Church*, Westminster 1957.

Gordienko, N. S., *Sovremennoe Pravoslavie* (Orthodoxy Today), Moscow 1968.

Harris, R. and Howard-Johnston, X. (ed.), *Christian Appeals from Russia*, London 1969.

Hauptmann, P., *Altrussischer Glaube*, Göttingen, 1963.

Hayward, M., and Fletcher, W. C. (ed.), *Religion and the Soviet State: a Dilemma of Power*, London, 1969.

Heyer, F., *Die Orthodoxe Kirche in der Ukraine von 1917 bis 1945*, Cologne 1953.

Hutten, K., *Christen hinter dem Eisernen Vorhang. Die Christlichen Gemeinden in der kommunistischen Welt*, 2 vols., Stuttgart 1962–3.

——, *Kampf des Glaubens. Dokumente aus der Sowjetunion*, Bern 1967.

Kischkowsky, A., *Die sowjetische Religionspolitik und die Russische Orthodoxe Kirche*, Munich 1960.

Klibanov, A. I. (ed.), *Konkretnie issledovania sovremennykh religioznykh verovanii* (Empirical researches on contemporary religious beliefs), Moscow 1967.

Kolarz, W., *Religion in the Soviet Union*, London 1961.

——, *Kratky nauchno-ateistichesky slovar* (Short scientific-atheist dictionary), Moscow 1964.

Kurochkin, *Evolyutsia sovremennogo russkogo pravoslavia* (The evolution of contemporary Russian Orthodoxy), Moscow 1970.

(Levitin-Krasnov, A. E.), *Dialog s Tserkovnoi Rossiei* (Dialogue with ecclesiatical Russia), Paris 1967.

(——), *Zashchita very v SSSR* (The defence of faith in the USSR), Paris 1966.

Marshall, R. H., Jr., (ed.), Bird, T., and Blane, A. Q., *Aspects of Religion in the Soviet Union, 1917–1967*, Chicago–London 1971.

Martin, A., *Les croyants en URSS*, Paris 1970.

Milovidov, V. F., *Staroobryadchestvo v proshlom i nastoyashchem* (Old Believers in past and present), Moscow 1969.

Mitrokhin, L. N., *Baptizm* (The Baptist Church), Moscow 1966.

Mourin, M., *Der Vatikan und die Sowjetunion*, Munich 1967.

Nastolnaya Kniga Ateista (Atheist's handbook), Moscow 1968.

Pantskhava, I. D. (ed.), *Konkretno-sotsiologicheskoe izuchenia sostoyania religioznosti i opyta ateisticheskogo vospitania* (An empirical sociological study of the state of religiosity and of experience in atheist education), Moscow 1969.

——, *Osnovnie voprosy nauchnogo ateizma* (Basic questions of scientific atheism), Moscow 1969.

Rössler, R., *Kirche und Revolution in Russland. Patriarch Tichon und der Sowjetstaat*, Cologne–Vienna 1969.

The Russian Orthodox Church: Organization, Situation, Activity, Moscow 1959.

Scheludkow, S., *Ist Gott in Russland tot?* transl. by E. Voss, Stuttgart–Berlin 1971.

Simon, G., *K. P. Pobedonoscev und die Kirchenpolitik des Heiligen Sinod 1880 bis 1905*, Göttingen 1969.

Situation des Chrétiens en l'Union Soviétique, 2 vols., Paris 1964–5.

Skoda, F., *Die sowjetische philosophische Religionskritik heute*, Basle–Vienna 1968.

Smolitsch, I., *Geschichte der russischen Kirche 1700–1917*, Vol. I, Leiden 1964.

Stroitelstvo kommunizma i preodolenie religioznykh perezhitok (The building of communism and the conquest of religious survivals), Moscow 1966.

Struve, N., *Christians in the USSR*, London 1967.

Stupperich, R. (ed.), *Kirche und Staat in der Sowjetunion. Gesetze und Verordnungen*, Witten 1962.

Theodorowitsch, N., *Religion und Atheismus in der UdSSR. Dokumente und Berichte*, Munich 1970.

Titov, V. Ye., *Pravoslavie* (Orthodoxy), Moscow 1967.

Tsameryan, I. P., *Kommunizm i Religia* (Communism and Religion), Moscow 1967.

Voprosy preodolenia religioznykh perezhitok v SSSR (Questions on the conquest of religious survivals in the U.S.S.R.), Moscow–Leningrad 1966.

de Vries, W., *Kirche und Staat in der Sowjetunion*, Munich 1959.

Journals and Series

(For list of abbreviations see page x)

Bratsky Vestnik (Fraternal Herald), Moscow.

Kirche im Osten, Göttingen.

Nauka i Religia (Science and Religion), Moscow.

Ostkirchliche Studien, Würzburg.

Religion in Communist Dominated Areas, New York.

Russia Cristiana, Milan.

Stimme der Orthodoxie, Berlin–Karlshorst.

Vestnik russkogo studencheskogo khristianskogo dvizhenia (Herald of the Russian Student Christian Movement), Paris.

Voprosy Nauchnogo Ateizma (Questions of Scientific Atheism), Moscow.

Zhurnal Moskovskoi Patriarkhii (Journal of the Moscow Patriarchate), Moscow.

INDEX

Guide Library

Hillwood Museum
Washington, D.C.